Also by Sarah Bell

The British Columbia Lodge & Resort Guide
Also includes the Banff/Jasper area and the Yukon

The British Columbia & Alberta Adventure Travel Guide
Guided outdoor trips and more

Gordon Soules Book Publishers Ltd.
West Vancouver, Canada
Seattle, U.S.

Canadian Cataloguing in Publication Data

Bell, Sarah.
The British Columbia bed & breakfast guide, also includes the
Banff/Jasper area

Includes index.
ISBN 1-894661-00-1

1. Bed and breakfast accommodations—British Columbia—
Guidebooks. 2. Bed and breakfast accommodations—Alberta—
Banff Region—Guidebooks. 3. Bed and breakfast
accommodations—Alberta—Jasper Region—Guidebooks. I. Title.
TX907.5.C22B73 2000 647.94711'03 C00-910858-0

Published in Canada by
Gordon Soules Book Publishers Ltd.
1359 Ambleside Lane
West Vancouver, BC V7T 2Y9
(604) 922-6588 or (604) 688-5466
fax: (604) 688-5442
email: books@gordonsoules.com
web site: www.gordonsoules.com

Published in the United States by
Gordon Soules Book Publishers Ltd.
PMB 620, 1916 Pike Place #12
Seattle, WA 98101-1097
(604) 922-6588 or (604) 688-5466
fax: (604) 688-5442
email: books@gordonsoules.com
web site: www.gordonsoules.com

Cover designed by Harry Bardal
Printed and bound in Canada by Printcrafters Inc.

Contents at a Glance

(for full contents, see pages 4 to 7)

Contents

Information for Users of This Book

1. Information in any guidebook is subject to change and error. It is advisable to confirm important information when making reservations.

2. While great care has been taken to ensure the accuracy of the information in this book, neither the author nor the publisher can accept responsibility for any outdated information, omissions, or errors.

3. Rates are in Canadian currency.

4. Distances are approximate.

5. For the B&Bs that accept credit cards for payment, the specific credit cards they accept are listed.

6. B&Bs are open year round unless otherwise indicated.

7. Ensuite bathroom describes a bathroom accessible directly from a guest room or from a bedroom in a suite or cottage, for the exclusive use of the guests in that room.

8. Private bathroom describes a bathroom for the exclusive use of the guests of one room or suite; the guests must exit their room or suite to get to it.

9. Bathroom in suite describes a bathroom in a suite, not accessible directly from a bedroom in the suite.

10. Bathroom in cottage describes a bathroom in a cottage, not accessible directly from a bedroom in the cottage.

11. Shared guest bathroom describes a bathroom shared by some or all guests; the hosts do not use this bathroom.

12. Shared bathroom describes a bathroom shared by guests and hosts.

13. Kitchen describes, at minimum, a sink, a stove, and a fridge.

14. Suite describes, at minimum, a bedroom with a large sitting area and a bathroom in the suite.

15. Honeymoon suite describes, at minimum, a bedroom with a bathroom in the suite.

16. Self-contained suite describes, at minimum, a bedroom with a large sitting area, a bathroom in the suite, and cooking facilities that include, at minimum, a sink, a hot plate, and a fridge.

17. Self-contained room describes, at minimum, a bedroom with an ensuite bathroom and cooking facilities that include, at minimum, a sink, a hot plate, and a fridge.

18. Examples of rates and bed types:

    Example 1: Four rooms. One person $60–70; two people $70–80. King-sized bed; queen-sized bed; twin beds. This means that the B&B has one or more rooms with a king-sized bed, one or more rooms with a queen-sized bed, and one or more rooms with twin beds.

    Example 2: Two rooms. One person $70; two people $75–85. Queen-sized bed. Ensuite bathroom. This means that each room has a queen-sized bed and an ensuite bathroom

    Example 3: Four rooms. One person $75–90; two people $90–100. Queen-sized bed, ensuite bathroom; double bed, shared guest bathroom; queen-sized bed and one twin bed, shared guest bathroom. This means that the B&B has one or more rooms with a queen-sized bed and an ensuite bathroom; one or more rooms with a double bed and a shared guest bathroom; and one or more rooms with a queen-sized bed, a twin bed, and a shared guest bathroom.

    Example 4: Three rooms. One person $60–65; two people $70–85. Queen-sized bed and one twin bed, ensuite bathroom; queen-sized bed and one twin day bed, private bathroom; double bed and one twin bed, private bathroom. This means that the B&B has one room with a queen-sized bed, a twin bed, and an ensuite bathroom; one room with a queen-sized bed, a twin day bed, and a private bathroom; and one room with a double bed, a twin bed, and a private bathroom.

    Example 5: Two rooms. One person $60; two people $70–80. Queen-sized bed; twin beds (or twin beds side by side with king-sized bedding). Ensuite bathrooms. This means that the B&B has one room with a queen-sized bed and an ensuite bathroom and one room with twin beds (or twin beds side by side with king-sized bedding) and an ensuite bathroom.

19. Maps of British Columbia are available from many sources, including bookstores, newsstands, gift shops, gas stations, automobile associations, tourist information offices, and the book's publisher, Gordon Soules Book Publishers Ltd. Information on how to obtain maps available from the book's publisher is included on the publisher's web site, www.gordonsoules.com. (Retailers, automobile associations, and tourist information offices can order maps of British Columbia from Gordon Soules Book Publishers Ltd. at wholesale prices; addresses are given on the copyright page of this book.)

MAP 1:
North America

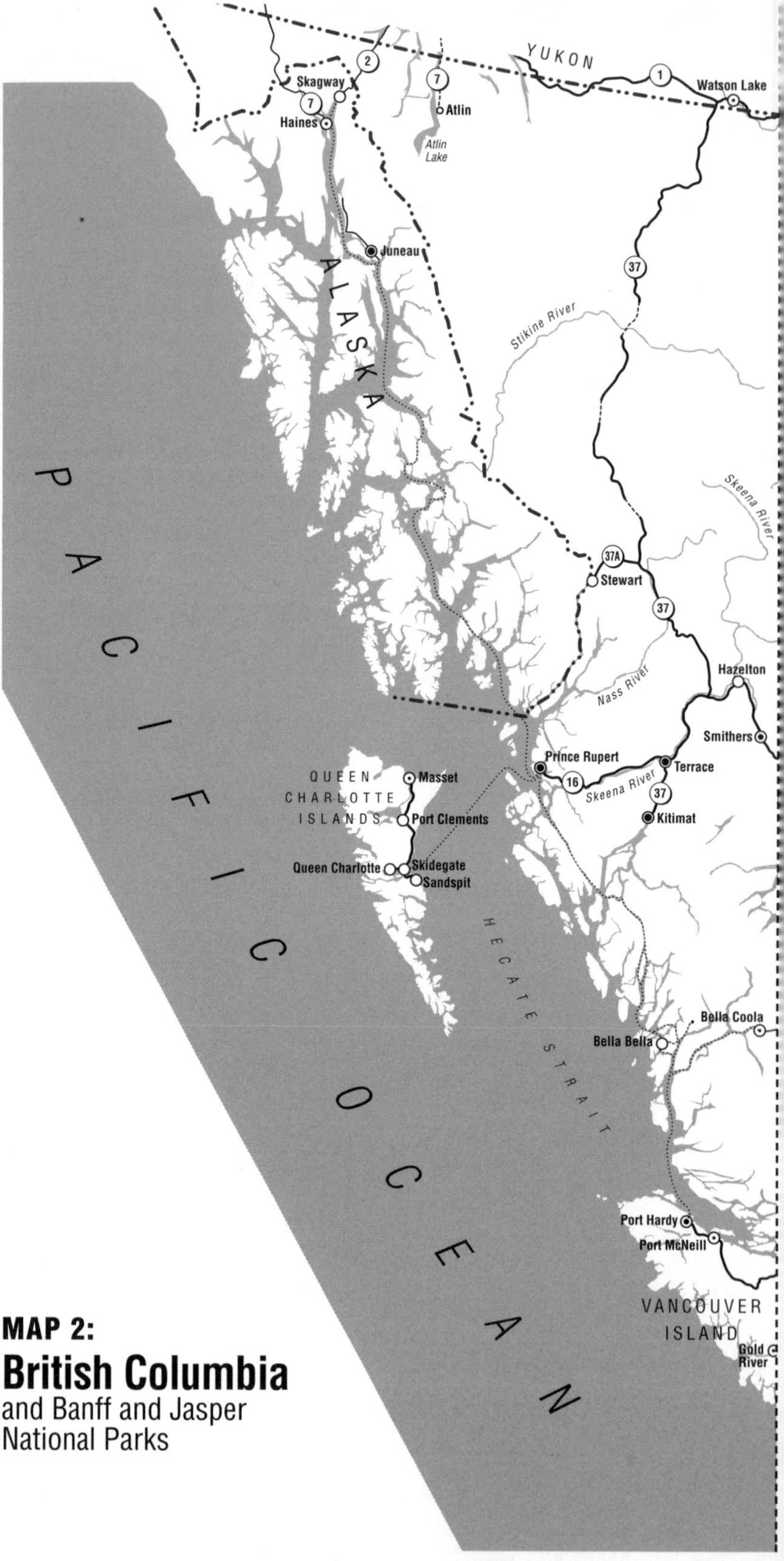
YUKON
Watson Lake
1
2
7
Skagway
7
Haines
Atlin
Atlin Lake
Juneau
ALASKA
37
Stikine River
Skeena River
PACIFIC OCEAN
37A
Stewart
37
Hazelton
Nass River
Smithers
Prince Rupert
Terrace
16
Skeena River
37
Kitimat
QUEEN CHARLOTTE ISLANDS
Masset
Port Clements
Queen Charlotte
Skidegate
Sandspit
HECATE STRAIT
Bella Coola
Bella Bella
Port Hardy
Port McNeill
VANCOUVER ISLAND
Gold River

MAP 2:
British Columbia
and Banff and Jasper
National Parks

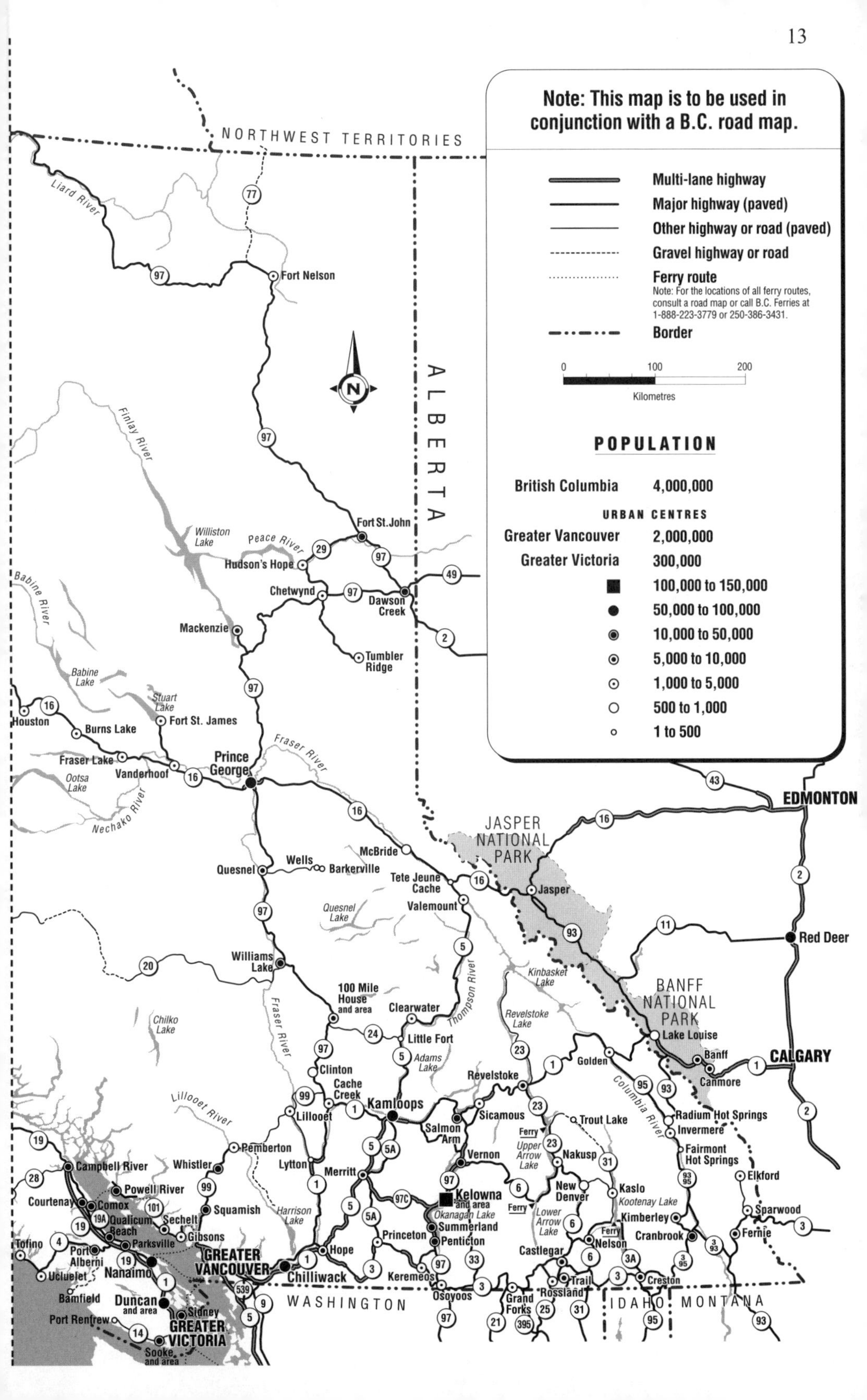
Note: This map is to be used in conjunction with a B.C. road map.
Multi-lane highway
Major highway (paved)
Other highway or road (paved)
Gravel highway or road
Ferry route
Note: For the locations of all ferry routes, consult a road map or call B.C. Ferries at 1-888-223-3779 or 250-386-3431.
Border
0
100
200
Kilometres
POPULATION
British Columbia 4,000,000
URBAN CENTRES
Greater Vancouver 2,000,000
Greater Victoria 300,000
100,000 to 150,000
50,000 to 100,000
10,000 to 50,000
5,000 to 10,000
1,000 to 5,000
500 to 1,000
1 to 500
NORTHWEST TERRITORIES
ALBERTA
WASHINGTON
IDAHO
MONTANA
Liard River
Fort Nelson
Finlay River
Williston Lake
Peace River
Fort St. John
Hudson's Hope
Chetwynd
Dawson Creek
Tumbler Ridge
Mackenzie
Babine River
Babine Lake
Stuart Lake
Fort St. James
Houston
Burns Lake
Fraser Lake
Vanderhoof
Ootsa Lake
Nechako River
Prince George
Fraser River
EDMONTON
JASPER NATIONAL PARK
Jasper
McBride
Wells
Barkerville
Quesnel
Tete Jeune Cache
Valemount
Quesnel Lake
Red Deer
Williams Lake
Kinbasket Lake
BANFF NATIONAL PARK
Lake Louise
Banff
Canmore
CALGARY
100 Mile House and area
Clearwater
Thompson River
Chilko Lake
Revelstoke Lake
Little Fort
Adams Lake
Golden
Columbia River
Clinton
Cache Creek
Revelstoke
Lillooet River
Lillooet
Kamloops
Sicamous
Salmon Arm
Trout Lake
Radium Hot Springs
Invermere
Fairmont Hot Springs
Ferry
Upper Arrow Lake
Nakusp
Pemberton
Lytton
Merritt
Vernon
Whistler
Campbell River
Powell River
Comox
Courtenay
Qualicum Beach
Squamish
Sechelt
Gibsons
Parksville
Harrison Lake
Kelowna and area
Okanagan Lake
Summerland
Penticton
Princeton
New Denver
Kaslo
Kootenay Lake
Lower Arrow Lake
Kimberley
Cranbrook
Elkford
Sparwood
Fernie
Castlegar
Nelson
Tofino
Port Alberni
Nanaimo
Ucluelet
Bamfield
Duncan and area
GREATER VANCOUVER
Hope
Chilliwack
Keremeos
Osoyoos
Grand Forks
Rossland
Trail
Creston
Sidney
GREATER VICTORIA
Port Renfrew
Sooke and area

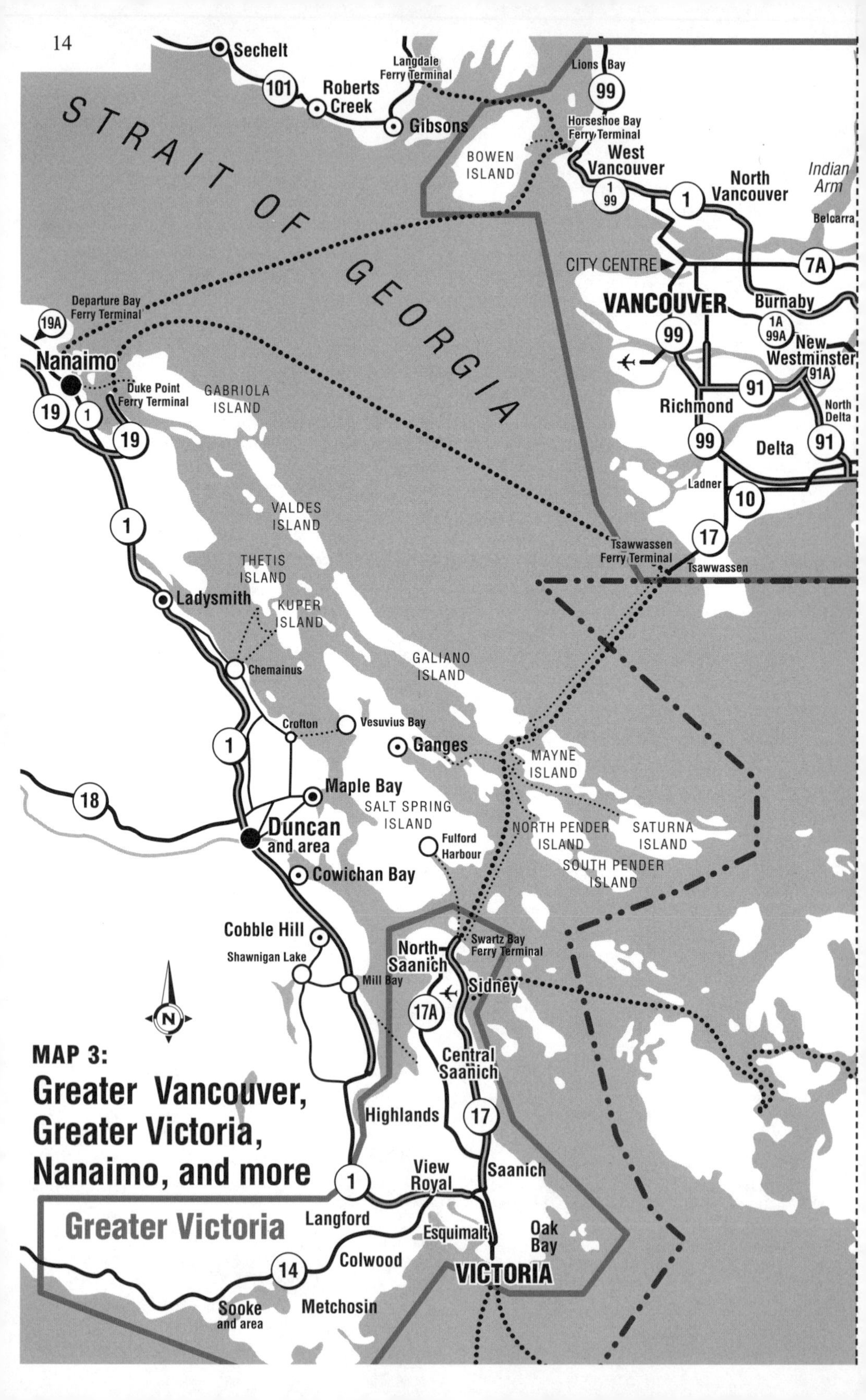

MAP 3:
Greater Vancouver, Greater Victoria, Nanaimo, and more

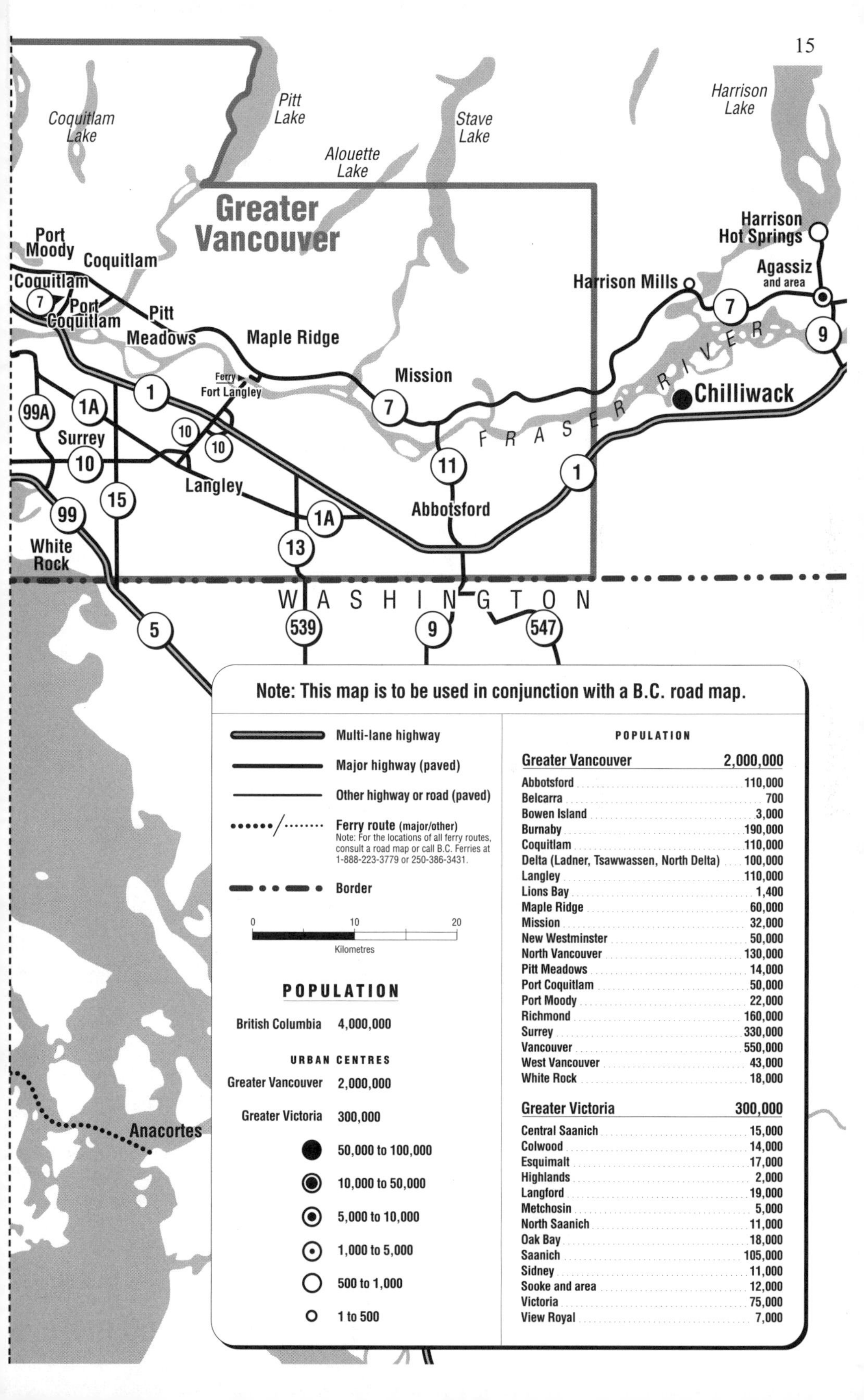
Coquitlam Lake
Pitt Lake
Alouette Lake
Stave Lake
Harrison Lake
Greater Vancouver
Port Moody
Coquitlam
Coquitlam
Port Coquitlam
Pitt Meadows
Maple Ridge
Mission
Harrison Hot Springs
Harrison Mills
Agassiz and area
Ferry
Fort Langley
Chilliwack
FRASER RIVER
Surrey
Langley
Abbotsford
White Rock
WASHINGTON
Anacortes
7
1
1A
99A
10
15
99
13
11
9
5
539
547
Note: This map is to be used in conjunction with a B.C. road map.
Multi-lane highway
Major highway (paved)
Other highway or road (paved)
Ferry route (major/other)
Note: For the locations of all ferry routes, consult a road map or call B.C. Ferries at 1-888-223-3779 or 250-386-3431.
Border
0
10
20
Kilometres
POPULATION
British Columbia 4,000,000
URBAN CENTRES
Greater Vancouver 2,000,000
Greater Victoria 300,000
50,000 to 100,000
10,000 to 50,000
5,000 to 10,000
1,000 to 5,000
500 to 1,000
1 to 500
POPULATION
Greater Vancouver 2,000,000
Abbotsford 110,000
Belcarra 700
Bowen Island 3,000
Burnaby 190,000
Coquitlam 110,000
Delta (Ladner, Tsawwassen, North Delta) 100,000
Langley 110,000
Lions Bay 1,400
Maple Ridge 60,000
Mission 32,000
New Westminster 50,000
North Vancouver 130,000
Pitt Meadows 14,000
Port Coquitlam 50,000
Port Moody 22,000
Richmond 160,000
Surrey 330,000
Vancouver 550,000
West Vancouver 43,000
White Rock 18,000
Greater Victoria 300,000
Central Saanich 15,000
Colwood 14,000
Esquimalt 17,000
Highlands 2,000
Langford 19,000
Metchosin 5,000
North Saanich 11,000
Oak Bay 18,000
Saanich 105,000
Sidney 11,000
Sooke and area 12,000
Victoria 75,000
View Royal 7,000

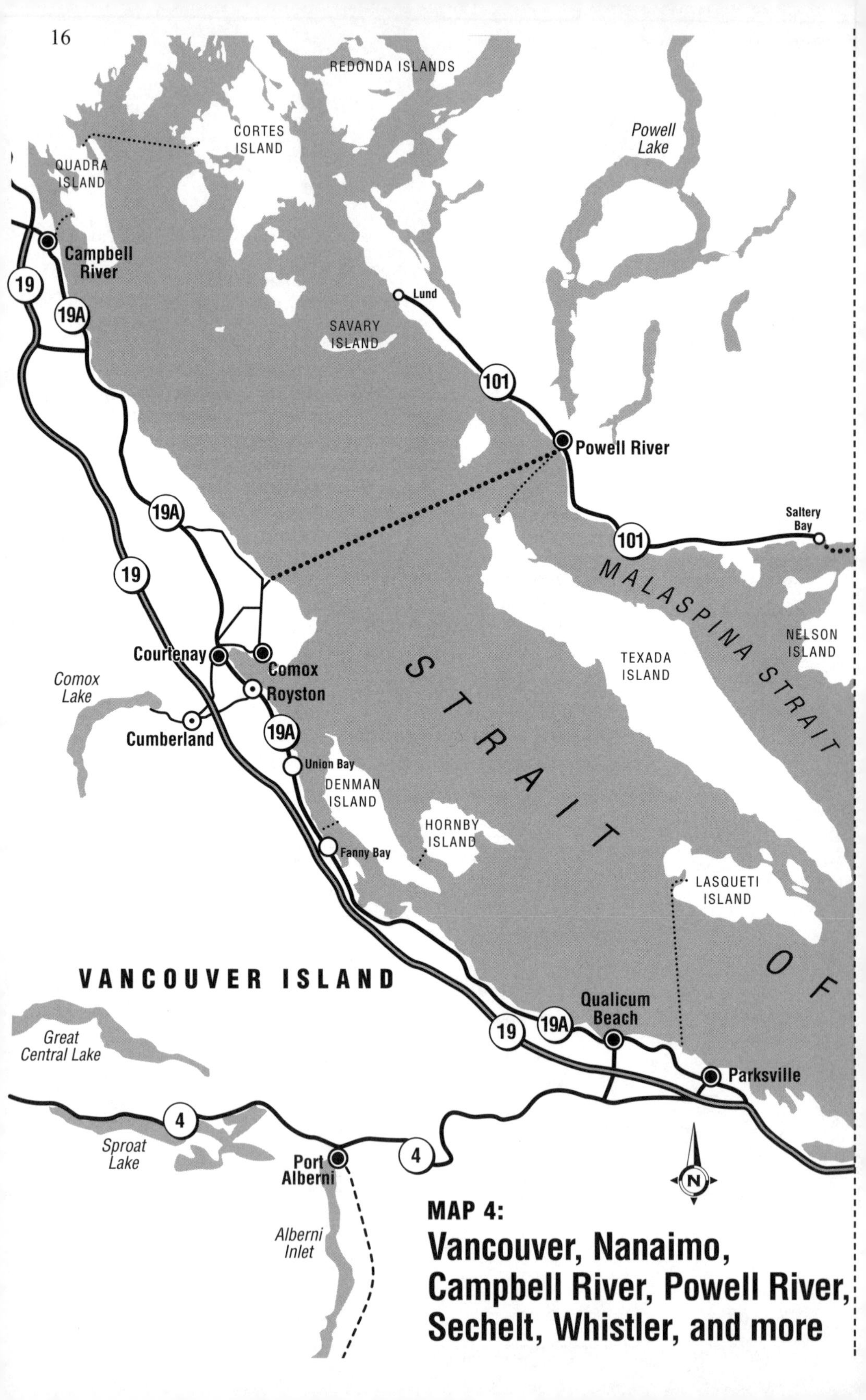

MAP 4:
Vancouver, Nanaimo, Campbell River, Powell River, Sechelt, Whistler, and more

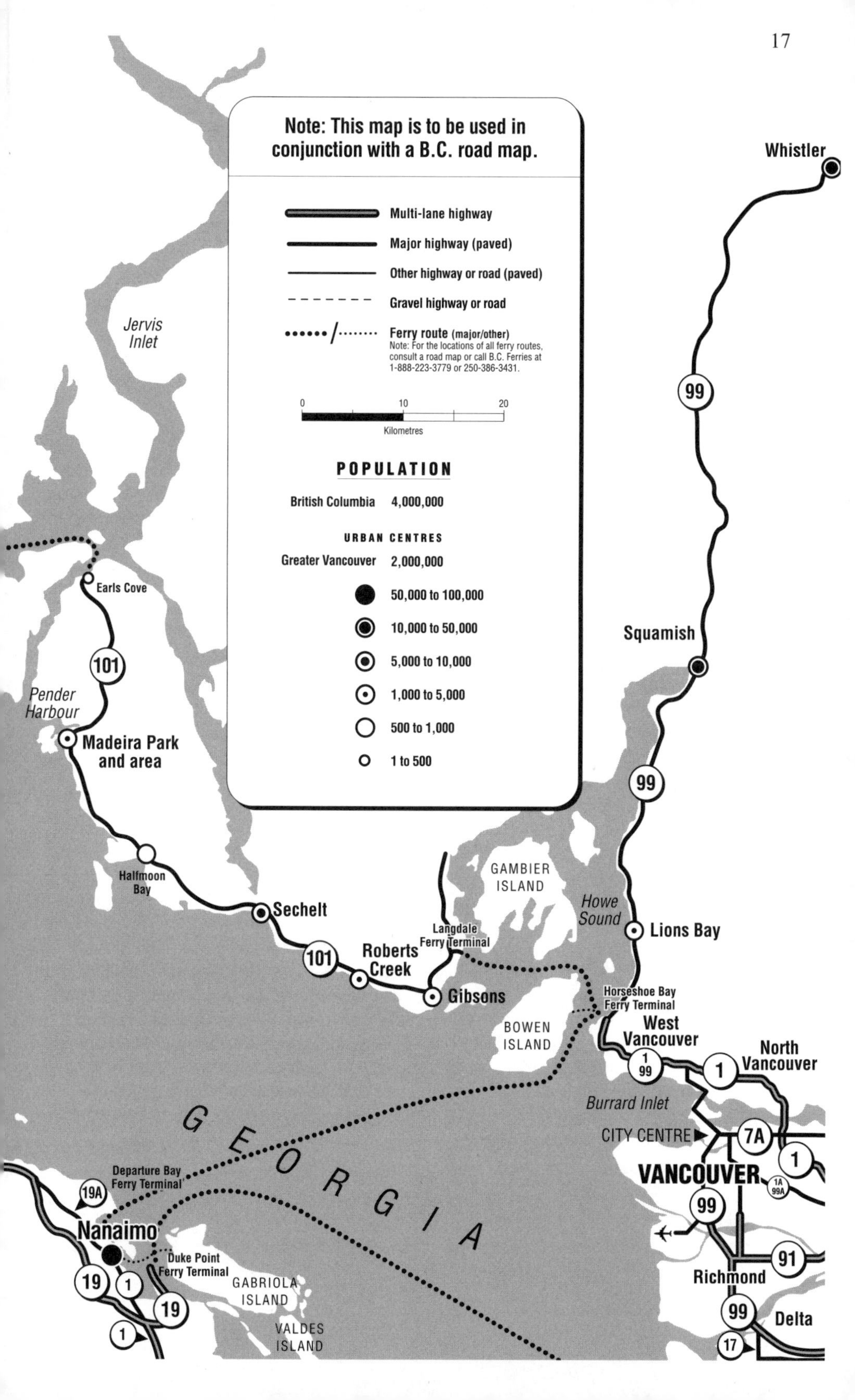

Note: This map is to be used in conjunction with a B.C. road map.
Multi-lane highway
Major highway (paved)
Other highway or road (paved)
Gravel highway or road
Ferry route (major/other)
Note: For the locations of all ferry routes, consult a road map or call B.C. Ferries at 1-888-223-3779 or 250-386-3431.
0
10
20
Kilometres
POPULATION
British Columbia 4,000,000
URBAN CENTRES
Greater Vancouver 2,000,000
50,000 to 100,000
10,000 to 50,000
5,000 to 10,000
1,000 to 5,000
500 to 1,000
1 to 500
Whistler
99
Jervis Inlet
Earls Cove
101
Pender Harbour
Madeira Park and area
Squamish
99
Halfmoon Bay
GAMBIER ISLAND
Howe Sound
Sechelt
Langdale Ferry Terminal
Lions Bay
101
Roberts Creek
Gibsons
Horseshoe Bay Ferry Terminal
BOWEN ISLAND
West Vancouver
North Vancouver
1 99
1
Burrard Inlet
CITY CENTRE
7A
1
GEORGIA
Departure Bay Ferry Terminal
19A
VANCOUVER
1A 99A
99
Nanaimo
91
Duke Point Ferry Terminal
Richmond
19
1
GABRIOLA ISLAND
19
99
Delta
1
VALDES ISLAND
17

Canada-West Accommodations B&B Registry

Ellison Massey
Mail: Box 86607
North Vancouver, BC V7L 4L2
(604) 990-6730 fax: (604) 990-5876
toll-free from within North America, for reservations: 1-800-561-3223
email: ellison@b-b.com
web site: www.b-b.com

• One person $50–85; two people $85–125.

• A B&B reservation service covering British Columbia and Alberta, including Greater Vancouver, Victoria, Vancouver Island, Whistler, the Okanagan, Prince George, and Prince Rupert in British Columbia and Jasper, Banff, and Calgary in Alberta. The B&Bs have one to three rooms; ensuite and private bathrooms; and full breakfasts. Most B&Bs are within fifteen to twenty minutes of city centres and are near shops, restaurants, and attractions. Weekly rates may be arranged. Credit card payment required to hold reservation. Cancellation notice seven days. Visa, MasterCard, American Express. **In the agents' own words:** "Travellers planning to visit many locations within British Columbia and Alberta will be pleased with our convenient, one-stop service plan and the hospitality offered by our personally chosen B&Bs. We extend an invitation to call on us to assist you with your travel plans."

Garden City B&B Reservation Service

Doreen Wensley
660 Jones Terrace
Victoria, BC V8Z 2L7
(250) 479-1986 fax: (250) 479-9999
email: gardencity@bc-bed-breakfast.com
web site: www.bc-bed-breakfast.com

• One person $45–75; two people $55–125. King-sized beds, queen-sized beds, and double beds. Additional person from $15. Child from $5.

• A B&B reservation service covering Victoria, Vancouver Island, and Gulf Island locations. Cottages and houses with ocean views, antiques, hot tubs, and swimming pools. All accommodations are inspected and are selected with attention to cleanliness, hospitality, and breakfasts. Many welcome families with children. Full descriptions are given over the phone or detailed brochures are mailed on request. No booking fees. Office is open Monday to Saturday from 8:00 a.m. to 9:00 p.m. and Sunday from 2:00 to 9:00 p.m. Visa, MasterCard, American Express. **In the agents' own words:** "We are pleased to offer country comfort and magnificent ocean views in a range of accommodations from rustic cottages to regal heritage houses. Our reservation service has been family owned since 1985. Your requirements are given caring, careful attention to ensure your satisfaction."

Old English B&B Registry

Vicki Tyndall
1226 Silverwood Crescent
North Vancouver, BC V7P 1J3
(604) 986-5069 fax: (604) 986-8810
email: sarahb@oldenglishbandb.bc.ca
web site: www.oldenglishbandb.bc.ca

• Rooms: Two people $85–225. Rate for one person is usually $10–20 less.
Minimum stay two nights on holiday weekends.
• A B&B reservation service covering Vancouver, North Vancouver, and West Vancouver. The B&Bs are within twenty minutes of the city centre. Visa or MasterCard required to hold reservation. Cancellation notice fourteen days. **In the agents' own words:** "All our B&Bs have been personally inspected with attention to cleanliness, ambience, and hospitality. Since 1985, we have been providing fast, reliable, informative service. Many of our clients return again and again. We would be delighted to assist you with your accommodation reservations. Don't waste time, when one call to us will do it all."

Reservations Jasper Ltd.

Debbie Taylor
Mail: Box 1840
Jasper, AB T0E 1E0
(780) 852-5488 fax: (780) 852-5489
email: resjas@incentre.net

• A reservation service covering Jasper, Banff, Lake Louise, Canmore, Edmonton, Calgary, and Mount Robson. B&Bs, in-house accommodation without breakfast, hotels, motels, cabins, and bungalows. Booking fee of $20 for one destination and $5 for each additional destination. Additional $5 fee for overseas clients. Visa. Non-commissionable. **In the agents' own words:** "We offer a fast, reliable, and informative service for our clients. You need only make one call for your Canadian Rockies vacation accommodations."

Town and Country B&B Reservation Service

Helen Burich
Mail: Box 74542
2803 West Fourth Avenue
Vancouver, BC V6K 1K2
(604) 731-5942 fax: (604) 731-5942
web site: www.townandcountrybedand breakfast.com

• One person $55–95; two people $85–190. Queen-sized beds, double beds, and twin beds. Private and shared bathrooms.

• A B&B reservation service covering Vancouver, Victoria, and Vancouver Island. Bookings for other areas in BC and the Banff/Jasper area for guests who are making reservations for Vancouver, Victoria, and/or Vancouver Island. B&Bs range from modest to luxurious. Character houses to contemporary. Most B&Bs in residential areas are within twenty minutes of city centres and within walking distance of neighbourhood shops, restaurants, and parks. Some self-contained units and cottages. Personally selected and inspected. Deposit required. Cancellation notice seven days. **In the agents' own words:** "Our service has been established since 1980. We know our hosts and houses personally and do our best to meet your requirements according to facilities and availability."

The Denniston by the Sea B&B

Drew and Rosemary Denniston
430 Grafton Street
Victoria, BC V9A 6S3
(250) 385-5195 or (250) 385-1962 fax: (250) 385-5100
toll-free from within North America: 1-888-796-2699
email: denniston@pacificcoast.net
web sites: www.bbcanada.com/1011.html
www.denniston.net

• From the Victoria airport, the Anancortes ferry, or the Swartz Bay ferry terminal, go south on Highway 17. Take the McKenzie Avenue exit and turn right onto McKenzie Avenue, which becomes Admirals Road. Turn right onto Esquimalt Road and left onto Grafton Street.
From Victoria's Inner Harbour, take Wharf Street to Johnson Street. Turn left onto Johnson Street and continue over the blue bridge. Johnson Street becomes Esquimalt Road after the bridge. Continue on Esquimalt Road and turn left onto Grafton Street.

• Three rooms and a suite: In summer, two people $95–125. In winter, two people $85–115. King-sized bed; queen-sized bed; double bed; twin beds. Each room has an additional twin bed, day bed, or hide-a-bed. Ensuite bathrooms.
Additional person $20.

• An early 1900s Tudor-style house on a hill with a view of the ocean and the Olympic Mountains. Seven minutes' drive from downtown and the Inner Harbour. Near transit to downtown, the Empress Hotel, ferries, the airport, and the University of Victoria. Above a waterfront walkway from which birds, marine life, ferries, and ocean-going ships can be seen. Guest living room with wood-burning fireplace has a view of the Juan de Fuca Straight. Guest rooms have TVs, coffee, and tea. Daily housekeeping. One of the hosts is from Hawaii, and the other host is a third-generation Victoria resident. Deposit required to hold reservation. Cancellation notice five days. Check-in 4:30 to 6:00 p.m. or by arrangement; check-out until 11:00 a.m. Credit cards for reservations only. No pets. Smoking in designated outdoor areas. **In the hosts' own words:** "We invite you to enjoy and rejuvenate in the peace and quiet of a serene, relaxing atmosphere—picturesque views in many directions will nurture your spirit."

The Gatsby Mansion

Rita Roy-Wilson
309 Belleville Street
Victoria, BC V8V 1X2
(250) 388-9191 fax: (250) 920-5651
toll-free from within North America, for reservations: 1-800-563-9656
email: huntingdon@bctravel.com
web site: www.bctravel.com/huntingdon/gatsby.html

• At Belleville and Oswego streets, one and a half blocks west of the Parliament Buildings.

• Twenty suites: One person \$85–329; two people \$95–329. King-sized bed; queen-sized bed; double bed; twin beds. Ensuite bathrooms. Additional person \$25. Off-season rates.
Romance, wedding, honeymoon, whale-watching, and golf packages.

• A restored Queen Anne–style mansion built in 1897 and a smaller house, both of which have views of the ocean, five minutes' walk from downtown, shopping, parks, and museums and one and a half blocks from the Parliament Buildings. Main house has antiques, frescoed ceilings, stained glass windows, mahogany panelling, and a large veranda with a view of the Inner Harbour. Rose and other flower gardens. Many of the guest suites have views of the harbour. Guest suites have TVs, movies, video games, and coffeemakers. Some of the suites have sofa beds. Fine dining restaurant that serves West Coast cuisine. Aromatherapy studio, gift shop, and currency exchange. Near golf courses. Across the street from the ferry terminals for the Clipper ferry, a passenger ferry that runs between Victoria and Seattle, and the Coho ferry, a passenger and vehicle ferry that runs between Victoria and Port Angeles. Full breakfast. Credit cards. No pets. Smoke-free environment. **In the hosts' own words:** "Our antiques, hand-painted ceilings, delicate stained glass windows, and mahogany panelling evoke a time of extravagance and prosperity; the fine dining restaurant completes the setting. Step back to a time when life was less complicated and pleasures were found at home."

Andersen House B&B

Janet and Max Andersen
301 Kingston Street
Victoria, BC V8V 1V5
(250) 388-4565 fax: (250) 388-4563
email: andersen@islandnet.com
web site: www.andersenhouse.com

• At Kingston and Pendray streets, one and a half blocks west of the Parliament Buildings.

• Four suites in a house and one suite in a classic motor yacht: In summer (May to mid-October), two people $195–250. In winter (mid-October to April), two people $95–145. Queen-sized bed; king-sized bed and twin beds; queen-sized bed and a bed narrower than a twin bed; double bed. Ensuite bathrooms; on the yacht, a shower and two washrooms with toilets and washbasins.

• A Victorian house built for a sea captain in 1891, with twelve-foot-high ceilings, stained glass windows, fireplaces, hardwood floors, and a garden with mature shrubs, fruit trees, and flowers. Three blocks from ferry and floatplane terminals. Antiques, original modern paintings, Peruvian rugs, and homemade Raku pottery throughout. Suites have private entrances, CD/cassette players, telephones, and books; some have views of mountains, gardens, the Parliament Buildings with passing horse-drawn carriages, or the downtown skyline. One of the suites has an ensuite bathroom with a two-person Jacuzzi tub. A second suite has a claw-foot soaker tub and a bar with sink, microwave, fridge, coffeemaker, and electric kettle. A third suite has an antique four-post bed, a window seat/bed, and French doors that lead to a private deck. Fifty-foot 1927 classic motor yacht is docked at a marina five minutes' walk from the B&B and has a double bed, art deco teak cabinetry, a shower, two bathrooms, a skylight, and views of ships, kayaks, floatplanes, and seals. Full breakfast includes homemade jam. **In the hosts' own words:** "We are ideally located a short walk from Victoria's most popular attractions, and we can ensure that you enjoy the secret Victoria so many visitors miss."

Marketa's B&B

Marketa and Tim Clark
239 Superior Street
Victoria, BC V8V 1T4
(250) 384-9844 fax: (250) 384-9848
email: info@marketas.victoria.bc.ca
web site: www.marketas.victoria.bc.ca

• Rooms: Two people $65–95. Queen-sized bed; twin beds. Private and shared bathrooms. Cribs and cots available.
Off-season rates. Carriage ride $50.

• A 1912 house in the James Bay area of Victoria, within walking distance of the Parliament Buildings, the Royal British Columbia Museum, the Inner Harbour, restaurants, shops, theatres, Dallas Road waterfront, Beacon Hill Park, a bus terminal, and a ferry terminal with ferries to the U.S. Deck with flowers. Parking behind the house. Full breakfast is served in the dining room, or, for a fee and with advance notice, is packed in a basket for guests to eat while they ride in a horse-drawn carriage. Cancellation notice three days. Check-in until 3:00 p.m. or by arrangement. **In the hosts' own words:** "Our home is your home. We do our best to help you get to know our beautiful city while staying in our affordable, centrally located B&B."

Medana Grove B&B

Noreen and Garry Hunt
162 Medana Street
Victoria, BC V8V 2H5
(250) 389-0437 fax: (250) 389-0425
toll-free from within North America: 1-800-269-1188
email: medanagrove@home.com
web site: www.medanagrove.com

• From Belleville Street at the Inner Harbour, go south on Menzies Street for three blocks. Turn left onto Simcoe and take the first right onto Medana.

• Three rooms: Two people $110–135. King-sized bed and roll-away cot; double bed and one twin bed; queen-sized bed. Ensuite bathrooms. Additional person $25.
Off-season rates.

• A traditionally decorated 1908 house with antiques, in a residential neighbourhood near downtown. Around the corner from shops, restaurants, and services. Guest living room on the main floor with TV and local guidebooks and tourist publications. Full breakfast is served on an oak table in the dining room. Diets accommodated with advance notice. Visa, MasterCard. No pets. Smoke-free environment. **In the hosts' own words:** "Our B&B is reminiscent of a traditional English B&B and is within easy walking distance of the Inner Harbour ferry terminals, downtown Victoria, Beacon Hill Park, and the ocean. We are helpful but not intrusive. Experience our genuine Irish hospitality and guest rooms that are comfortable and tastefully decorated."

Battery Street Guest House

Pamela Verduyn
670 Battery Street
Victoria, BC V8V 1E5
(250) 385-4632
web site: www.bbcanada.com/340.html

- Near Battery and Douglas Streets.
- Four rooms: $65–105. Queen-sized bed; two double beds; queen-sized bed and one twin bed. Additional person $20.
- An 1898 house on a quiet street, within walking distance of downtown, the Inner Harbour, the Royal British Columbia Museum, and the Empress Hotel. One block from Beacon Hill Park and the ocean. Two of the guest rooms have views of the ocean. Full breakfast, including a hot entrée, homemade baked goods, fresh-squeezed juice, cheese, whole wheat bread, coffee, and tea, is served between 7:00 and 9:00 a.m. Children welcome. Cat in hosts' quarters in the attic. Cheques, traveller's cheques. Dutch spoken. Nonsmoking. **In the hosts' own words:** "Our comfortable, established heritage guest house is centrally located in a quiet, peaceful area."

The Henderson House

Cliff Whitehead
522 Quadra Street
Victoria, BC V8V 3S3
(250) 384-3428
email: henderson@coastnet.com
web site: www.coastnet.com/~henderson

• Three rooms: $85–135. Queen-sized bed. Ensuite bathrooms. Additional person $40.

• An 1897 Queen Anne–style house, within walking distance of downtown and ferry terminals. One block from Beacon Hill Park. Two blocks from the Inner Harbour, the Royal British Columbia Museum, and the Empress Hotel. In the area are the Butchart Gardens, art galleries, antique shops, whale watching, and golf. Guest rooms have a Jacuzzi, a soaking tub, a shower, a TV, and/or a fridge. Garden. Full breakfast, with a choice of traditional dishes, is served between 7:30 and 9:00 a.m. Visa, MasterCard. **In the hosts' own words:** "At our B&B, the service is good and the atmosphere is friendly. Our rooms are suitable for special occasions—especially honeymoons and anniversaries."

Humboldt House B&B

Mila Werbik and David and Vlasta Booth
867 Humboldt Street
Victoria, BC V8V 2Z6
(250) 383-0152 fax: (250) 383-6402
toll-free from within North America: 1-888-383-0327
email: rooms@humboldthouse.com
web site: www.humboldthouse.com

• In downtown Victoria, on Humboldt Street at Quadra.

• Five rooms: One person or two people $140–315. Queen-sized bed. Ensuite bathrooms.
Honeymoon and celebration packages available.

• An 1895 Victorian house on a quiet, tree-lined street, with guest rooms that have fireplaces and Jacuzzi tubs. One block from Beacon Hill Park. Three blocks from the Inner Harbour and the Royal British Columbia Museum. Guest rooms have down duvets, CD players, and flowers. Sitting room with fireplace, books, and telephone. Sherry and baked goods are served in the library in the afternoon. Full breakfast with champagne is delivered to guest rooms. Cash, Visa, MasterCard. Not suitable for children. No pets. Nonsmoking. **In the hosts' own words:** "Our B&B is a perfect choice for honeymoons, anniversaries, and retreats. Enjoy Victorian luxury, just steps from the heart of downtown."

Beaconsfield Inn

Con and Judi Sollid
998 Humboldt Street
Victoria, BC V8V 2Z8
(250) 384-4044 fax: (250) 384-4052
toll-free from within North America: 1-888-884-4044
email: beaconsfield@islandnet.com
web site: www.islandnet.com/beaconsfield/

- At the corner of Vancouver and Humboldt streets.
- Rooms, suites, and cottage.

Six rooms and three suites: One person or two people $200–350. Queen-sized bed. Ensuite bathrooms. Additional person $65. Off-season rates.
Self-contained cottage: Two people $395. King-sized bed. Ensuite bathroom.
Minimum stay two nights.

- A 1905 English-style manor in a residential area, one block from Beacon Hill Park's 120 acres and four blocks from the Inner Harbour, downtown shops, galleries, and restaurants. Sixteen-foot beamed ceilings and mahogany floors. Ten minutes from downtown. Guest rooms and suites have down comforters, canopied feather beds, antiques, and flowers. Most of the guest rooms and suites have fireplaces, Jacuzzi tubs, and stained glass windows. Sun room with a view of an English cottage–style front garden. Oceanfront cottage has king-sized pine sleigh beds, a two-person Jacuzzi tub, a kitchen, and a sitting room with fireplace, TV, and VCR. Beach is twelve metres from garden patio. Afternoon tea and sherry served by a fireplace in the library. Full breakfast is served in the dining room. Visa, MasterCard. Cancellation notice seven days. Full payment required to hold reservation. No children. No pets. No smoking. **In the hosts' own words:** "We offer fine service and luxury for discerning travellers. The style of our inn attracts many people celebrating special occasions."

Abigail's Hotel

Frauke and Daniel Behune
906 McClure Street
Victoria, BC V8V 3E7
(250) 388-5363 fax: (250) 388-7787
toll-free from within North America: 1-800-561-6565
email: innkeeper@abigailshotel.com
web site: www.abigailshotel.com

• At the corner of Quadra and McClure streets. From Vancouver Street, turn onto McClure Street.
• Twenty-two rooms: One person or two people $199–329. Ensuite bathrooms. Celebration and honeymoon packages. Off-season rates.
• A European-style inn with a garden, in a residential area, three blocks from downtown and the Inner Harbour. Guest rooms have antique furniture, telephones, robes, hair dryers, down duvets and pillows, and flowers. Some guest rooms have fireplaces, sitting areas, Jacuzzis or soaker tubs, and four-post beds. In the evening, hors d'oeuvres and beverages are served in the library. Full breakfast is served in the dining room or on the patio. Cash, Visa, MasterCard, American Express. German spoken. No children under ten. No pets. No smoking. **In the hosts' own words:** "We greet you with smiling faces at our Tudor-style mansion, which has been lovingly restored. Charm, comfort, and sophistication make staying at our heritage inn a quality experience."

Prior House B&B Inn

Candis Cooperrider and Julie Usher
620 St. Charles Street
Victoria, BC V8S 3N7
(250) 592-8847 (250) 592-8223
toll-free from within North America: 1-877-924-3300
email: innkeeper@priorhouse.com
web site: www.priorhouse.com

- Ten blocks from the Inner Harbour.
- Five rooms and three one-bedroom or two-bedroom suites: One person or two people $145–275. King-sized bed; queen-sized bed. Private bathrooms. Additional person $45. Off-season rates and packages October to June.
- A house built in 1912 as the private residence of E.G. Prior, lieutenant governor of British Columbia. Fireplaces, chandeliers, oak floors, and oak-panelled walls. Within walking distance of Government House, Craigdarroch Castle, an art gallery, Victoria's antique row, and ocean beaches. Five minutes' drive from the Inner Harbour. Afternoon tea is served between 4:00 and 6:00 p.m. by a fireplace in the library, in a sitting room, or on a stone deck that has a view of landscaped gardens. Suites and rooms have down duvets, antiques, and views of the gardens. Some rooms have fireplaces, spa tubs, and views of the ocean and the Olympic Mountains. Robes. Full breakfast. Cancellation notice fourteen days. Check-in 4:00 to 6:00 p.m. or by arrangement; check-out until 11:00 a.m. Visa, MasterCard. Smoking outdoors. **In the hosts' own words:** "We delight in taking care of our guests and making sure that your vacation is everything you hoped for and more."

Beacon Hill

Sherrin Pryce
608 Trutch Street
Victoria, BC V8V 4C5
(250) 388-4485 fax: (250) 381-4401
email: bhbb@home.com
web site: www.bhbb.net

• One block east of Cook Street. The B&B is the third house from the corner of Richardson and Trutch.
• Four rooms: $85–100. Additional person $30. Child $20.
• An 1908 Edwardian house on a quiet, tree-lined street, with antiques, stained glass windows, and three wood-burning fireplaces. Fifteen minutes' walk from Beacon Hill Park, ocean beaches, and downtown. Six blocks from the Inner Harbour and the Empress Hotel. Ten minutes' walk from the lieutenant governor's official residence. Sun room. Down duvets. Full breakfast is served on fine bone china in the dining room. **In the hosts' own words:** "Our B&B is centrally located on a quiet street of well-maintained historical houses. All of our lovely rooms are exquisitely furnished with antiques, and you can be assured of a restful sleep on comfortable beds."

Dogwood Manor

Anne-Marie and Haji Dawood
1124 Fairfield Road
Victoria, BC V8V 3A7
(250) 361-4441 fax: (250) 382-1618
toll-free from within North America: 1-888-309-9706
email: dogwoodmnr@coastnet.com
web site: www.coastnet.com/home/dogwoodmnr/

• Between Cook and Trutch streets.

• Eight suites: One person $75–105; two people $95–155. Queen-sized bed and sofa bed. Ensuite bathrooms. Breakfast ingredients supplied. Additional person $20–30. Child under 13 $20. Off-season rates October to May. Extended stay rates in winter.

• A 1910 house with a garden, six blocks from the Empress Hotel and the Inner Harbour and two blocks from Beacon Hill Park. Suites have private entrances, kitchens, TVs, and telephones. Some of the suites have fireplaces. Coin laundry. Suites are supplied with ingredients for Continental breakfast. Reservations recommended. Deposit of one night's rate required to hold reservation. Cancellation notice three days. Check-in 1:00 to 6:00 p.m. or by arrangement; check-out until 11:00 a.m. Visa, MasterCard. French, German, and Spanish spoken. No pets. No smoking. **In the hosts' own words:** "We offer our house as your home away from home."

Marion's B&B

Thomas and Marion Simms
1730 Taylor Street
Victoria, BC V8R 3E9
(250) 592-3070

• Five minutes from downtown Victoria. From the Victoria airport or the Swartz Bay ferry terminal, take the Patricia Bay Highway, which becomes Blanshard Street. Turn left onto Hillside Avenue. Turn right onto Shelbourne Street and take the first left onto Myrtle, which becomes Taylor. The B&B is the fifth house on the left.

• Three rooms: One person $35–40; two people $50–60. Queen-sized bed; double bed. Shared guest bathroom and shared bathroom. Additional person $20. Child $10.

• A B&B on a quiet street, five minutes from downtown. Breakfast is served in a dining room that has a view of a field that was originally part of Victoria's first airport, with Mount Tolmie in the distance. Living room with a view of the Olympic Mountains. Beds with comforters, percale sheets, and homemade quilts. Full breakfast is served on bone china with silver cutlery. Reservations recommended. Cancellation notice two days. Cash, traveller's cheques. Smoking outdoors. **In the hosts' own words:** "We offer home accommodation with a friendly atmosphere."

Chez Raymonde

Raymonde Lortie
1762 Midgard Avenue
Victoria, BC V8P 2Y7
(250) 472-1768
email: chezraymonde@home.com

• Two rooms: One person $65; two people $95. Queen-sized bed; twin beds. Shared bathrooms. Additional person $20. Roll-away beds and playpen available.

• A quiet split-level house with large trees in the university district of Victoria, half a block from the University of Victoria. Close to shopping centres, bus route, and beach. Fifteen minutes from downtown. Guest lounge with TV. Sun deck and large backyard. Parking. French cuisine is served on silver tableware. Visa, MasterCard. French spoken. Children welcome. A nonsmoking house. **In the hosts' own words:** "We are renowned for the quality of our food; many guests book for one night and stay for more. Come see us soon. You will not be disappointed."

Seabird House B&B

Ilima Szabo
1 Midwood Road
Victoria, BC V9B 1L4
(250) 479-2930 fax: (250) 744-2998
web site: www.travelguides.com/inns/full/B.C./18937.html

• Ten minutes from downtown. From Highway 1, take exit 8. Turn left onto Helmcken. Turn left onto Midwood. Alternatively, from Highway 1A, turn right onto Helmcken, and turn right onto Midwood.

• Two rooms: In summer (June to September), one person $60–70, two people $65–75. In winter (October to May), one person $50–60, two people $55–65. Twin beds (or twin beds side by side with king-sized bedding). Shared guest bathroom. Full breakfast ingredients supplied.
Closed December to February.

• A quiet house on the edge of Portage Inlet, a tidal bird sanctuary connected to the ocean by the Gorge Waterway. Ten minutes from downtown. The second floor, which is one-thousand-square-feet, is for guests. One of the guest rooms has a private deck and a view of the ocean. The other guest room has a partial ocean view. Living room, patio, and garden. Sitting area with TV, fridge, coffee, and tea. Kitchen and laundry facilities available, December to February. Full or Continental breakfast. Cancellation notice three days. Small pets. A nonsmoking house. **In the hosts' own words:** "We offer you a home away from home on scenic Portage Inlet."

Swan Lake Chalet

Alan and Linda Donohue
948 McKenzie Avenue
Victoria, BC V8X 3G5
(250) 744-1233 fax: (250) 744-2510
toll-free: 1-888-345-1233
email: swanlake@pacificcoast.net
web sites: www.bctravel.com/swanlake.html
www.swanlakechalet.net

- Five kilometres from downtown Victoria, near Saanich Road, between Highway 17 and Quadra Street.
- Three rooms: Two people $65–130. Queen-sized bed and double bed; queen-sized bed; double bed. Ensuite and private or shared guest bathrooms. Additional person $25.
- A modern chalet-style house across from Swan Lake nature sanctuary. The nature sanctuary has walking areas and views of the city, ocean, and mountains from Christmas Hill. Within walking distance of the Galloping Goose Trail, a neighbourhood pub, restaurants, shops, and public transit to downtown. The guest room with a queen-sized bed and a double bed has an ensuite bathroom, a sitting room with a TV, and sliding glass doors that lead to a deck. The guest room with a queen-sized bed has an ensuite bathroom and access to the deck through a gallery. The guest room with a double bed has a private or shared guest bathroom with a Jacuzzi tub. Full breakfast, including homemade muffins, homemade preserves and with different entrée choices each day, is served in the dining room, which has antique furnishings. Children welcome. No pets; cat in residence. No smoking.

Bender's B&B

Glenda Bender
4254 Thornhill Crescent
Victoria, BC V8N 3G7
(250) 472-8993 fax: (250) 472-8995

- Eight kilometres from the city centre. From downtown, take Johnson Street east. As Johnson curves north, its name changes to Begbie and then to Shelbourne. Turn east onto Kenmore. At the first right, turn onto Thornhill Crescent.
- Six rooms: Two people $55–65. Two double beds, shared guest bathroom; queen-sized bed, shared guest bathroom; double bed, ensuite bathroom; double bed and one twin bed, shared guest bathroom; double bed and one twin bed, ensuite bathroom. Additional person $25.
- A B&B with six guest rooms, eight kilometres from the city centre. Two minutes' walk from a bus stop. Two of the guest rooms have TVs and ensuite bathrooms. Living room, deck, and guest family room. Full breakfast is served in a solarium before 10:00 a.m. Check-in by 10:00 p.m.; check-out until 10:00 a.m. Children welcome. No smoking. **In the hosts' own words:** "A friendly atmosphere."

Eagle's Nest B&B

Pat and Kathy McGuire
4769 Cordova Bay Road
Victoria, BC V8Y 2J7
(250) 658-2002 fax: (250) 658-0135
toll-free: 1-877-658-2002
email: eagle@islandnet.com
web site: www.victoriabc.com/accom/eagles.htm

• Fifteen minutes from downtown Victoria. From the Victoria airport or the Swartz Bay ferry terminal. Highway 17 (Patricia Bay Highway), take the exit for Royal Oak Drive, turn left at the stop sign, and cross over an overpass. Continue on Royal Oak Drive to the intersection of Blenkinsop Road and Cordova Bay Road. Turn left onto Cordova Bay Road, continue for half a kilometre, and turn right into the B&B's driveway.

• Two rooms and one self-contained suite: Two people $75–125. King-sized bed, ensuite bathroom; queen-sized bed and sofa bed, private bathroom.
Use of kitchen facilities in the suite $15. Additional person $15. Weekly and seasonal rates.
Honeymoon packages.

• A new house with a deck and ocean views, five minutes' walk from beachcombing by the ocean. Six kilometres from Cordova Bay. Five minutes' drive from three golf courses, the Commonwealth Games pool, and a shopping centre. A few minutes from downtown, the Butchart Gardens, the Victoria airport, and the University of Victoria. Near Mount Douglas Park, which has more than five hundred acres for walking and hiking. Deer, raccoons, and squirrels can be seen on the property. On bus route. Most beds have duvets. One of the guest rooms has a king-sized bed and an ensuite bathroom with Jacuzzi. Self-contained suite has kitchen facilities, a TV, a private deck with a view of the ocean, and a private entrance. Use of kitchen facilities in self-contained suite for an additional fee. Coffee available in the sun room. Full breakfast is served between 7:30 and 9:00 a.m. Most diets are accommodated. Reservations recommended. Cancellation notice seven days. Check-in 3:00 to 6:00 p.m. or by arrangement; check-out until 10:30 a.m. Cash, cheques, Visa, MasterCard, American Express. Children welcome. No pets. Smoking on the deck. **In the hosts' own words:** "We offer luxury, modern accomodation at an affordable price. Our home is truly your home away from home."

Iris Garden Country Manor B&B

Dave and Sharon Layzell
5360 West Saanich Road
Victoria, BC V9E 1J8
(250) 744-2253 fax: (250) 744-5690
for reservations: 1-877-744-2253
email: irisgarden@home.com
web site: www.irisgardenvictoria.com

• From downtown Victoria, go north on Highway 17 for 12 kilometres to the Royal Oak exit.

• Four rooms: One person $90–155; two people $95–160. Queen-sized bed. Ensuite bathrooms.

• A house on three rolling acres, surrounded by mixed gardens and large Douglas fir trees. Guest rooms are decorated in bold colours and have flowers, antiques, contemporary furniture, and views of pastures and wooded hillsides. Guest rooms have down duvets. Three of the guest rooms have Jacuzzi tubs; one of these rooms has a soaker tub in the room and a canopied bed. Two guest living rooms with fireplaces. One of the guest living rooms has books and games; the other has twelve-foot ceilings and large beams. Outdoor terrace with tables and sitting areas with views of gardens and pastures. Seasonally heated indoor pool. Within walking distance of biking and hiking trails, tennis courts, and Prospect Lake beach. Ten minutes from the Butchart Gardens, display gardens at the Horticultural Centre of the Pacific, the Victoria Butterfly Gardens, four public golf courses, restaurants, and shopping. Full breakfast, including homemade muffins or scones, fruit from local farms, and an entrée such as German puffed pancakes, crêpes, herb and cheese omelettes, French toast with warm berry sauce, or locally made sausage, is served in the living room that has a high ceiling. Menu changes daily. Cash, traveller's cheques, Visa, MasterCard. Adult oriented. Nonsmoking. **In the hosts' own words:** "At our B&B, we provide the charm of yesterday with the amenities and casual comfort of today. Breakfast—decadent and delicious—is always an adventure."

Gazebo B&B

Linda and Martin Vernon
5460 Old West Saanich Road
Victoria, BC V8X 3X1
(250) 727-2420 fax: (250) 727-6605
toll-free from within North America: 1-877-211-2288
email: stay@gazebo-victoria.com
web site: www.gazebo-victoria.com

• From Victoria, take Highway 17 north to the Quadra Street/West Saanich Road exit. Follow West Saanich Road (Highway 17A) for 3.2 kilometres. Turn right onto Old West Saanich Road and continue for 2.4 kilometres. The B&B is on the left, after a sharp bend in the road.

• Room, suite, and cottages.
Room: $75. Twin beds. Private bathroom.
Suite: $95. Queen-sized bed. Ensuite bathroom.
Two cottages: $120–150. Queen-sized bed. Ensuite bathrooms.
Additional person $25. Roll-away cots available. Extended stay and off-season rates.

• A manor-style house surrounded by farms and forested hills, with three-quarters of an acre of landscaped gardens. Ponds, waterfalls, fruit trees, patio, and gazebo. Twenty minutes' drive from downtown, the Victoria airport, and ferry terminals. Ten minutes' drive from the Butchart Gardens, the Butterfly Gardens, shops, restaurants, golf courses, ocean and lake beaches, parks, cycling, hiking trails, kayaking, and a sport, swim, and spa centre. Whale-watching tours can be arranged by the hosts. Guest sitting room and dining room with fireplace, hardwood floors, and beamed ceilings. Furnished with antiques and tapestries. TV, CDs, and books. Laundry facilities, fridge, and barbecue. One of the cottages has cedar-clad walls, vaulted ceilings, a single Jacuzzi tub, kitchen facilities, recliner chairs, a TV, a VCR, and videos. Both cottages are in the garden. Tea and coffee any time. Full, multi-course breakfast. Diets are accommodated. Cancellation notice seven days. Reservations recommended. Visa, MasterCard. Children welcome. Dogs welcome. Smoking outdoors. **In the hosts' own words:** "Enjoy our peaceful garden setting with its charming house and cottages. While you savour a delicious breakfast, allow us to provide local knowledge and insights to make your stay memorable."

Island View Beach B&B

Sylvia Nicholson
7242 Highcrest Terrace
Saanichton, BC V8M 1W5
(250) 652-6842
cel: (250) 744-7413

• Fifteen minutes from the Swartz Bay ferry terminal. From the ferry terminal, take Highway 17 (Patricia Bay Highway). Turn left onto Island View Road and continue for one block. Turn left onto Puckle. Turn right onto Lamont Road, which becomes Highcrest Terrace.

• Self-contained suite: Two people $79. Additional person $20.

• A B&B with a self-contained suite that has a view of Haro Strait and Mount Baker. Suite has a private entrance, a kitchen, a bathroom, a sun room, and a living room with TV and VCR. Fifteen minutes' drive from ferries and the Butchart Gardens. Twenty minutes' drive from Victoria. Coffee and tea supplies and homemade cakes and cookies are provided in the suite. Breakfast is served at guests' convenience in the sun room, which has a view of the ocean and a bird sanctuary. Breakfast includes blackberry muffins, fresh fruit with yogurt, and pancakes. Smoking outdoors. **In the hosts' own words:** "An ideal location for a quiet holiday, birdwatching, or just walking on our beach."

Lovat House Seaside B&B

Fran and Chris Atkinson
9625 Second Street
Sidney, BC V8L 3C3
(250) 656-3188 fax: (250) 656-3188
email: sailing@telus.net
web sites: www.pixsell.bc.ca/bb/1224.htm
www.bbcanada.com/3981.html

• Three rooms: In summer (May to October), one person $45–79, two people $59–79. Queen-sized bed; double bed and one twin bed. Ensuite and private bathrooms. Additional person $20. Off-season rates.

• A B&B in a quiet area of Sidney, within walking distance of shopping, restaurants, and marinas and with a view of the ocean, islands, and mountains. A few minutes from B.C. and U.S. ferries, the Victoria airport, and the Butchart Gardens. Near beach access. Boat charters, lessons, and whale watching can be arranged. Guest rooms have TVs. Two of the guest rooms have sea views. Sitting area and patio. Full breakfast is served in summer. Continental breakfast is served in guest rooms the rest of the year. Children over eleven welcome. No pets. No smoking.

Orchard House

Gerry Martin
9646 Sixth Street
Sidney, BC V8L 2W2
(250) 656-9194
toll-free: 1-888-656-9194
web site: www.gerrymartin.com

• From Highway 17, turn east onto Beacon Avenue. Turn south onto Fifth Street and continue for three blocks. Turn west onto Orchard Avenue and continue for one block to Sixth Street.

• Four rooms: One person $69; two people $79. Queen-sized bed; double bed. Additional person $20. Off-season rates October to April.

• A house built in 1914 by the founding family of Sidney, with beamed ceilings, built-in wooden cabinets with leaded glass windows, and English-style gardens. Ten minutes' drive from the Butchart Gardens. Five minutes' walk from beaches and parks and from shops and restaurants in Sidney. Two blocks from ferries to Anacortes, Washington. A short drive from the airport and from ferries to Vancouver. Twenty minutes' drive from downtown Victoria. Full breakfast is served in a formal dining room. MasterCard. Children over twelve welcome. No pets. Smoking outdoors. **In the hosts' own words:** "Come stay with us in our beautiful heritage house and enjoy our large, healthy breakfasts and the small-town character of Sidney by the Sea. Sidney's main street comes alive with arts and crafts during Sidney days, on the first weekend in July."

Atop Triangle Mountain

Loreen and Jim Gardner
3442 Karger Terrace
Victoria, BC V9C 3K5
(250) 478-7853 fax: (250) 478-2245
toll-free: 1-877-353-6887
email: loreen@hospitalityvictoria.com
web site: www.hospitalityvictoria.com

- From Highway 1, go west on Highway 14 for 5.5 kilometres. Turn left onto Fulton Road. At the top of the hill, keep left on Fulton. Turn left onto Karger and continue to the cul-de-sac.
- Two rooms and one suite: One person $65–105; two people $80–120. Queen-sized bed, ensuite bathroom; queen-sized bed and double hide-a-bed, bathroom in suite. Additional person $20. Child under 10 $5; child 10 to 15 $10. Roll-away bed and crib $10. Off-season rates.
- A cedar house surrounded by fir and arbutus trees, on a small mountain, with views of Victoria, the Juan de Fuca Strait, Mount Baker, and the Olympic Mountains. Twenty minutes from downtown. Fifteen minutes from golf, fishing, swimming, hiking trails, and provincial and regional parks. Ten minutes' drive from a bird sanctuary and the ocean. Garden and wrap-around deck. Pool table, hot tub, piano, and books. Sitting area on the ground floor has a fridge, a kettle, and hot and cold drinks. Guest rooms and suite have TVs. Suite has a sitting room with a double hide-a-bed. One of the guest rooms and the suite face a back garden with trees. Another guest room has a view of the ocean and mountains and sliding glass doors that lead to the deck. Full hot breakfast is served in the solarium or in the dining room, both of which have a view of the ocean and mountains. Visa, MasterCard. No pets; cat and dog in residence. Smoking on the deck. **In the hosts' own words:** "At our B&B, we offer a tranquil setting with spectacular views of mountains, ocean, and city. The quiet location assures a peaceful sleep, and each day begins with a delicious, hearty breakfast."

Wayward Navigator B&B

Nancy Fry and Barry Rinas
337 Damon Drive
Victoria, BC V9B 5G5
(250) 478-6836 fax: (250) 478-6850
toll-free from within North America: 1-888-478-6808
email: nancy@wayward.com
web site: www.wayward.com

•From Victoria, go north on Douglas Street, which becomes Highway 1. Take exit 10 (the Colwood/Sooke exit). At the Six Mile House Pub, turn right onto Six Mile Road. Turn right onto Damon Drive. The B&B is at the top of the hill.

•Two rooms: One person $85; two people $95. Queen-sized bed. Ensuite and private bathrooms.
Getaway packages.

•A B&B with a nautical theme, with passenger liner memorabilia, including paintings, etchings, and seafaring books, in the guest rooms and living areas. A few minutes' walk from hiking, swimming, and boating at Thetis Island. Near the Galloping Goose Trail. English pub-style room with hundred-year-old mahogany bar, antique mirrors, and pump organ. Guest living room with fireplace, TV, VCR, stereo, wet bar, fridge, microwave, and pin-ball machine. Guest rooms have down comforters. A three-level cedar deck leads to a California redwood gazebo with a hot tub among arbutus and maple trees. Full breakfast is served in the dining room. Diets are accommodated with advance notice. One of the hosts is a registered nurse. Cancellation notice forty-eight hours. Check-in 3:00 to 6:00 p.m.; check-out until 11:00 a.m. Visa, MasterCard. **In the hosts' own words:** "Our B&B offers a taste of classic passenger ship opulence with modern conveniences. Let us pamper you with our full gourmet breakfasts. Ask about our five-course candlelit dinner, part of our getaway special. We have dedicated over twelve hundred square feet of our house to your comfort and enjoyment."

Cycle-Inn B&B

Joanne and Chris Cowan
3158 Anders Road
Victoria, BC V9B 4C4
(250) 478-6821
cel: (250) 216-5465
email: stay@cycleinn.com
web site: www.cycleinn.com

• From the Swartz Bay ferry terminal, go south on Highway 17. Turn right onto MacKenzie Avenue. Turn right onto Highway 1. At exit 10, take Highway 1A to Highway 14. Continue for 7.5 kilometres. Turn right onto Anders Road. The B&B is at the end of the road.

• Rooms and suite.

Two rooms: One person $60–70; two people $65–75. Queen-sized bed; extra long twin beds (or twin beds side by side with king-sized bedding). Shared guest bathroom. Additional smaller room with one twin bed available for use by additional person travelling with guests staying in one of the guest rooms $50.

Self-contained two-bedroom suite: Two people $125. Double bed, double/single bunk, and day bed. Weekly or extended stay rates.

• A country-style house adjacent to the Galloping Goose Trail, with guest rooms that have views of Glen Lake. Twenty minutes' drive from downtown. Recreation room with VCR, books, games, and pool table. Living room with stone fireplace. Self-contained suite has a separate entrance and a kitchen. Deck with views of the lake. Boats, dock, swimming, and rope swing. Bicycles for use on the trail. Yard with cultivated fruit trees, perennial flowers, shrubs, and natural wild section. Wildlife viewing on the property. Breakfast often includes fruit from the yard. **In the hosts' own words:** "We enjoy sharing our outdoor paradise with guests of all ages. Our suite is a haven for family retreats. Our guests will sleep well because of the privacy of our location and will start each day with a fine, healthy breakfast."

Hummingbird Lane B&B

Virginia and Keith Kupitz
3963 Metchosin Road
Victoria, BC V9C 4A5
(250) 478-4095
email: hummingbird@lodgingvictoria.com
web site: www.lodgingvictoria.com/hummingbird

• From downtown Victoria, turn left at the Metchosin and Sooke intersection onto Metchosin Road. Continue for about ten minutes to the Green Acres driving range. The B&B is across the street from the driving range.

• Three rooms: Two people $55–95. Queen-sized bed; double bed. Ensuite, private, and shared guest bathrooms. Additional person $15. Roll-away cot and playpen available. Children under 6 free.

• A B&B on four acres, with an indoor swimming pool. Fifteen minutes' walk from a beach that has mountain views. Twenty-five minutes' drive from downtown. In the area are beaches, golf, fishing, kayaking, hiking trails, forests, the Galloping Goose Trail, the Butchart Gardens, country dining, and whale watching and other marine wildlife viewing. Five to fifteen minutes' drive from a lighthouse and four parks. Thirty-five minutes' drive from the Victoria airport. One of the guest rooms has a queen-sized canopied bed, a two-person Jacuzzi, and candles. The indoor swimming pool is heated to 85 degrees Farenheit and is locked for safety at all times. Full breakfast. Cash, traveller's cheques. Children welcome. No pets; pets in residence. No smoking. **In the hosts' own words:** "Our B&B is close enough to the city centre for you to enjoy all the downtown attractions, yet far enough removed to feel like you've left the city far behind. We are in a tranquil rural setting, with affordable prices, and attractive, bright, cheerful, and comfortable rooms. We cater to everyone from honeymooners to families on vacation."

Wooded Acres B&B

Elva and Skip Kennedy
4907 Rocky Point Road
Victoria, BC V9C 4G2
(250) 478-8172
email: ekennedy@pacificcoast.net
cabin@lodgingvictoria.com
web site: www.LodgingVictoria.com/countryside

• From Victoria, take Highway 1 north to Highway 1A. Take Highway 1A to Highway 14. From Highway 14, turn left onto Metchosin Road, right onto Happy Valley Road, and left onto Rocky Point Road.

• Two suites: Two people $110–130. Queen-sized bed. Bathrooms in suites.

• A log house built by the hosts on three treed acres in the country. Each suite has a hot tub, a sitting area, flowers, antiques, and down duvets. Thirty minutes from downtown. Twenty minutes from Sooke. Near beaches, wilderness parks, golf courses, fishing, birdwatching, tennis, museums, artisans' studios, whale watching, and trails for walking, hiking, and mountain biking. Full breakfast, including homemade baked goods, is served at guests' convenience. **In the hosts' own words:** "Welcome to our home built with logs from our forested acreage. We take great pride in giving warm and friendly hospitality, comfort, relaxation, and helpful information to make our guests' holiday in Victoria's countryside a memorable occasion."

A B&B at Swallow Hill Farm

Gini and Peter Walsh
4910 William Head Road
Victoria, BC V9C 3Y8
(250) 474-4042 fax: (250) 474-4042
email: info@swallowhillfarm.com
web site: www.swallowhillfarm.com

• Thirty minutes from Victoria. Take Highway 1 north to exit 10. Take Highway 1A west to Highway 14. Turn left onto Metchosin Road, which becomes William Head Road in the town of Metchosin. Continue for 2 kilometres past the town centre to the B&B.

• Two suites: One person $80–85, two people $85–95. King-sized bed, ensuite bathroom; queen-sized bed and twin beds, private bathroom.

• A B&B on an apple farm, with views of the ocean, mountains, and sunrises. Suites have decks. Two-bedroom suite has feather beds and down duvets. Whales, otters, seals, deer, and eagles and other birds can be seen. Five minutes from hiking, cycling, swimming, fishing, diving, kayaking, and golf. Twenty minutes from whale watching. Adjacent to the Galloping Goose Trail. Antique Canadiana. Handmade furniture made by one of the hosts. Sauna. Tea, coffee, and homemade cookies. Farm-style breakfast. Cancellation notice seven days. Reservations preferred. Cash, credit cards. No pets; dog in residence. Nonsmoking. **In the host's own words:** "You'll find a peaceful country getaway at our little farm on Vancouver Island's beautiful southwest coast."

Lilac House Country B&B

Gail Harris
1848 Connie Road
Victoria, BC V9C 4C2
(250) 642-2809 or (250) 389-0252
email: lilac@pinc.com
web site: vvv.com/~lilac/

• Twenty-six kilometres west of Victoria, on the road to Sooke.
• Rooms and cottage.
Three rooms: One person $45–75; two people $60–90. Ensuite and shared bathrooms.
Cottage: $109–149.
Discount of 10 percent on stays of three or more nights. Other discounts available.
• A traditional-style custom-built house with hill views, vaulted ceilings, antiques, feather beds, and skylights, on five acres of wooded trails and moss-covered hills. A creek runs through the property. Living room with wood stove. Hot tub, garden, and walking trails. Cottage is next to creek and has vaulted ceilings, a gas fireplace, a Jacuzzi tub, and french doors that lead to a veranda and deck which have pastoral views. In the area are hiking, swimming, fishing, cycling, horseback riding, whale watching, and bird and wildlife viewing. Llama hiking trips available. Five minutes' drive from the Galloping Goose Trail. Twenty-five minutes from Victoria. Ten minutes from Sooke. Ten minutes from lake, river, and ocean beaches. One kilometre from a historical pub. Deposit required to hold reservation. Cancellation notice seven days. Visa, MasterCard. Adult oriented. No pets; cat in residence, and llamas, ducks, and rabbits on the farm. Nonsmoking. **In the hosts' own words:** "In the heart of the Sooke Hills, high on a rock bluff with a view of Veitch Creek, our B&B extends warm hospitality to the discerning traveller. We offer all the comforts of a home away from home in an atmosphere of warmth and elegance. Enjoy a cool drink on the wrap-around veranda or soak in the hot tub under the stars."

Cape Cod B&B

Gwen Utitz and Peter Ginman
5782 Anderson Cove Road
Sooke, BC V0S 1N0
(250) 642-3253 fax: (250) 642-3253
email: capecodbb@home.com
web site: members.home.com/capecodbb

• Self-contained suite: Two people $125. Queen-sized bed. Ensuite bathroom. Roll-away beds available for an additional fee. Off-season rates.
• A Cape Cod–style house on two wooded acres, with views of Sooke Basin, the Sooke Hills, and sunsets. Suite has a private entrance, a kitchen, a dining area, a living room with TV, videos, and books, a bedroom with queen-sized bed, an ensuite bathroom with robes and hair dryers, and a private patio with barbecue. Ten minutes from hiking, kayaking, biking, swimming, beachcombing, and tennis courts. In the area are horseback riding, llama trekking, golf, birdwatching, and wildlife viewing. Transportation to and from hiking in East Sooke Park can be provided by the hosts. Salmon fishing charters, whale-watching tours, reflexology, and massages can be arranged by the hosts. Restaurant reservations can be made by the hosts. Twenty minutes' drive from Sooke. Forty minutes' drive from Victoria. Full breakfast includes fresh fruit. Diets are accommodated. Deposit of one night's rate required to hold reservation. Cash. French, German, and Dutch spoken. Smoking outdoors. **In the hosts' own words:** "Enjoy total tranquillity at our B&B. Watch for eagles from the privacy of your own patio and catch a glimpse of deer walking through the forest. Explore or relax—the choice is yours."

Burnside House B&B

Renata Wuersch-Tilly
1890 Maple Avenue
Sooke, BC V0S 1N0
(250) 642-4403 fax: (250) 642-4403
toll-free from within North America:
1-877-688-1122
email: pharmeng@pacbell
web site: www.sookenet.com/burnside

• Less than 1 kilometre past Sooke; 37 kilometres west of Victoria.

• Four rooms: One person $65–85; two people $75–95. Queen-sized bed; double bed. Private bathroom. Additional person $20.
Off-season rates October 1 to May 1, excluding weekends and holidays.

• A restored 130-year-old Georgian-style country house on two acres of lawn and gardens. Built by John Muir in 1870, the B&B is the oldest inhabited house in Sooke. A bottle of wine is provided in each guest room. Two of the guest rooms have couches to accommodate an additional person. Some guest rooms have ocean and mountain views. Gazebo with Jacuzzi. Near golf, swimming, hiking, and trout and salmon fishing. Picnic lunches available for a fee. Whales and seals can sometimes be seen from nearby beaches. Accessible by public transit. Full breakfast is served in the guest living room, which has a fireplace, a TV, and games. Vegetarian breakfast available. Deposit of one night's rate required to hold reservation. Cancellation notice three days. Visa, MasterCard. German spoken. Children over eleven welcome. Pets welcome. Nonsmokers preferred. **In the hosts' own words:** "Our B&B is an ideal base for exploring the Sooke area. We'd love to spoil you."

Salty Towers Oceanfront Retreat and Vacation Homes

Linda and Glenn Thibault
1581 Dufour Road
Sooke, BC V0S 1N0
(250) 642-7034 fax: (250) 642-7034
toll-free: 1-877-374-8944
email: saltyg@islandnet.com
web site: www.sookenet.com/saltytowers

• Thirty-eight kilometres west of Victoria. One and one-half kilometres past Sooke, turn left onto Whiffen Spit Road. Turn left onto Dufour Road.

• Suites, cottages, and houses.
Two suites and three self-contained cottages: Two people $95–150. Additional person $15–20. Weekly and off-season rates. Pet $10 per day.
Four vacation houses: $225–325.

• Cottages, suites, and vacation houses on the ocean with a private wharf for moorage and views of Sooke Harbour, East Sooke, and Whiffin Spit Park. Hot tubs, fireplaces, ensuite Jacuzzis or steam showers, skylights, and kitchens. Private decks with sea views, fishing charters, whale watching, kayaking, mountain biking, and hiking. Deposit of fifty percent of total price required to hold reservation. Suitable for honeymooners, large families, or corporate retreats. **In the hosts' own words:** "We offer luxurious and romantic oceanfront accommodation with spectacular scenery, fabulous décor, and seafood from the ocean."

House on the Bay

Nargis and Amir Jamal
7954 West Coast Road
Sooke, BC V0S 1N0
(250) 642-6534 fax: (250) 642-1545
toll-free: 1-888-805-8800
email: hotb@home.com
web site: members.home.net/hotb

• Seven kilometres west of Sooke. Forty kilometres from Victoria.
• Room, suite, and honeymoon suite: $95–135. Queen-sized bed. Ensuite and private bathrooms.
• A B&B with views of Juan de Fuca Strait and the Olympic Mountains. Whales, deer, and eagles can be seen from guest rooms. Forty-five minutes' drive from beaches, rainforest trails, the Butchart Gardens, and the giant Red Creek fir tree, one of Canada's largest Douglas firs. Fishing and whale-watching charters can be arranged by the hosts. Near golf courses and bicycle and kayak rentals. Guest room, suite, and honeymoon suite have four-post beds and fireplaces. The guest room and suite have Jacuzzis in their bathrooms and private entrances from the patio. The honeymoon suite is on the upper floor and has a two-person Jacuzzi tub in the bedroom by a window with a view. Guest living room with fireplace. Snacks and beverages. Guest dining room. Outdoor patio. Gazebo. Full breakfast is served in the dining room or in the guests' room or suite by request. **In the hosts' own words:** "We enjoy catering to our guests and offer a romantic and peaceful getaway with spectacular views of mountains and ocean. Enjoy the peace and quiet and explore Canada's hidden West Coast."

Eagle Cove Guest Suite

Blythe Barlow and Des Thompson
8061 West Coast Road
Sooke, BC V0S 1N0
(250) 642-4885 fax: (250) 592-6357
email: djlt@telus.net

- From Victoria, take Highway 1 north. Take the Colwood-Sooke exit (Highway 1A, which leads to Highway 14). Continue for 8 kilometres, past the traffic light in Sooke.
- One-bedroom self-contained suite: One person or two people $90–100. Twin beds (or twin beds side by side). Bathroom in suite.
Breakfast ingredients supplied.
Extended stay rates.
- A B&B on half an acre, twenty-four steps above a sheltered cove, with a private beach and views of Juan de Fuca Strait and the Olympic Mountains. Whales, sea lions, river otters, deer, and eagles can be seen from the property. Near the Sooke Museum, salmon fishing charters, golf courses, and mountain biking and hiking trails. The self-contained suite is on the level below the hosts' quarters and has a separate entrance and a sitting room. Light cooking facilities include a coffee maker, a kettle, a microwave, a hot plate, a small fridge, a sink, and a barbecue. Living room/dining area with picture windows, a telescope, décor from Bali, books, and board games. Bedroom has a TV, a radio, a telephone, and sliding glass doors that lead to a private deck, which has a view of the ocean. Guests can bring their own kayaks and canoes. Bottle of wine and Continental breakfast ingredients supplied. Cancellation notice three days. Visa, MasterCard, American Express. No smoking indoors. **In the hosts' own words:** "At our B&B, enjoy sunrises, the sea breeze, beachcombing, birdwatching, or boating. In the evening, unwind under the stars with your own campfire on the beach, and then be lulled to sleep, soothed by the sound of the surf."

Gordon's Beach Farmstay B&B

Robyn Evans
4530 Otter Point Road
Sooke, BC V0S 1N0
(250) 642-5291 fax: (250) 642-5291
toll-free: 1-888-852-8881
email: gordonsbeachbandb@home.com
web site: gordonsbeachbandb.com

• Ten kilometres west of Sooke's only traffic light. From Highway 14 (West Coast Road), turn right onto Otter Point Road. The B&B is the second house on the left.

• Room and Suites.

Room: One person $55–75; two people $75–80. Double bed. Private bathroom.
Two suites: One person $55–75; two people $75–80. Queen-sized bed. Ensuite bathroom.

• A B&B across the road from an ocean beach, on ten acres with views of Juan de Fuca Strait and the Olympic Mountains. Suites and room have views of the ocean. Whales, sea lions, deer, and eagles can be seen from the B&B. Near hiking, biking, and nature trails. Suites have queen-sized beds, ensuite bathrooms, private entrances, patios, sitting areas, antiques, TVs, and coffeemakers. One of the suites has a sink and a microwave. Outdoor gazebo hot tub, barbecue, and bicycles. Full breakfast is served in the dining room, on the patio, or in the suites. Check-in after 3:00 p.m; check-out until 11:00 a.m. Visa, MasterCard. **In the hosts' own words:** "We offer hospitality, privacy, and comfort."

The Beach House

Ellie Thorburn
369 Isabella Point Road
Salt Spring Island, BC V8K 1V4
(250) 653-2040 fax: (250) 653-9711
for reservations: 1-888-653-6334

• Fifteen kilometres from Ganges. Two kilometres from the Fulford Harbour ferry terminal and village. Follow the road up the hill to the left and around the end of the harbour. Go straight along the water's edge, pass the Fulford Inn, which is on the right, and continue for 1.3 kilometres. The B&B is on the left.

• Rooms and suite.

Two rooms: One person $105–140; two people $140–160. King-sized bed; queen-sized bed. Ensuite bathrooms. Additional person $40–50 in an adjoining room with a double bed.

Self-contained one-bedroom suite: Two people $130–$154. Queen-sized bed, one twin bed, and queen-sized sofa bed. Breakfast is optional.

Additional person $15–25. Weekly and off-season rates.

• A B&B with beach access, on the shore of Fulford Harbour, in a rural setting. Country décor, local artwork, and a seashell theme. Outdoor oceanside hot tub. Eleven steps lead down to a shell beach for beachcombing, crabbing, kayaking, swimming, and birdwatching. Each guest room has a private entrance, a sitting area with views of the sea and marine life, and French doors that lead to a sitting area and the beach. The guest room with a king-sized bed has a two-person Jacuzzi tub. An adjoining room with a double bed is available for a third person accompanying the guests staying in that guest room. Common area with bar, fridge, and facilities for making hot beverages. One-bedroom suite is on the top floor and has a deck with a view of the harbour, a kitchen, a dining area, a living room, a TV, a VCR, and a gas barbecue. Outdoor fire pit. Guests are requested to refrain from wearing toxic products including perfume. Full breakfast. Diets are accommodated. Reservations recommended. Credit cards. Rooms are adult oriented; suite is suitable for families. Rooms are not suitable for pets; pets in suite by arrangement. Smoking outdoors. **In the hosts' own words:** "Either before or after a day of hiking, kayaking, golfing, or browsing in studios, relax in our oceanside hot tub. Enjoy the magnificent sunrise or the glistening reflections of the harbour by moonlight."

Weston Lake Inn B&B

Susan Evans and Ted Harrison
813 Beaver Point Road
Salt Spring Island, BC V8K 1X9
(250) 653-4311 fax: (250) 653-4340
toll-free from within North America: 1-888-820-7174
email: westonlake@saltspring.com
web site: www.westonlakeinn.com

• Take the ferry from Vancouver (Tsawwassen), Victoria (Swartz Bay), or Crofton to Salt Spring Island. Located 3.6 kilometres from Fulford Harbour, on the road to Ruckle Provincial Park. Eleven kilometres from Ganges.

• Three rooms: One person $90–115; two people $105–130. Queen-sized bed; queen-sized bed and one twin bed. Ensuite bathrooms. Additional person $25. Charters on the hosts' 36-foot sailboat.

• A country house surrounded by gardens, with a view of Weston Lake. A long driveway beside a split-rail fence winds past cows grazing in a pasture. Guest rooms have down duvets, robes, sitting areas, and flowers. Antiques, art, and needlepoint throughout. Guest living room with stone fireplace, piano, CD player, and CDs. Second guest living room with wood stove, books, movies, satellite TV, VCR, and collection of African musical instruments. Fridge and microwave. Hot tub. Decks, sitting areas, and paths through the gardens (rock, alpine, wildflower, rhododendron, herb, heather, cut flower, vegetable, and fruit). Pond, woodlands, pastures, birds, and wildlife on the ten-acre property. Full breakfast includes home-grown organic produce; menu changes daily. Cancellation notice seven days. Check-out until 11:00 a.m. Visa, MasterCard. Children over thirteen welcome. No pets; sheep dog in residence. No smoking indoors. **In the hosts' own words:** "Our B&B offers serenity, privacy, outstanding food, and warm hospitality. We invite you to share our bit of heaven."

Daffodil Cove Cottage

John Gilman
146 Meyer Road
Salt Spring Island, BC V8K 1X4
(250) 653-4950
email: sabine@interchange.ubc.ca
web site: www.interchange.ubc.ca/sabine

• Seven kilometres from the Fulford Harbour ferry terminal, on the south end of Salt Spring Island.

• Self-contained cottage (sleeps four or five): Two people $80–110. Queen-sized bed, twin beds in a loft, and double sofa bed. Private bathroom. Additional person $20. Weekly rates.
Minimum stay two nights. In July and August, minimum stay one week (Saturday to Saturday).

• A self-contained cedar and glass cottage on the ocean, adjacent to a nature reserve. Living room with glass-front wood stove, wrap-around deck, and view of the ocean and forest. Adjoining kitchen and sun room dining area. Electric heat. Cedar, ceramic tile, and floor-to-ceiling windows. Linen, stove, fridge, microwave, and coffee maker. Food staples, including tea, coffee, sugar, flour, and condiments, are provided for guests to prepare meals. Deposit required to hold reservation. Cancellation notice four weeks. Children welcome. No pets. Nonsmoking establishment. **In the hosts' own words:** "Our cottage has a spectacular setting and is completely private, with arbutus and Douglas fir forest, a garry oak meadow, and wildflowers. The nature and marine reserves provide an array of wildlife at the door and many hiking opportunities."

Beddis House B&B

Terry and Bev Bolton
131 Miles Avenue
Salt Spring Island, BC V8K 2E1
(250) 537-1028 fax: (250) 537-9888
email: beddis@saltspring.com
web site: www.saltspring.com/beddishouse

- Eight kilometres south of Ganges. Call for directions.
- Three suites in a coach house separate from the hosts' house: In winter, two people $130–160. In summer, two people $150–180. King-sized bed; queen-sized bed; twin beds. Ensuite bathrooms. One-person and weekly rates.
- A restored turn-of-the-century farmhouse on the ocean with a clam-shell beach. The house is between the ocean and an apple orchard and is surrounded by one and a quarter acres of flower gardens, lawns, and fruit trees. Deer, otters, seals, and eagles can be seen. Suites are in a coach house separate from the hosts' house. Each suite has a private deck that faces the ocean, a fireplace, a sitting area, flowers, wine glasses, sweets, candles, and an ensuite bathroom with claw-foot tub, shower, toiletries, and robes. Afternoon tea is served in the sitting room or on the decks. Guest sitting room in the main house has a fireplace, a games table, and books. Multi-course breakfast, including homemade baked goods, is served in the dining room in the main house; specialties include poached pear in blueberry sauce, apple pan puff, and barbecued salmon with scrambled eggs. Visa, MasterCard. Adult oriented. No pets. Nonsmoking. **In the hosts' own words:** "At our B&B, whether you choose rest, romance, or revitalization, you'll escape to quieter times in a spot that is truly magical all year round."

A Perfect Perch B&B

Libby and Michel Jutras
225 Armand Way
Salt Spring Island, BC V8K 2B6
(250) 653-2030 fax: (250) 653-2045
toll-free: 1-888-663-2030
email: ljutras@saltspring.com
web site: www.saltspring.com/perfectperch/

• Six kilometres south of Ganges. Three kilometres from the highway.

• Three rooms: $135–175. Queen-sized bed. Ensuite bathrooms.

• A West Coast–style contemporary house, with private entrances and decks, one thousand feet above sea level. Views of sunrises, the Sunshine Coast, and the San Juan Islands. At night, the lights of Vancouver, White Rock, and Bellingham can be seen fifty-five kilometres away across the Strait of Georgia. Guest rooms have ensuite bathrooms with double Jacuzzis, twin shower heads, or double soaker tubs. Beds have duvets and feather pillows. One of the hosts is a watercolour artist and instructor. Bookings and rentals for sailing, scuba diving, boating, fishing, horseback riding, kayaking, tennis, golf, mopeds, theatre, and artists' studio tours can be arranged by the hosts. Five-course breakfast includes farm-fresh eggs, homemade jam, and seafood or vegetarian alternatives. Check-in 4:00 to 6:00 p.m. Visa, MasterCard. Adult oriented. No pets. Smoke-free environment. **In the hosts' own words:** "For a romantic escape, we offer luxury accommodation in a dramatic setting."

The Barn Swallow B&B

Edie and Graham Fishlock
237 Bulman Road
Salt Spring Island, BC V8K 1X5
(250) 653-9577 fax: (250) 653-9576
web site: www.saltspring.com/barnswallow

• Four and a half kilometres from the Fulford ferry terminal, on the way to Ruckle Provincial Park.

• Two rooms: Two people $95–110. Queen-sized bed and sofa bed; queen-sized bed. Ensuite bathroom. Additional person $15.

• A new post-and-beam log house on five acres, surrounded by gardens and pastures, with ocean and mountain views. Guest rooms have duvets, private entrances, and views of Pender and Mayne Islands, Ruckle Provincial Park, Swanson Channel, Mount Baker, and sunrises. Near hiking, beachcombing, and artists' studios. Deck with hot tub. One of the guest rooms has a Jacuzzi-style tub and a window seat. The other guest room has a garden-level private deck and a fireplace. Multi-course breakfast, including local farm products, is served on the deck or in the great room. Diets are accommodated by arrangement. Cancellation notice seven days. Check-in after 3:00 p.m. Visa, MasterCard. Adults only. No pets; dog in residence and horses on the property. Smoke-free environment. **In the hosts' own words:** "Come to our B&B, and enjoy country elegance with an ocean view and meet our heritage breed Canadian horse."

Water's Edge B&B

Helen Tara
327 Price Road
Salt Spring Island, BC V8K 2E9
(250) 537-5807 fax: (250) 537-2862
toll-free from within North America: 1-877-537-5807
web sites: www.islandnet.com/saltspring/
www.pixsell.bc.ca/bb/1114.htm

• Four kilometres south of Ganges. Take Fulford-Ganges Road, turn southeast onto Beddis Road and continue for 2 kilometres. Turn left onto Price and continue for 1 kilometre to the waterfront.

• Room and one two-bedroom suite: One person $95–130; two people $115–150. King-sized bed and one twin day bed; two queen-sized beds. Ensuite bathroom and bathrooms in suite. Additional person $35–45.

• A contemporary house with a country garden and fish and lily ponds, on Ganges Harbour, a few steps from a beach. Guest rooms have views of the ocean. Guest living room with books, games, CD player, leather couches, dining area, paintings, a fireplace, a fridge, a microwave, and dishes for preparing light meals. Guest entrance. Rowboat. Covered brick patio and open seaside patio with views of birds, sea life, boats, and other islands. Seven minutes' drive from shops, restaurants, pubs, galleries, a market, and golf. The hosts share their knowledge of the area. Breakfast, including fresh fruit, juice, homemade cereal, fresh bread, yogurt, muffins, bacon, ham, and eggs, is served on local pottery on the patio or in the guest sitting room. Diets are accommodated. MasterCard. Adult oriented. Smoking outdoors. **In the hosts' own words:** "Special diets receive careful consideration. We invite you to watch the sun rise over the water, stroll the beach, or row the boat along the peaceful shore."

White Fig Orchard B&B and Cottage

Cathie and John Wellingham
135 Goodrich Road
Salt Spring Island, BC V8K 1L2
(250) 537-5791
web site: www.pixsell.bc.ca/bb/1313.htm

• From the Vesuvius Bay ferry terminal, take Vesuvius Bay Road for two blocks. Turn right onto Bayview and continue for one block. Turn left onto Goodrich. From the Fulford Harbour or the Long Harbour ferry terminal, take Vesuvius Bay Road. Turn left onto Bayview and left onto Goodrich.

• Rooms and cottage.

Rooms: One person $70; two people $80. Queen-sized bed; twin beds. Private and shared guest bathrooms.

Cottage (sleeps four): Two people $95. Private bathroom. Breakfast not included.

• A B&B with a view of the ocean, on two acres of landscaped grounds with an orchard. Two minutes' walk from a swimming beach, a pub, a restaurant, and a store. Guest sitting room in the main house has a stone fireplace, a TV, and a VCR. Cottage has kitchen facilities, a bedroom, a living room with TV, a deck with barbecue, and a ground-level entrance. Cancellation notice fourteen days. Visa, MasterCard. Smoking restricted.

Anchor Point B&B

Lynn and Ralph Bischoff
150 Beddis Road
Salt Spring Island, BC V8K 2J2
(250) 538-0110 fax: (250) 538-0120
email: info@anchorpointbb.com
web site: www.anchorpointbb.com

• Room and suites.
Room: $95. Double bed. Private bathroom.
Two suites: $125. Queen-sized bed. Bathrooms in suites.
Additional person $30. Extended stay and group rates.
Packages. Gift certificates.

• A Cape Cod–style house on a wooded acreage with harbour views, meadows, and gardens, within walking distance of Ganges. Across the street from a sailing club and a beach. Near wooded trails. Guest room and suites have reading and writing areas. The suites have views of the harbour and islands and loveseats that convert to twin beds. One of the suites has Sheraton and Queen Anne–style furniture. The other suite is decorated in a country style. The guest room's private bathroom has a claw-foot tub. Outdoor hot tub. Robes provided. Guest living room. Guest reading area. Books, classical and jazz CDs, and videos. Pickup and drop-off for guests arriving by ferry or float plane. Luggage can be stored until afternoon ferry service. Choice of three-course breakfast, served from 8:30 to 9:30 a.m. in the dining room or on the deck, or continental breakfast, served in guests' room or suite. Deposit of one night's rate required to hold reservation. Cancellation notice seventy-two hours. Minimum stay two nights on summer weekends and on long weekends. Check-in 3:00 to 7:00 p.m.; check-out until 11:00 a.m. Visa, MasterCard. No pets. **In the hosts' own words:** "Our B&B is yours to enjoy. You'll be pampered and relaxed—our amenities will make you want to stay for days."

Giselle's Place

Stephan and Giselle Harstall
410 Langs Road
Salt Spring Island, BC V8K 1N3
(250) 537-2636 fax: (250) 537-2608

• Eight kilometres north of Ganges. From Ganges, go north on Lower Ganges Road, which becomes North End Road, and continue along St. Mary Lake. Turn left onto Langs Road. The B&B is at the end of the road. Park against the laurel hedge in the B&B's paved driveway.

• Two rooms: One person $60; two people $70. Queen-sized bed; twin beds. Ensuite bathrooms. Family rates.

• A country-style B&B, with a view of Trincomali Channel, two minutes from a public beach on St. Mary Lake. Five minutes from a golf course, tennis courts, and a cinema. Guest rooms have TVs, ceiling fans, and thermostats for individually controlled heat. Sitting area with fridge, coffee maker, writing desk, paper, envelopes, and tourist information on Salt Spring Island is accessible from each guest room through a sliding glass door. Balcony with glass-topped table, chairs, bench, a view of Trincomali Channel, and a guest entrance that leads to another sitting area with books. Hot tub. Robes, extra towels, and thongs provided. Badminton and croquet equipment, lawn lounge chairs, and tables with chairs. Full breakfast is served in the dining room. Cash, cheques, Visa. Reservations appreciated. Children over five welcome. No pets. Smoking on the balcony. **In the hosts' own words:** "Come and enjoy the tranquillity at our B&B. Watch the birds, the visiting deer, and the soothing fountain while eating your breakfast. The experience is both Canadian and European, and both the familiar and the different are well worth a try."

Anne's Oceanfront Hideaway B&B

Rick and Ruth-Anne Broad
168 Simson Road
Salt Spring Island, BC V8K 1E2
(250) 537-0851 fax: (250) 537-0861
toll-free from within North America: 1-888-474-2663
email: annes@saltspring.com
web site: www.bbcanada.com/annesoceanfront

• Eight kilometres north of Vesuvius, off Sunset Drive; beside Stone Cutter's Bay on the northwest shore of Salt Spring Island.
• Three rooms and one honeymoon suite: In winter, $150–195. In summer, $180–230. Queen-sized bed; twin beds. Ensuite bathrooms.
• A seven-thousand-square-foot house with an elevator, a guest library with a fireplace, and a guest living room with a TV and a VCR. Covered veranda and outdoor hot tub are for guest use only. Guest entrance and east-facing deck. Guest rooms have ocean views, small fridges, thermostats for individually controlled heat, recliners, down duvets, percale sheets, fruit trays, and terry robes. Ensuite bathrooms have hydromassage tubs and showers. Honeymoon suite has a balcony overlooking the ocean, a fireplace, a canopied queen-sized bed, a hydromassage tub for two, and a separate shower for two. Canoe and bicycles. Refreshments served when guests arrive. Coffee is served to guests' rooms before breakfast. Full breakfast. Allergy aware; most diets are accommodated with advance notice. Reservations recommended. Cancellation notice seven days. Visa, MasterCard, American Express. Wheelchair accessible. Adult oriented. No pets. Smoke-free establishment. **In the hosts' own words:** "Enjoy the ever-changing ocean views, the sunsets, and our luxurious house. Come and share the experience of peace and tranquillity."

Stonecutter's Rest B&B

Chris Gosset and Irene Heron
170 Simson Road
Salt Spring Island, BC V8K 1E2
(250) 537-4415 fax: (250) 537-4462
email: stonecuttersrest@saltspring.com

•Eight kilometres north of Vesuvius, off Sunset Drive.
•Rooms and cottage.
Two rooms: One person $85; two people $95. Queen-sized bed; twin bed.
Ensuite bathrooms.
Cottage: $160, $900 per week. Minimum stay two nights.
•A B&B on five acres with rooms that face the water, private decks, and views of Stonecutter's Bay and islands. A path winds down to three hundred feet of private shore. Swimming, fishing, and kayaking. Guest entrance with stair glide for those who have difficulty negotiating stairs. Near golf, walking and biking trails, horseback riding, and tennis. In the area are a farmers' market, a craft market, an art studio, galleries, shops, and fine dining. Guest cottage is new and has a deck and a hot tub in a gazebo with a view of the ocean. Full breakfast is served on the deck. Deposit or credit card number required to hold reservation. Cancellation notice seven days. Visa, MasterCard. Smoke-free.

Arbutus Point Oceanfront B&B

Nancy and Simon Gould
215 Welbury Point Drive
Salt Spring Island, BC V8K 2L7
(250) 537-9510 fax: (250) 537-9521
toll-free from within North America: 1-888-633-9555
email: nancy@saltspring.com
web site: www.saltspringisl.com

- Six kilometres northeast of Ganges. One kilometre from Long Harbour ferry terminal.
- Three suites: In winter, two people $100–165. In spring/fall, two people $125–185. In summer, two people $145–225.
Self-contained suite (sleeps four): In winter, two people $190. In spring/fall two people $225. In summer, two people $275. Additional person $50. King-sized beds. Ensuite bathrooms.
Senior, student, and auto club rates.
- A lowbank oceanfront B&B on one acre, with a one-hundred-foot private point. Seven stairs lead to one mile of beachfront. Views of sunrises. Wildlife. Outdoor hot tub. Rowboats. Bicycles and kayaks available with advance notice. Suites may have private entrances, living rooms with gas fireplaces, seating for two inside and out, and/or Jacuzzis. Two of the suites have kitchens, dining areas, living rooms, sofas, and beds that swing up into a cabinet when not in use. Suites have ocean views, TVs, VCRs, showers, stereos with CD players, irons and ironing boards, hair dryers, bar fridges, coffee makers, glasses, wine buckets, barbecues, and private decks with patio furniture. Down duvets. Breakfast is served between 8:30 and 10:30 in the dining room or on the deck. Adult oriented. Enquire about pets. Non-smoking. **In the hosts' own words:** "Your hosts and the deer look forward to seeing you. Our luxurious B&B is perfect for the outdoor enthusiast or just for relaxing."

Sunrise/Sunset B&B

Donna Good
RR 1 Site 14 C–37
219 Sticks Allison Road
Galiano Island, BC V0N 1P0
(250) 539-5693
web site: www.aebc.com/~sunrise

• Suites: Ensuite bathrooms. Continental breakfast ingredients supplied.

• An oceanside B&B with a hot tub in an oceanside gazebo and new suites that have private entrances, balconies, and views of the ocean. Near swimming. Videos and books. Barbecue. Continental breakfast ingredients supplied. **In the hosts' own words:** "You'll enjoy our homey hospitality and our deluxe sunny suites. Our B&B is close to all amenities. We'll make sure your visit to our island home is enjoyable and memorable."

Wildeflower B&B

Suko and Christopher Starkey
212 Mariners Way
Mail: C–24 Quadrant RR 1
Mayne Island, BC V0N 2J0
(250) 539-2327 fax: (250) 539-2624
email: jstarkey@axion.net
web site: www.bbcanada.com/106.html

• Three rooms: $50–70. Queen-sized bed; twin beds. Shared guest bathroom.

• A Victorian-style house with a view of Village Bay, close to fishing, hiking, canoeing, biking, and beachcombing. Bicycles. Picnic lunches available. Evening tea, coffee, and snacks. Guest living room. Five minutes from the Village Bay ferry terminal. Pickup and drop-off for guests arriving by ferry. Full breakfast is served in the breakfast room or on the patio, both of which have a view of the bay. Deposit required to hold reservation. Cancellation notice seventy-two hours. Visa, MasterCard, American Express. French, German, and Spanish spoken. Children welcome. No pets. No smoking indoors. **In the hosts' own words:** "Relax in the comfort of our B&B and enjoy creative breakfasts and tastefully decorated rooms. During your stay with us, you may wish to explore Mayne Island and other islands nearby."

Saturna Lodge

Steve and Rebecca Cozine
130 Payne Road
Saturna Island, BC V0N 2Y0
(250) 539-2254 fax: (250) 539-3091
toll-free from within North America: 1-888-539-8800
email: saturnalodge@hotmail.com
web site: www.saturna-island.bc.ca

• Two rooms and five suites: In summer, $120–175. In winter, $135–195. Queen-sized bed and double sofa bed; queen-sized bed; twin beds. Ensuite and shared guest bathrooms.

• A newly refurbished country-style house overlooking Boot Cove, with guest suites that have ocean and garden views. Licensed restaurant and lounge on the main floor, with a fireplace and a wrap-around deck. Hot tub on the deck. Living room with fireplace, books, and satellite TV. One of the suites is a honeymoon suite that has an ensuite bathroom with a soaker tub and a private balcony. Garden with croquet and bocce in summer. Mountain bicycles. Near a vineyard. Five minutes from the ferry terminal; there is bus service from and to the terminal. West Coast–style Continental breakfast. Visa, MasterCard. Smoking on the balconies. **In the hosts' own words:** "Tour our nearby vineyard."

Ocean-Breeze B&B

Bev and Alan Birchard
2585 Seaview Road
Mail: RR 1
Mill Bay, BC V0R 2P0
(250) 743-0608 fax: (250) 743-0603
toll-free from within North America: 1-877-743-0654
email: oceanbreeze@telus.net
web site: www.oceanbreeze.bc.ca

•Thirty-five minutes north of Victoria. Fifty-five minutes south of Nanaimo. From Highway 1, turn east (towards the ocean) onto Frayne Road. Turn left onto Partridge Road and continue for two blocks. Turn right onto Sea View Road.

•Three rooms: One person $70–80; two people $85–95. Queen-sized bed; twin beds. Ensuite bathrooms. Extended stay and off-season rates.

•A seventy-five-year-old recently renovated house with views of Mill Bay, the Gulf Islands, and Mount Baker. Five minutes' walk from the ocean, a marina, shopping, and Brentwood College. In the area are private schools, restaurants, and artisans. Near hiking, cycling, golf, fishing, kayaking, whale watching, and marine animal viewing. Thirty minutes' drive from winery tours, Chemainus's murals, the B.C. Forestry Museum, Duncan's totem poles, and the Butchart Gardens. Mountain bikes. Guest rooms have Shaker pine beds, armoires, and down duvets. Guest areas with antiques, original art, Persian rugs, and hardwood floors. Guest reading room. Coffee and tea any time. Guest living room with brick fireplace, TV, VCR, videos, CDs, and radio. Sun room. Two outdoor guest patios with tables and chairs. Gardens and orchard area. On-site parking. Full breakfast is served in the dining room on Wedgwood china. Diets are accommodated. Cancellation notice seventy-two hours. Visa, MasterCard. Not suitable for children under ten years. No pets. Smoking outdoors. **In the hosts' own words:** "Our warm hospitality, breathtaking scenery, luxurious guest rooms, and gourmet breakfasts make for a memorable experience. Arrive as our guests and leave as our friends."

Norton's Green B&B

Clifford and Mary Norton
663 Frayne Road, RR 1
Mill Bay, BC V0R 2P0
(250) 743-8006
email: nortonsgreen@seaside.net

- Forty minutes from Victoria. Forty-five minutes from Nanaimo.
- Three rooms: One person $50; two people $55–60. Queen-sized bed; double bed. Ensuite, shared, and private bathrooms.
- A green farm-style house near the ocean, with a wrap-around balcony and flowers. Forty minutes from Victoria. Near beaches, Chemainus's murals, a marina, fishing, golf, Brentwood College, shopping, and the ferry to the Butchart Gardens. TV and garden. Terry robes. Beverages. Parking. Full English-style breakfast or breakfast of choice, including fruit, is served by a fireplace in the dining room. No pets. No smoking. **In the hosts' own words:** "Stay with us—we love to spoil you."

Shirley's Cozy Nest B&B

Shirley and Paul Chmielewski
2502 Fawn Road
Mill Bay, BC V0R 2P0
(250) 743-8286
toll-free: 1-877-743-8286
email: pchmiele@cow-net.com
web site: www.cow-net.com/pchmiele

- Forty minutes north of Victoria. One hour south of Nanaimo. From Victoria, go north on Highway 1 towards Mill Bay for 40 minutes. Just before Mill Bay, turn left onto Frayne Road (into Deer Park). Turn right onto Fawn Road. The B&B is a few hundred metres down the road, on the left.
- Two rooms: One person $55; two people $65. Queen-sized bed. Shared guest bathroom. Extended stay rates.
- A B&B in a modern residential area, within walking distance of shopping, a marina, and Brentwood College. In the area are many family restaurants. Near the Mill Bay ferry terminal's ferries to Brentwood Bay, which is near the Butchart Gardens and the Victoria airport. Fifteen minutes' drive from a golf and country club and a golf course. Thirty minutes' drive from Chemainus's murals. An hour's drive from the Nanaimo ferry terminals' ferries to Vancouver. Guest rooms have sitting areas, TVs, VCRs, and movies on request. Covered patio in backyard. Hot tub. Full or Continental breakfast. Cancellation notice forty-eight hours. Check-out until 11:00 a.m. Cash, cheques, traveller's cheques, Visa. Children welcome. Small pets welcome but must be kept in guest room; cat in residence. Smoking in designated areas. **In the hosts' own words:** "A warm welcome awaits you at our B&B. In the morning, enjoy a Continental or home-cooked breakfast with all the fixings. At the end of the day, relax in the secluded hot tub while enjoying the quiet atmosphere."

Maple Tree Lane B&B

Dot and Jim Garbet
440 Goulet Road, RR 2
Mill Bay, BC V0R 2P0
(250) 743-3940 fax: (250) 743-3959
toll-free: 1-877-854-2643
email: mapletree@cvnet.net
web site: www.cvnet.net/cowb&b/maple

• From Highway 1, turn east onto Hutchinson Road, towards Arbutus Ridge. Turn right onto Telegraph, left onto La Fortune Road, right onto Kilipi Road, and left onto Goulet Road. Watch for signs on all corners.

• Two rooms: One person $50–60; two people $75–85. Twin beds (or twin beds side by side with king-sized bedding); queen-sized bed. Bathrooms in suite. Additional person $25. Child 6 to 14 $10. Double hide-a-bed. Crib and cot. Family and weekly rates.

• A house on the ocean, thirty-five minutes from Victoria, with a beach and, in summer, a swimming pool. Canoeing and kayaking from the B&B. Five to ten minutes from golf, fishing charters, hiking trails, Brentwood and Shawnigan College schools, shopping, and restaurants. Twenty minutes from Duncan. Thirty minutes from Chemainus. Fifty-five minutes from Nanaimo. Garden-level guest room has a queen-sized bed and a private entrance. Adjoining family room has a double hide-a-bed and a TV. Main-floor guest room has twin beds and is wheelchair accessible. Full breakfast. Diets are accommodated. MasterCard. Children welcome. Pets by arrangement; two cats in residence. Smoking outdoors. **In the hosts' own words:** "Enjoy our country hospitality and scrumptious breakfasts in a beautiful setting on Vancouver Island. Stroll the beach and collect shells and driftwood, canoe on calm waters, and enjoy tea in the gazebo."

Shawnigan Shores B&B

Elly Ruge
2374 Renfrew Road
Mail: RR 1
Shawnigan Lake, BC V0R 2W0
(250) 733-2233 fax: (250) 733-2234
toll-free: 1-877-937-7722
email: lakeBB@hotmail.com
web site: www.lakeBB.com

• From Highway 1, turn onto Mill Bay Road, towards Shawnigan Lake. At the four-way stop in Shawnigan Lake Village, turn right onto Renfrew Road and continue for 3.4 kilometres. The B&B is on the left.

• Self-contained three-bedroom suite (sleeps six): In summer (June 15 to September 15), $299. King-sized bed, queen-sized bed, and two twin beds.
Bathroom in suite.
Breakfast ingredients supplied.
Extended stay rates. Weekend rates May to October.

• A B&B on one and a half acres, on Shawnigan Lake, with a private beach and surrounded by evergreens. Dock with kayaks, canoes, fishing boat, and waterski boat. Outdoor hot tub under trees. Living room with stone fireplace and patio doors that lead to the grounds and the lake. Satellite TV, DVD player, VCR, stereo, CD player, computer, and Internet access. Kitchen with fridge, built-in oven, microwave, coffee maker, toaster, blender, dishwasher, and cookware for guest meals. Private entrance. Duvets and robes. Jacuzzi tub and river rock double shower in bathroom. Ingredients for full breakfast supplied. Deposit required to hold reservation. Cancellation notice seven days. Check-in after 2:00 p.m.; check-out until 11:00 a.m. Cash, Visa, MasterCard, American Express, traveller's cheques, Interac. Adult oriented; children over twelve welcome. No pets; a cat and a golden retriever in residence. Smoking outdoors. **In the hosts' own words:** "Discover paradise at our B&B, tucked away in a grove of whispering pines. For fun and recreation or romance and relaxation, our three-bedroom suite on a lake is a great setting. Our private beach, water sports, outdoor hot tub, and luxurious suite with gourmet breakfast ingredients make this your ideal getaway."

Whistlestop Shawnigan Lakeside B&B

Ken and Shirley Charters
1838 Baden Powell Road
Mail: Box 39
Shawnigan Lake, BC V0R 2W0
(250) 743-4896 fax: (250) 743-3301
email: whistle@cvnet.net
website: www.cvnet.net/cowb&b/whistlestop

• Forty minutes north of Victoria, on the east shore of Shawnigan Lake.
• Rooms and honeymoon suite.
Four rooms: Two people $139, $250 for two nights. Ensuite bathrooms.
Honeymoon suite: Two people $250, $425 for two nights. King-sized bed. Ensuite bathroom.
Extended stay, group, and off-season rates.

• A B&B on the east shore of Shawnigan Lake, accessible by car and float plane. Docks for boats and float planes are a sixty-metre walk from the B&B. Close to E & N passenger train station. A few minutes' walk from the village of Shawnigan and a provincial park with walking/jogging trails and a beach. Guest rooms have down quilts, TVs, VCRs, and private decks with views of sunsets and the lake. Guest hot tub in a gazebo has a view of the lake, privacy glass windows, and a keyed entrance. Robes provided. Croquet sets and rowboats. Living room with stone fireplace, sun room, library, ice machine, and bar area. Suite has a private dining/bar area, a four-post king-sized bed, a two-person Jacuzzi, and a marble fireplace. Hosts help arrange small weddings, honeymoons, anniversaries, birthdays, and conferences. A karafe of fresh-ground coffee and assorted baked goods are served on a tray left at guests' doors before breakfast. Full breakfast; guests choose either an 8:30 or a 10:00 a.m. seating. Diets are accommodated by arrangement. Deposit of fifty dollars required to hold reservation. Cancellation notice seven days. Check-in 2:00 p.m. to midnight; check-out until noon. Visa, MasterCard, American Express. Smoking on decks and in the courtyard. **In the hosts' own words:** "We invite you to rediscover the country spirit of days gone by on southern Vancouver Island. Our house is set amongst magnificent ivy-covered maples on a secluded, sandy-beached acreage. We offer rooms decorated in a railroad theme, warm hospitality, and privacy. Curl up by the fireplace or relax on the balcony and enjoy the beautiful grounds, courtyard, and lakeside views. Our full breakfasts will satisfy even the heartiest appetites. The perfect romantic getaway."

Cobble House B&B

Ingrid and Simon Vermegen
3105 Cameron-Taggart Road, RR 1
Cobble Hill, BC V0R 1L0
(250) 743-2672 fax: (250) 743-2672
email: stay@cobble-house.com
web site: www.cobble-house.com

• Forty-five minutes north of Victoria. One hour south of Nanaimo. Fifteen minutes south of Duncan. Near Mill Bay and Shawnigan Lake.

• Three rooms: One person $65–75; two people $79–89. Queen-sized bed; queen-sized bed and double futon; twin beds. Ensuite bathrooms. Additional person $20.
Packages.

• A new one-level house with a cedar deck, on forty forested acres with a creek. Guest rooms have sitting areas. One of the guest rooms has an ensuite bathroom with Jacuzzi. Living room with Russian fireplace. In the area are wineries, private boarding schools, golf, kayaking, swimming, hiking, mountain biking, and fishing. Thirty minutes from Chemainus's murals. A base for exploring southern Vancouver Island. One of the hosts is a former executive chef. Full breakfast includes homemade baked goods. Deposit of 30 percent required to hold reservation. Cancellation notice four days. Visa, MasterCard. Dutch and German spoken. Two dogs in residence. No smoking. **In the hosts' own words:** "Our two friendly dogs would like to take you for a walk. We pride ourselves on offering a quiet, relaxing environment and on giving attention to every detail."

Dream Weaver B&B

Cathy and Ken McAllister
1682 Botwood Lane
Cowichan Bay, BC V0R 1N0
(250) 748-7688 fax: (250) 748-4519
toll-free from within North America: 1-888-748-7689
email: dreamwvr@islandnet.com
web site: www.vancouverisland-bc.com/dreamweaver/

• Forty-five minutes north of Victoria. Fifty-five minutes south of Nanaimo. From Duncan, go south on Highway 1, following the signs for Cowichan Bay. The B&B is in the township of Cowichan Bay, at the corner of Cowichan Bay Road and Botwood Lane.

• Four suites: One person $55–75; two people $70–130. Queen-sized bed; queen-sized bed and double hide-a-bed. Ensuite bathrooms. Additional person $15.

• A new Victorian-style house with river rock walls, planters, and stairs. Near restaurants, a marine ecology centre, a wooden boat museum, and a government wharf. In the area are kayak and bike rentals, sailing, and whale-watching and fishing tours. Fifteen minutes' drive from a Native heritage centre and a forestry museum. Within fifteen kilometres of vineyards, Mill Bay, Duncan, and Chemainus. Suites have private entrances, TVs, VCRs, radios, CD players, fridges, coffee makers, telephones, books, games, robes, and room-darkening blinds. One of the suites is a honeymoon suite and is on the top floor. Two of the suites have bedrooms with double-jetted Jacuzzi tubs. One of the suites has a bathroom with a single-jetted tub. Three of the suites have fireplaces. Guest veranda, covered deck, and patio. Full breakfast is served in the dining room. Diets are accommodated. Reservations recommended. Visa, MasterCard, Interac. No pets. No smoking indoors. **In the hosts' own words:** "Spoil yourself."

Old Farm B&B

Barbara and George MacFarlane
2075 Cowichan Bay Road
Cowichan Bay, BC V0R 1N0
(250) 748-6410 fax: (250) 748-6410
toll-free from within Canada and the U.S.: 1-888-240-1482
email: oldfarm@seaside.net
web site: www.cvnet.net/cowb&b/oldfarm

• Forty-five minutes north of Victoria. Five minutes south of Duncan. From Highway 1, turn onto Cowichan Bay Road. The B&B is 1 kilometre north of Cowichan Bay Village, on the side of the road closer to the water.

• Three rooms: One person $75–115; two people $85–125. Queen-sized beds. Ensuite bathrooms. Additional person $25.

• A restored century-old three-storey house, designed by architect Samuel Maclure for a retired English sea captain. On two acres that slope down to tidal water. An estuary provides a sanctuary for resident and migrating birds. Gazebo, garden spa, badminton, and horseshoes. Guest sitting/reading room with fireplace, TV, and VCR. Guest rooms are decorated in Laura Ashley–style. Coffee or tea is delivered to guest rooms before breakfast. Full breakfast includes farm produce. Check-in and check-out times are flexible. Visa, MasterCard. Children over eleven welcome. Dog and cats in residence. Smoking outdoors. **In the hosts' own words:** "We try to make sure that every guest will want to come back."

Bird Song Cottage B&B

Larry and Virginia Blatchford
9909 Maple Street
Mail: Box 1432
Chemainus, BC V0R 1K0
(250) 246-9910 fax: (250) 246-2909
email: birdsong@island.net
web site: www.romanticbb.com

• In Chemainus (one hour north of Victoria).

• Rooms and cottage.

Three rooms: $85–115. Queen-sized bed; queen-sized bed and one twin bed; double bed and one twin bed. Ensuite bathrooms. Additional person $20.

One-bedroom cottage: $325. Queen-sized bed. Ensuite bathroom.

• A 1905 character house with antiques and oil paintings, half a block from the ocean, gift and antique shops, restaurants, Chemainus's murals, and a dinner theatre. Guest living room with fireplace, baby grand piano, pump organ, Celtic harp, and collection of fancy hats. Evening tea and cookies. Guest rooms have duvets, flowers, and lace-trimmed cotton linen. Medieval-style cottage has a fireplace, a double soaker tub, and two balconies. Breakfast is served on fine china in a sun room surrounded by a garden. Diets are accommodated. Visa, MasterCard, American Express, Interac. No pets; birds and cats in residence. Nonsmoking.
In the hosts' own words: "Warmth, gracious service, and unique décor make our B&B what dreams are made of."

Island View B&B

Darlene and Russ Dillon
5391 Entwhistle Drive
Nanaimo, BC V9V 1H2
(250) 758-5536 fax: (250) 758-5536
email: rdmts@islandnet.com
web site: www.bbcanada.com/1017.html

• From the Departure Bay ferry terminal, take Highway 19A north for fifteen minutes. Turn right onto Rutherford, right onto Hammond Bay, and left onto Entwhistle.
From the Duke Point ferry terminal, take Highway 19. Turn right onto Mostar, which becomes Rutherford. Turn right onto Hammond Bay and left onto Entwhistle. The B&B is halfway down the hill, on the left.
• Room and suite.
Room: Two people $60. Twin beds. Private bathroom.
Self-contained suite: Two people $85. Queen-sized bed and queen-sized sofa bed. Bathroom in suite. Additional person $20. Call for one-person rates.
• A B&B on half an acre with a garden and views of the Strait of Georgia and the Sunshine Coast. Guest room has a TV and a view of the garden. Eight-hundred-square-foot one-bedroom suite has a view of the ocean, a private entrance, a kitchen, a living room with queen-sized sofa bed, a gas fireplace, a TV, a VCR, and a collection of videos. Fresh fruit, snacks, and refreshments. Sunsets can be seen from a deck. Half a block from a shoreline to walk on. Laundry facilities. Full breakfast is served in the dining room. Children welcome. Smoke-free environment. **In the hosts' own words:** "Enjoy quiet surroundings, tastefully served breakfasts, and magnificent sunsets in our garden paradise."

Madrona Point Waterfront B&B

Lise and Reg Johanson
1344 Madrona Drive
(Nanoose Bay)
Parksville, BC V9P 9C9
(250) 468-5972 fax: (250) 468-5976
email: madronap@island.net

• From Nanaimo, take Highway 19 to Parksville. Take the north exit onto Highway 19A. At the traffic light, turn right onto Franklin Gull Road, which becomes Northwest Bay Road. Turn left onto Beaver Creek Wharf Road and left onto Madrona Drive. The B&B is on the right side.

• Room and suite.
Room: In summer (May to October), two people $95. In winter (November to April), two people $75. King-sized bed. Ensuite bathroom.
Suite: In summer (May to October), two people $95. In winter (November to April), two people $75. Queen-sized bed. Bathroom in suite.
Additional person $20. Roll-away and pull-out sofa beds available. Additional rooms for larger parties available.

• A B&B on the ocean with a private beach and views of Georgia Strait and mountains from the guest rooms. Eagles, whales, sea lions, and other marine life can be seen. Three kilometres from golf, swimming, fishing, and shopping. Near beachcoming and birdwatching. Windsurfer, Laser sailboats, kayaks, canoes, and bikes for rent on the property. Hosts share knowledge of the area. Guided salmon fishing can be provided by hosts. Guest room and suite have separate patio or deck entrances, down comforters, and feather beds. Suite has a living room. Guest room has a fireplace. Antique furniture. Hot tub with a view of the beach. Full breakfast is served in a solarium kitchen, which has views of the ocean, mountains, and wildlife. Visa, MasterCard. French spoken. Children welcome. Friendly pets welcome; golden retriever in residence. Smoking outdoors. **In the hosts' own words:** "Make yourself at home in our warm, spacious, and comfortable house, which offers spectacular views, elegantly furnished rooms, and delicious breakfasts. This is a birdwatcher's and beachcomber's haven. Whether you are coming for business or pleasure, a wedding party or a romantic getaway, our attention to detail provides a welcoming and relaxing atmosphere. We are experienced travellers who understand the needs of our guests."

The Maclure House Inn

Penny and Michael McBride
1015 East Island Highway
Parksville, BC V9P 2E4
(250) 248-3470 fax: (250) 248-5162
email: stay@maclurehouse.com
web site: www.maclurehouse.com

• From the Nanaimo ferry terminal, go north on Highway 19 for 24 kilometres. Take the Parksville exit and continue for three minutes. At Beach Acres Resort, turn right into the resort's driveway. The B&B is just past the office of the resort.

• Four rooms: Two people $95–140. Queen-sized bed; twin beds. Ensuite and private bathrooms. Additional person $21. Child $12. Off-season rates.

• A Tudor-style house on Rathtrevor Beach, a beach known for its sheltered warm waters. Views of islands and the snowcapped mountains of the Sechelt Peninsula. A few steps from a sandy beach and walking trails. Light afternoon tea served when guests arrive. Coffee and juice outside guest room doors in the morning. Restaurant, tennis, pool, hot tub, sauna, and shuffleboard on the property. Five minutes from golf, kayaking, and horseback riding. Three-course breakfast is served on the patio, which has a view of the ocean, or by a fireplace in the dining room. Visa, MasterCard, American Express, Interac. **In the hosts' own words:** "Our heritage inn, frequented in the 1920s by Rudyard Kipling, who was a friend of the then owners, is full of charm and history. Our unobtrusive pampering brings guests back year after year."

Marina View B&B

Bob Hetherington and Linda Teshima
895 Glenhale Crescent
Parksville, BC V9P 1Z7
(250) 248-9308 fax: (250) 248-9408
email: marinaview@bcsupernet.com
web site: www.vancouverisland-bc.com/MarinaViewBB/

• Take Highway 19A north through Parksville. Past the French Creek Market, turn right onto Wright Road (at the traffic light) and take the first left onto Glenhale Crescent. Follow the B&B's signs.

• Three rooms: One person $70–90; two people $85–95. Queen-sized bed; twin beds. Ensuite bathrooms. Additional person $20. Roll-away bed available.

• A B&B on the ocean with a view of the Strait of Georgia, the Gulf Islands, and mountains. Deck and solarium with views of Alaska cruise ships, sailboats, eagles, herons, seals, and otters. Guest sitting room with books, TV, VCR, movies, and games. Breakfast, including homemade baked goods, homemade preserves, and fresh fruit, is served in the dining room. Reservations recommended. Cancellation notice seven days. Check-in 3:00 to 6:00 p.m.; check-out until 10:30 a.m. Cash, traveller's cheques, Visa, MasterCard. Adult oriented. No pets; two cats in residence. No smoking. **In the hosts' own words:** "We offer views to soothe your soul and breakfasts to please your palate."

Hollyford B&B

Jim and Marjorie Ford
106 Hoylake Road East
Qualicum Beach, BC V9K 1L7
(250) 752-8101 fax: (250) 752-8102
toll-free from within Canada and the U.S.: 1-877-BBHOLLY (224-6559)
email: mail@hollyford.ca
web site: www.hollyford.ca

• From Highway 19 or Highway 19A, turn onto Memorial Avenue and continue to Hoylake Road. The B&B is on the corner.
From Tofino or Port Alberni, take Highway 4, which becomes Memorial Avenue and continue to Hoylake Road.

• Rooms: In summer, two people $140–165. In winter, two people $115–120. King-sized bed; queen-sized bed; twin beds. Ensuite bathrooms.

• A cottage surrounded by holly hedges and a half acre of fruit trees, herbs, and flower gardens. Five minutes' walk from the ocean and downtown. Forty minutes' drive from the ferry terminals in Nanaimo. Guest rooms are sound-proofed and have private entrances, patios, fine linen, duvets, robes, toiletries, TVs, VCRs, fireplaces, telephones, thermostats for individually controlled heat, and ensuite bathrooms with soaker tubs and heritage furniture. Guest lounge, guest breakfast lounge with fireplace, and two guest libraries. Morning trays with coffee, tea, and/or juice and evening trays with chocolates and bottled water or sherry. Full, three-course breakfast is served to guests at separate tables in the dining room with Irish linen, sterling silver, and Waterford crystal. Cash, traveller's cheques, Visa, MasterCard. Children over eleven welcome. No pets; cat in residence. Smoke-free. **In the hosts' own words:** "Welcome to our heritage cottage. We offer Irish hospitality—casual elegance and haute cuisine. The essence of executive lodging."

Blue Willow B&B

Arlene and John England
524 Quatna Road
Qualicum Beach, BC V9K 1B4
(250) 752-9052 fax: (250) 752-9039
email: bwillow@island.net
web site: www.bluewillow.bc.ca

• From Highway 19, turn west onto Qualicum Road and then right onto Quatna Road.

• Rooms and suite.
Rooms: One person \$85; two people \$95. Additional person \$25.
Suite: Two people \$105. Queen-sized bed and three twin beds. Additional person \$25.
Off-season rates November to March.

• A Tudor-style house with beamed ceilings, leaded windows, and garden views, surrounded by evergreens. Five minutes' walk from an ocean beach. Fifteen minutes' walk from the village of Qualicum Beach. Suite has a separate entrance. Garden, patio, and guest sitting room with TV. Full breakfast. Visa, MasterCard. French and German spoken. Children welcome in the suite. Pets welcome by arrangement. Dachshund in residence. Nonsmoking house. **In the hosts' own words:** "We offer hospitality, comfort, quiet, and relaxation. Breakfast is a very special event."

Shoreline B&B

Dave and Audrie Sands
4969 Shoreline Drive
Deep Bay, BC
Mail: RR 1 Site 152 C–4
Bowser, BC V0R 1G0
(250) 757-9807 fax: (250) 757-9807
email: sands@nanaimo.ark.com
web site: www.pixsell.bc.ca/bb/1439.htm

• In Deep Bay, off Highway 19A. From Highway 19, take the Cook Creek exit. From Highway 19A, turn at the Deep Bay signs. Turn right at the E & N railway tracks. Turn left three times, the third time onto Shoreline Drive.

• Room: Two people $75. Queen-sized bed. Private bathroom. Additional person $35. Twin bed in family room adjacent to the bathroom is available for additional person.

• A house on a walk-on ocean beach, with a guest room that has a view of a garden, Baynes Sound, the Chrome Island lighthouse, and Denman and Hornby islands. Guest family room with TV, books, and fireplace. Private entrance. Robes provided. Garden and beach chairs. Near golf, charter fishing, cave exploration at Horne Lake Caves, birdwatching, and boat charters. Within ten minutes' drive of restaurants. Full breakfast is served on the deck, which has a view of the ocean. Diets are accommodated. Visa. Adult oriented. Pets welcome; dog in residence. No smoking indoors. **In the hosts' own words:** "We have a lovely location and we are happy to share it with you."

Seahaven B&B

Carol and Roy Richards
6660 South Island Highway
Mail: Site 3 C–12
Fanny Bay, BC V0R 1W0
(250) 335-1550 fax: (250) 339-1283
toll-free from within North America:
1-888-335-1550
email: seahaven@island.net
web site: www.seahaven.org

- At Fanny Bay (20 minutes south of Courtenay; 3 hours north of Victoria), 1 kilometre from the Buckley Bay ferry terminal. Midway between Victoria and Port Hardy.
- Three rooms: One person $50; two people $65. Double bed; queen-sized bed; twin beds. Private and ensuite bathrooms. Additional person $10.
- A two-level house on two hundred feet of waterfront, with a deck that has a view of sunrises, eagles, herons, seals, and otters. Guest sitting room has books, a selection of videos, and a view. In the area are Denman and Hornby islands, golf courses, hiking, swimming, kayak tours, and skiing at Mount Washington. One kilometre from the Buckley Bay ferry terminal's ferries to Denman Island. Barbecue and picnic tables. Full breakfast includes fresh fruit, homemade bread, jam, and free-range eggs. Visa, MasterCard. Children over ten welcome. Smoking on the deck and in the garden. **In the hosts' own words:** "Take in our fantastic views. Our house is a very friendly and comfortable place to visit and an excellent place to take a relaxing break."

Wellington House B&B

Shelagh Davis and Doug Jackson
2593 Derwent Avenue
Mail: Box 689
Cumberland, BC V0R 1S0
(250) 336-8809 fax: (250) 336-2455
email: cma_chin@island.net
web site: www.vquest.com/wellington

• On Vancouver Island. Take Highway 19 north to Cumberland. At the T junction, turn left towards Cumberland. Turn right onto Dunsmuir Avenue. Turn left onto Sutton. Turn right onto Derwent Avenue.

• Room and suites.
Room: One person $65. Double bed. Private bathroom.
Suite (sleeps three): $75.
Suite (sleeps four): $85.
Additional person $25.
Extended stay rates.

• A modern house in the foothills of the Beaufort Mountains, in the historical mining village of Cumberland. Garden-level guest entrance. Suites have sitting rooms with TVs, VCRs, and books. One of the suites has a kitchen. Deck, covered patio, perennial garden, and grape arbour. Five to forty-five minutes' drive from golf courses, Forbidden Plateau and Mount Washington ski areas, sport fishing, and fresh and saltwater activities. Biking and hiking trails from the B&B. Full breakfast is served in a country-style kitchen. Visa. Children welcome. No pets. Smoking outdoors. **In the hosts' own words:** "This is one area where you can golf and ski on the same day. Come relax and watch many species of birds, share our peaceful surroundings, and enjoy our tranquil garden and our hospitality."

Greystone Manor B&B

Mike and Maureen Shipton
4014 Haas Road
Mail: RR 6 Site 684 C–2
Courtenay, BC V9N 8H9
(250) 338-1422
email: greyston@island.net
web site: www.bbcanada.com/1334.html

• From Courtenay, take Highway 19A south for 3 kilometres to Royston. Turn left onto Hilton and left onto Haas Road.

• Three rooms: One person $60; two people $80. Queen-sized bed; double bed; twin beds. Ensuite and private bathrooms.

• A 1918 house on the ocean, on one and a half acres with English flower gardens and old maples and firs. Perennial beds, rockeries, and herb and vegetable gardens. View across Comox Bay to mainland mountains. Seals, herons, sea birds, and eagles can be seen. Guest sitting room with fireplace, piano, books, and magazines. Twenty minutes from ferries to Denman and Hornby islands. Forty minutes from Mount Washington and Strathcona Provincial Park. Eight minutes from Courtenay. Ten minutes from golf courses. Halfway between Port Hardy and Victoria; a stopover point on the Sunshine Coast circle tour. The hosts, who came to Canada from Bath, England, share their knowledge of the local area and hiking and walking trails. Full breakfast. Visa, MasterCard. Children over twelve welcome. No pets. No smoking. **In the hosts' own words:** "A friendly welcome awaits you. Relax in our lovely heritage house and spectacular gardens."

Forest Glen B&B

Art and Lois Enns
5760 Sea Terrace Road
Mail: RR 2 Site 280 C–37
Courtenay, BC V9N 5M9
(250) 334-4374 fax: (250) 334-4396
toll-free from within North America: 1-888-349-2332
email: forestgl@island.net
web site: forestglen.bc.ca

• Fifteen minutes north of Courtenay. Ten minutes north of the Powell River ferry. From Courtenay, go north on Highway 19 for 6 kilometres. Turn right onto Hardy Road. Turn right onto Coleman. Turn right onto Loxley and continue to the end. Turn left onto Avonlea. Turn right onto Sea Terrace.

• Rooms and suite.

Two rooms: One person $50–60; two people $70–80; three people $100. Queen-sized bed and one twin bed, private bathroom; queen-sized bed, ensuite bathroom.
Two-bedroom suite: In summer (May to September), $90–170. Queen-sized bed; twin beds. Bathroom in suite. Additional person $20.
Winter rates.

• A Cape Cod–style house in the Seal Bay Forest with walking trails from the B&B through Seal Bay Regional Park to Seal Bay. Deer, seals, eagles, and herons can be seen on the walking trails. Thirty minutes from skiing and hiking at Mount Washington in Strathcona Park. Five minutes' drive from fishing and kayaking at Bates Beach. Fifteen minutes' drive from ocean beaches. Living room with fireplace. Sun room with TV and view of flower gardens leads to a deck with guest hot tub and outdoor fireplace. Guest rooms have sitting areas. Suite has a living room, a TV, a VCR, a fireplace, books, and a private entrance. Full breakfast includes fresh fruit, juice, and homemade baked goods. Visa, MasterCard. Nonsmoking house. **In the hosts' own words:** "We've built our dream home, and now we invite you to come and enjoy it with us. Have a glass of wine or cup of tea with us by the fireplace."

Foskett House B&B

Dove and Michael Hendren
484 Lazo Road
Comox, BC V9M 3V1
(250) 339-4272 fax: (250) 339-4272
toll-free from within North America: 1-800-797-9252
email: foskett@island.net
web site: www.vquest.com/foskett/

• At Point Holmes, 5 kilometres east of Comox.

• Two rooms: One person $65–75; two people $80–90. Queen-sized bed and one twin hide-a-bed; queen-sized bed. Ensuite bathrooms. Additional person $20. Seasonal rates.

• A 1920 South African–style ranch house with wrap-around verandas, on five acres of wind-sculpted oaks and pines, across the road from the ocean. Views of the ocean, the Gulf Islands, and winter storms. Interior is finished with cedar. Antiques. Beach-stone fireplace. Guest rooms have private entrances. Ten minutes from ferries to Powell River. Full breakfast includes homemade baked goods, fresh fruit, and an entrée. Border collie in residence. Nonsmoking. **In the hosts' own words:** "After the sound of the ocean has lulled you to sleep, awake from a wonderful night's rest to our gourmet breakfast."

Tudor Acres B&B

Betty and Peter Cartwright
2065 Endall Road
Black Creek, BC V9J 1G8
(250) 337-5764 fax: (250) 337-5764
toll-free from within British Columbia and Washington State:
1-888-326-4411
email: tudoracres@telus.net
web site: www3.telus.net/tudoracres

• From Courtenay, go north for 15 minutes. Pass Black Creek Building Supply, which is on the right, and continue for 2 kilometres. Turn left onto Endall Road.
• Rooms and suite.
Two rooms: One person $50; two people $65. Queen-sized bed; two double beds. Two-piece ensuite and shared guest tub and shower.
Self-contained suite: Two people $75. Queen-sized bed and twin day beds. Private bathroom. Additional person $15. Extended stay rates.
• A modern house on a twelve-acre sheep farm. Living room with brick fireplace, organ, piano, TV, and VCR. French doors in the dining room lead to a deck with hot tub, outdoor furniture, and barbecue. Lawns, fruit and vegetable gardens, orchard, and grape arbour. Suite has a private entrance. Five minutes from Miracle Beach Provincial Park. Fifteen minutes from ferries to Powell River. Thirty minutes from skiing at Mount Washington and hiking trails at Strathcona Provincial Park. Midway between Courtenay and Campbell River. Near Crown Isle and Storey Creek golf courses. Full breakfast includes a hot entrée, fruit and juices made from the hosts' garden produce, and homemade bread and preserves. Beverages and homemade baked goods are served when guests arrive. Visa. All ages welcome. No pets. Smoking outdoors. **In the hosts' own words:** "Enjoy a variety of scrumptious breakfast creations and congenial conversation in our spacious lounge. Our aim is to help you enjoy our home and surrounding area as much as we do."

Rivers Ridge B&B

June and Frank Greens
2243 Steelhead Road
Campbell River, BC V9W 4P3
(250) 286-9696 fax: (250) 286-9605

• Two rooms: Two people $55–75. Queen-sized bed, ensuite bathroom; queen-sized bed or extra long twin beds, private bathroom. Cot-sized bed $15. Off-season and senior rates.

• A house on half an acre with rose gardens, a fish pond, and mature fir trees. One hundred feet of riverfront. Gated trail to a private picnic area on the river bank. Backyard with arbour. Snorkeling and fly-fishing in the river. Near two golf courses, hiking trails, kayaking, skiing, salmon fishing, and whale-watching, snorkeling, and eco tours. Guided fishing trips and eco tours can be arranged by the hosts. Guest rooms have TVs. One guest room has a queen-sized four-post bed and an ensuite bathroom. Living room with fireplace, bay window, swivel rockers, love seat, reading lamps, stereo, CD and cassette player, and books on the area. TV room. Tea and coffee any time. Dinner and picnic lunches available for a fee. Barbecue. Kitchen available on request. Full breakfast, including farm-fresh eggs, seasonal fruit, muffins, scones, waffles, hot cakes, and homemade bread, jam, and preserves, is served at guests' convenience in the breakfast room or the dining room, both of which have a view of the river. Diets are accommodated. Reservations appreciated; although not required. Traveller's cheques, Visa, MasterCard. Cat and duck toller dog in residence. Smoking on the deck. **In the hosts' own words:** "Enjoy the serenity of our house overlooking the Campbell River, surrounded by tall trees and tranquil gardens with paths and resting places. We will greet you upon arrival and ensure your stay is a pleasant experience."

The Lighthouse B&B

Dennis and Eleanor Hansen
Hansen Road, Smelt Bay
Mail: Box 244
Manson's Landing
Cortes Island, BC V0P 1K0
(250) 935-6389 fax: (250) 935-6389
toll-free from within North America: 1-888-246-5005

• Seventeen kilometres from the Whaletown ferry dock. Half a kilometre from Smelt Bay Provincial Park.

• Rooms and suite.

Five rooms: One person $40–65; two people $55–85. King-sized bed; queen-sized bed; twin beds. Private bathrooms.

Self-contained suite: Queen-sized hide-a-bed and one twin bed. Ensuite bathroom.

• A southwest-facing house with a view of Georgia Strait and mountains on Vancouver Island from all the rooms and the deck. Two minutes' drive from sand dollar picking, clam digging, oyster gathering, fishing, sunbathing, and white sandy beaches at Smelt Bay. Guest family room with pool table. Guest rooms with king-sized and queen-sized beds have private patios. Self-contained suite has laundry facilities, a kitchen, and a private patio. New furnishings. Heated swimming pool. Crib, highchair, playpens, swing set, sand box, small children's swimming pools, and a hot water tap for the children's pools. Decks have wire mesh and gates for the protection of small children. Full breakfast includes fresh-ground coffee, herbal tea, farm-fresh eggs, Texas potatoes, homemade bread or Norwegian crêpes, and a choice of bacon, sausage, or ham. Reservations required. Deposit of one night's rate required to hold reservation. German and Norwegian spoken. No pets. No smoking indoors.

In the hosts' own words: "Our luxurious, casually elegant, executive-style house has been designed with your comfort in mind. Enjoy our specialty Norwegian crêpes, as part of our gourmet breakfast. Bask in the sun around the heated pool and swim under the stars at night, and don't forget your camera for magnificent, unforgettable sunsets."

Blue Heron B&B

Gunnar and Emilia Hansen
Potlatch Road
Mail: Box 23
Manson's Landing
Cortes Island, BC V0P 1K0
(250) 935-6584

• Twenty kilometres from the Whaletown ferry landing; one kilometre from Smelt Bay Provincial Park.

• Two rooms: One person $40–65; two people $45–70. King-sized bed; twin beds. Ensuite and shared bathrooms. Additional person $15.

• A country-style house on the ocean with a garden and a view of Sutil Channel and Vancouver Island, a few steps from a sand and rock beach. Guests can walk along the beach, explore tidal pools, and watch sunsets. Living room and deck with views of ocean and mountains. Wood-fired sauna available for a fee. Guest entrance. Full breakfast includes fresh fruit, homemade baked goods, free-range eggs, and homemade preserves. Cancellation notice seven days. Cash, cheques, traveller's cheques. Danish spoken. No pets; dog and cat in residence. No smoking in the guest rooms. **In the hosts' own words:** "We invite guests to relax and read in our pleasant living room and enjoy the view deck."

Imperial Eagle Lodge

Jim and Karen Levis
Mail: Box 59
Bamfield
Vancouver Island, BC V0R 1B0
(250) 728-3430 fax: (250) 728-3430
email: impeagl@cedar.alberni.net
web site: www.imperialeaglelodge.com

• From Port Alberni, 1½ hours on logging roads. From Duncan, 2½ hours on logging roads.

• Rooms, suites, and cottage.

Two rooms in the main lodge and four rooms in two duplex cottages: One person $56–76; two people $86–119. Ensuite bathrooms. Additional person $30–45. Self-contained two-bedroom cottage (sleeps four): In winter (November 1 to March 30) $129. In spring/fall (April 1 to June 30 and October 1 to October 31) $149. In summer (July 1 to September 30) $169. Queen-sized bed; double bed; twin beds. Breakfast not included.

Sport fishing charters. Kayak rentals. Adventure packages.

Meal plans available.

Group and family rates.

• A country-style lodge and cottage with a garden and a view of the harbour, on the west side of Bamfield Inlet, which is in Barkley Sound. Sport fishing packages, guided charters, guided marine tours, and kayaking and hiking excursions can be arranged by the hosts. Guest dining and living area in the lodge has a fireplace, books, cards, a cribbage board, and a view of the harbour. Deck with hot tub. Cottage has a kitchen, a dining and sitting area, and a harbour view. Guest rooms have private entrances. Four of the guest rooms are in two duplex cottages adjacent to the lodge. Five of the guest rooms look out onto a garden. Full breakfast. Free parking in a lot on the east side of the harbour. Ferry transportation across the harbour to the B&B can be arranged by the hosts. Reservations recommended. Cancellation notice thirty days; in April, May, June, and October, sixty days. No refunds in July, August, and September. Thirty percent deposit required to hold reservation. Visa, MasterCard. Adult oriented; children over eleven welcome in the cottage. No pets. Smoking outdoors. **In the hosts' own words:** "Whether you are looking for an outdoor adventure or a quiet retreat, we are pleased to accommodate your West Coast vacation getaway. Come and experience our special brand of hospitality."

The Tide's Inn B&B

Valerie and James Sloman
160 Arnet Road
Mail: Box 325
Tofino, BC V0R 2Z0
(250) 725-3765 fax: (250) 725-3325
email: tidesinn@island.net
web site: www.island.net/~tidesinn

• In Tofino, turn left onto First Street. Turn right onto Arnet Road. The B&B is a brown house, the first house after the Y in the road.

• Three rooms: In summer (mid-May to mid-October), one person $85–100, two people $95–110. Queen-sized bed; twin beds. Private bathrooms. Minimum stay two nights. Additional $25. Off-season rates.

• A house on Duffin Cove, with views of the cove, Duffin Passage, and the mountains and islands of Clayoquot Sound. Shoreline with tidal pools. Ten minutes' walk from Tonquin Beach, a sandy beach protected from the open ocean by Wickaninnish Island. Five to fifteen minutes' drive from other beaches in Tofino and from Long Beach in Pacific Rim National Park. Ten minutes' walk from Tofino's galleries, restaurants, and charters and tours including whale watching, kayaking, hot springs, Clayoquot Sound harbour, and Meares Island hiking. Guest rooms have views of the ocean, private entrances, TVs, VCRs, fridges, and facilities for making coffee and tea. One of the guest rooms has a Jacuzzi. Another guest room has a fireplace and a steam bath and shower for two. Guest sitting room with beverage bar and pool table. Two guest rooms can be rented with the guest sitting room as a two-bedroom, two-bathroom suite. Decks and guest hot tub. Full breakfast includes baked goods, a hot entrée, fruit, juice, and fresh-ground coffee. Cancellation notice seven days, with $25 nonrefundable. Children over ten welcome. No pets; cat in residence. Smoking on decks. **In the hosts' own words:** "We welcome you to Tofino and our home. We'll help in every way we can to make sure your visit to Clayoquot Sound is a comfortable and memorable one."

Wilp Gybuu (Wolf House) B&B

Wendy and Ralph Burgess
311 Leighton Way
Mail: Box 396
Tofino, BC V0R 2Z0
(250) 725-2330 fax: (250) 725-1205
email: wilpgybu@island.net
web site: www.island.net/~wilpgybu

• In Tofino, turn left onto First Street. Turn right onto Arnet Road. Turn left onto Leighton Way. The B&B is the first driveway on the right.

• Three rooms: One person $70–90; two people $85–105. Queen-sized bed; twin beds. Ensuite bathrooms. Minimum stay of two nights may apply. Off-season rates.

• A West Coast–style contemporary cedar house with a view of Duffin Passage and islands in Clayoquot Sound. Within walking distance of restaurants, galleries, kayaking, whale watching, sea plane tours, hot springs tours, Tonquin Beach, and buses to Nanaimo. Fifteen minutes' drive from golf and Pacific Rim National Park's beaches and rainforest trails. Guest sitting room with TV, books, piano, and CD player. Guest refreshment area with cookies and facilities for making coffee and tea. Guest rooms have sitting areas. Two of the guest rooms have fireplaces and private entrances. Pickup from bus and plane. One of the hosts is a Native artist. Coffee or tea is delivered to guest rooms before breakfast. Full breakfast is served in the dining room, which has a view of the inside waters of Duffin Passage. Reservations recommended. Cancellation notice seven days. Visa, MasterCard. Adult oriented. No pets; cat in residence. No smoking. **In the hosts' own words:** "We welcome you to our home with warm hospitality and invite you to share the extraordinary beauty of Tofino and Pacific Rim National Park in all seasons."

Ocean on the Beach Retreat—Ch-ahayis

St. Clair McColl and Sandra Snetsinger
1377 Thornberg
Mail: Box 629
Tofino, BC V0R 2Z0
(250) 725-2710 fax: (250) 537-9678
web site: www.islandnet.com/~chahayis/

• Three hours from Nanaimo.

• House (sleeps four): $175. Queen-sized bed, twin beds, and sofa bed. Private bathroom.
Three-bedroom house (sleeps six): $275. Two queen-sized beds, twin beds, and sofa bed. One and a half bathrooms.
Breakfast not included.

• Two two-storey houses on the ocean joined by a covered walkway and surrounded by two-hundred-year-old spruce trees. Both houses are a few steps from a beach and have ocean views, kitchens, wood stoves, laundry rooms, and outside deck showers. One house sleeps four and has a bath and a shower. The other house sleeps six and has a Jacuzzi tub and a shower. Five minutes from Tofino, Pacific Rim National Park, whale watching, kayaking, hot springs, and hiking in a rain forest. Five minutes' walk from a restaurant. **In the hosts' own words:** "Cedar walls inside both our houses bring the West Coast experience into the comfort of the restful interiors. Our retreat on beautiful Chesterman Beach is ideal for weddings on the beach and surfers' holidays."

Watercolour I Dockside B&B

Marie Simmons and Bill Massey
750 Pacific Boulevard A-4
Vancouver, BC V6B 5E7
(604) 609-0311 fax: (604) 602-1290
email: marie@onwater1.com
web site: www.onwater1.com

• Dockside at a downtown Vancouver Marina near Granville Island.
• Self-contained suite (sleeps up to 6): Two people $475-550. Queen-sized bed. Ensuite and shared guest bathrooms. Additional person $75. Queen-sized beds, sofa bed, and pull-out sitting area available.
Honeymoon suite: One person or two people $175-250. Two twin beds side by side with king-sized bedding. Ensuite bathroom.
Weekly and off-season rates.
• A one-hundred-and-twenty-seven-foot European canal barge built in 1929, with views of the mountains. A few minutes walk from rapid transit and water taxis to restaurants, professional sport venues, shopping, and sightseeing. Within walking distance of Yaletown, BC Place, GM Place, Granville Island, and a grocery store. Canopied guest deck with cushioned pillows and Adirondack chairs. Honeymoon suite is an authentic 1929 Captain's quarters with stained-glass, panelled walls, wooden-dowel floor, wooden shutters, and ten foot beamed ceilings. Honeymoon suite has a TV, a VCR, a CD player, a small fridge, a coffeemaker, an oversized platform bed with king-sized pillows and bedding, a tiled bathroom with French sitting tub, and a stairway that leads to a wheelhouse and office decorated in WWII navigational charts and a private upper deck with leather sling-back chairs. The self-contained suite has a four-post fabric queen-sized bed and a bathroom decorated with teak and black marble with a two-person Jacuzzi tub, double sinks, a wall mosaic of sky and clouds made of blue and white hand-cut tiles, and a blue ceiling with teak beams. It also has a 65 foot multi-level living room with two sitting areas, a wet bar, a large screen TV, a VCR, a CD player, a custom glass and metal dining table on a canvas rug with a hand painted underwater scene, a full size kitchen galley with black granite counters and flooring, a dishwasher, an ice maker, an oven, a microwave, two fridges, and a washer and dryer. Visa, MasterCard, American Express. Adult oriented. No pets. No smoking indoors. **In the hosts' own words:** "Artistry creates an aura throughout the yacht with unique brushstrokes enveloping the walls. Combine the beauty and serenity of sleeping on water aboard our B&B with the enjoyment of downtown Vancouver."

Jolie Maison

Dimka and Louis Gheyle
1888 West Third Avenue
Vancouver, BC V6J 1K8
(604) 730-8010 fax: (604) 730-8045
email: joliemaison@direct.ca

- One block west of Burrard Street. One block north of Fourth Avenue.
- Four rooms: In summer, one or two people $90–145. In winter, one person $65–115, two people $75–125. Ensuite, private, and shared guest bathrooms. Additional person $20.
Off-season and extended stay rates.
- A restored 1901 house in Kitsilano, four blocks from Kitsilano Beach Park and one block from shops and restaurants. Ten minutes' drive from downtown, Stanley Park, and Granville Island. Fifteen minutes' drive from the University of British Columbia. Around the corner from a bus stop. Sitting room with fireplace and TV. One of the guest rooms has a Jacuzzi tub and a walk-in shower. The other guest rooms have views of mountains. Breakfast is served in the dining room. Deposit of one night's rate required to hold reservation. Cancellation notice three days. French, Dutch, and German spoken. Smoking on the porch.

In the hosts' own words: "We are located in Kitsilano, Vancouver's truly original and trendy neighbourhood. Put your feet up in front of the fire to read a book, watch TV, or visit with other guests. The relaxed and tranquil atmosphere of our charming B&B will make you feel right at home."

View of the Bay B&B

Helen Kritharis
2588 Cornwall Avenue
Vancouver, BC V6K 1C2
(604) 731-3290 fax: (604) 739-4379
email: krithabo@tjm.com
web site: www.vancouver-bc.com/viewofthebay

- In Kitsilano, at Cornwall Avenue and Trafalgar Street.
- Room and one suite: $95–125. Queen-sized bed; queen-sized bed and twin beds. Private bathrooms. Additional person $25.
- A B&B with a view of English Bay and Stanley Park, across the street from an ocean beach and a park with an outdoor pool. A few minutes' drive from the University of British Columbia and downtown. Within walking distance of Granville Island, Stanley Park, Jericho Beach, restaurants in the Kitsilano Beach area, and shopping and dining on West Fourth Avenue. Near the Vancouver Museum and Planetarium. Suite is on the main floor and has a sitting area, a TV, a private entrance, a loft bedroom and access to a roof patio that has a view of mountains, ocean, and city. Guest room is on the second floor and has a deck with a view of mountains, ocean, and city. Nonsmoking house. **In the hosts' own words:** "Enjoy our new, comfortable, contemporary house, tasty breakfasts, and gracious hospitality. When you stay here, Vancouver is at your doorstep."

Heritage Harbour B&B

Debra Horner
1838 Ogden Avenue
Vancouver, BC V6J 1A1
(604) 736-0809 fax: (604) 736-0074
email: dhorner@direct.ca
web site: www.vancouver-bc.com/HeritageHarbour

- Five minutes from downtown Vancouver.
- Two rooms: Two people $115–165. Queen-sized bed. Private bathrooms.
- A traditional-style house in Kitsilano Point across the street from a beach, with views of the ocean, heritage boats, mountains, and downtown. Five minutes' walk along the waterfront from tennis courts and a heated outdoor swimming pool. Two minutes' walk along the waterfront from Vanier Park's museum, planetarium, observatory, and moorage for heritage boats. Fifteen minutes' walk from Granville Island, boutique shopping, and fine dining restaurants on Fourth Avenue. Five minutes by bus, or fifteen minutes by small passenger ferry, or thirty minutes by foot from downtown, Stanley Park, and English Bay beaches. Fifteen minutes' drive from the University of British Columbia. One of the guest rooms has a view of the ocean, mountains, and downtown. The other guest room has French doors that lead to a private veranda overlooking a garden. Guest living room with oak wainscoting, TV, VCR, bar fridge, marble fireplace, and a view of the city and the ocean. Full breakfast is served in the dining room, which has a view of the harbour. Dietary allergies are accommodated. Check-in after 3:00 p.m. or by arrangement; check-out until 11:00 a.m. Not suitable for small children or pets. Smoking in front garden sitting area or on balconies. **In the hosts' own words:** "We encourage guests to enter our home as visitors and to leave as friends. Enjoy our B&B's quiet, seaside location and the convenience of being near downtown."

Kenya Court Oceanfront Guest House

Dr. and Mrs. H. R. Williams
2230 Cornwall Avenue
Vancouver, BC V6K 1B5
(604) 738-7085
email: d&hwilliams@telus.net

• Five self-contained suites: Two people $95–165. King-sized bed; queen-sized bed; twin beds. Ensuite bathrooms.

• A three-storey building across the street from Kitsilano Beach Park, which has an Olympic-sized outdoor saltwater heated pool. Seaside paths in Kitsilano Beach Park lead to Granville Island, a maritime museum, and a planetarium. Thousand-square-foot self-contained suites have private entrances and views of the ocean, city, and mountains. Five minutes' walk from tennis courts and ethnic restaurants. Ten minutes by bus from downtown. Near Jericho Beach and the University of British Columbia's Museum of Anthropology. Within walking distance of restaurants and boutiques on Fourth Avenue. Full buffet breakfast is served in a rooftop solarium that has a view. Check-in times are flexible. No smoking. **In the hosts' own words:** "Our house is a heritage building and has a spectacular view."

Kitsilano Heritage House B&B

Jocelyn Krug and Steve Stroich
2455 West Sixth Avenue
Vancouver, BC V6K 1W2
(604) 732-8004
email: bandb@axionet.com
web site: vancouver-bc.com/kitsilanoheritagehouse/

• Rooms and suite.
Rooms: $100–130. Queen-sized bed and twin bed; queen-sized bed. Ensuite and private bathrooms.
Suite: $120. Queen-sized bed; double bed and pull-out queen-sized bed. Bathroom in suite. Continental breakfast ingredients supplied.
• A 1912 character house with stained glass windows and antique furniture. Two blocks from boutiques, cafés, restaurants, and public transit on Fourth Avenue. Within walking distance of Kitsilano Beach. Ten minutes' drive from the University of British Columbia, downtown, and Stanley Park. Near Granville Island. Living room with fireplace and grand piano. Guest rooms have small fridges, sinks, and TVs. Guest suite has two bedrooms, a TV, and a kitchen. Guest entrance. Continental breakfast ingredients supplied. Smoking on covered veranda. **In the hosts own words:** "Enjoy the character, comfort, and convenience of our heritage home in the heart of Kitsilano. Our guest suite is ideal for families."

Camilla House B&B

Camilla Wang
2538 West Thirteenth Avenue
Vancouver, BC V6K 2T1
(604) 737-2687 fax: (604) 737-2586
email: camillaw@lynx.bc.ca
web site: www.vancouver-bb.com

• Rooms and suites.

Two rooms: One person \$65–85; two people \$70–95. Queen-sized bed; twin beds. Shared guest bathroom.

Four suites: One person \$75–135; two people \$85–145. King-sized bed; queen-sized bed; twin beds side by side with king-sized bedding. Ensuite bathrooms.

• A New York–style house in tree-lined Kitsilano, three blocks from shopping, restaurants, and public transit on Broadway. Ten minutes from the University of British Columbia, a golf course, the Museum of Anthropology, a botanical garden, the Nitobe Japanese gardens, Spanish Banks beach, Jericho beach, and Kitsilano beach. Ten minutes from downtown. Twenty minutes' drive from the Vancouver airport. Guest rooms and suites have TVs and telephones. One of the suites has a Jacuzzi and a small fridge. Another suite has a fridge and a fireplace. Guest living room with fireplace. Full breakfast is served in the dining room, which has a view of a garden. **In the hosts' own words:** "Let our warm, friendly hospitality greet you. Come and enjoy your vacation with us."

Graeme's House

Ms. Graeme Elizabeth Webster
2735 Waterloo Street
Vancouver, BC V6R 3J1
(604) 732-1488 fax: (604) 926-7046
toll-free: 1-888-732-6660
email: graeweb@telus.net
web site: www.graemewebster.com

• Near West Broadway and Alma Street.

• Rooms: $70–120. Queen-sized bed; twin beds; double bed.
Ensuite and shared bathrooms. Additional person $20. Child under 12 $15.
Additional bed available. Rates are based on stays of two or more nights; additional charge of $5 for one-night stays.

• A renovated 1926 country-style house with gardens and a deck, on a quiet street, one kilometre from Jericho Beach and ten minutes' drive or twenty minutes by bus from the University of British Columbia, an aquatic centre, Granville Island, and downtown. Within two blocks of restaurants, shops, and a movie theatre on Broadway. Down the hill from the village at Tenth Avenue and Sasamat Street. Living room with fireplace, kitchen/family room with TV, and roof garden. Country décor. Guest rooms have skylights, stained glass bay windows, and french doors that lead onto private decks or a balcony. No pets; cat in residence. Smoking outdoors. **In the hosts' own words:** "We welcome you to country-cottage charm in the city, great conversation, homemade muffins, and comfortable beds."

Collingwood Manor B&B

Stefanie and Howie Todd
1631 Collingwood Street
Vancouver, BC V6R 3K1
(604) 731-1107 fax: (604) 731-9443
toll-free from within North America: 1-888-699-1631
email: info@collingwoodmanor.com
web site: www.collingwoodmanor.com

- In Kitsilano, between Alma and MacDonald streets.
- Rooms and suite.

Four rooms: $95–125. Queen-sized bed. Private and shared guest bathrooms.
Honeymoon suite: $150–165. King-sized bed. Ensuite bathroom.

- A restored 1912 house with a modern interior, one block from an ocean beach and three blocks from Jericho Park. Guest living room is on the upper floor and has hardwood floors, vaulted ceilings, a fireplace, two chesterfields, armchairs, hot and cold beverages, books, magazines, and a view of the ocean, city, and mountains. Near kayak, bicycle, and windsurfer rental shops. Four blocks from public transit. Five minutes' drive from downtown. Guest rooms are on the main floor and have Egyptian cotton linen and down comforters. Honeymoon suite has a king-sized bed, a three-sided fireplace, and an ensuite bathroom with two sinks, a makeup table, and a two-person Jacuzzi. Breakfast includes fresh-squeezed juice, a fresh fruit plate, homemade muffins or scones, scrambled eggs with lox and cream cheese, French toast or pancakes, and coffee or tea; entrées change daily. Cancellation notice two days. Visa, MasterCard. Adult oriented; children welcome by arrangement. Smoke-free environment. **In the hosts' own words:** "Our beautifully restored heritage house, which has a sophisticated contemporary interior, is in one of Vancouver's most desirable and safe neighborhoods, a few blocks from first-class beaches and parks and a five-minute drive from major attractions—a B&B that is a delightful retreat."

B&B by Locarno Beach

Elke Holm
4505 Langara Avenue
Vancouver, BC V6R 1C9
cel: (604) 341-4975
web site: www.bbcanada.com/locarnobeach

- Twelve minutes from downtown. Five minutes from the University of British Columbia.
- Rooms: In summer, one person $75-85, two people $95-105. In winter, one person $55-65, two people $65-75. Queen-sized bed and sofa bed. Ensuite bathrooms. Additional person $25.
- A B&B on a quiet side street in West Point Grey, across the street from a city park and two minutes' walk from a three-kilometre sandy ocean beach and seaside trail. The beach and trail have views of the North Shore and Howe Sound mountains, downtown, and Stanley Park. The B&B is within walking distance of tennis courts, boat rentals, fine dining on the waterfront, and beachside food services. Five minutes' drive from the University of British Columbia's Museum of Anthropology and a public golf course. Fifteen minutes' walk from restaurants, a cinema, and shops on Tenth Avenue. Near bus routes. Twenty minutes by bus or twelve minutes by car from downtown. Telephone in hallway. All water in the house is filtered. Full breakfast, including free-range eggs and organically grown food, is served in the dining room. Cancellation notice 10 days. Cash, traveller's cheques. German and French spoken. Nonsmoking guests. **In the hosts' own words**: "Enjoy our resort-like setting, within minutes of downtown Vancouver."

Johnson Heritage House B&B

Sandy and Ron Johnson
2278 West Thirty-fourth Avenue
Vancouver, BC V6M 1G6
(604) 266-4175 fax: (604) 266-4175
email: fun@johnsons-inn-vancouver.com
web site: www.johnsons-inn-vancouver.com

- Near West Thirty-third Avenue and Arbutus Street.
- Three rooms: One person $75–145; two people $85–175. King-sized bed; queen-sized bed; twin beds. Ensuite and shared guest bathrooms.
- A 1920s Craftsman-style house on a quiet tree-lined street, with interior woodwork and antique furniture including iron and brass beds, Persian carpets, carousel horses, and gramophones. Guest living room with oak floors, French doors, brick fireplace, TV, and VCR. Telephones, hair dryers, and toiletries in guest rooms. Guidebooks, maps, list of recommended restaurants, and a weekly-events calendar. Covered front porch with a partial view of Grouse Mountain. Rhododendron and rock garden with stone sculptures. Five minutes' walk from buses, restaurants, shops, and banks. Fifteen minutes from the airport, downtown, Stanley Park, Granville Island, and the Museum of Anthropology at the University of British Columbia. Ten minutes from ocean beaches and the University of British Columbia. Five minutes from Queen Elizabeth Park and the VanDusen Gardens. Breakfast, including coffee, tea, juice, fruit, a hot entrée, and homemade muffins, scones, or cinnamon buns, is served from 8:15 to 9:30 a.m. Cash, cheques. Children over twelve welcome. No pets. Smoke-free. **In the hosts' own words:** "Our B&B offers comfortable beds, helpful hosts, satisfying breakfasts, and a wonderful neighbourhood—what you should expect from a quality B&B."

Arbutus House B&B

Gus and Lani Mitchell
4470 Maple Crescent
Vancouver, BC V6J 4B3
(604) 738-6432 fax: (604) 738-6433
email: stay@arbutushouse.com
web site: www.arbutushouse.com

• West of Granville Street, between Thirty-third Avenue and King Edward Avenue, at Twenty-ninth Avenue and Maple Crescent.

• Rooms: One person $95–155; two people $100–165. Queen-sized bed. Ensuite and shared guest bathrooms. Additional twin beds available.
Suite: One person $155; two people $165. Queen-sized bed and one twin bed. Ensuite bathroom.
Additional person $25. Off-season rates. May to October, minimum stay two nights. Open March 1 to October 31.

• A 1920s character house in Shaughnessy, with leaded windows, oak floors, cove ceilings, and original fireplaces. Guest living room with fireplace and tourist information. Den with TV and VCR. Some guest rooms have one or more of the following: private deck, fireplace, soaker tub, writing desk. Suite is six hundred square feet and has a TV, a telephone, a fridge, a sitting area with gas fireplace, and an ensuite bathroom. Decks and traditional flower gardens. Ten minutes' drive from downtown, Stanley Park, airport, beaches, the University of British Columbia, Granville Island, Queen Elizabeth Park, and General Motors Place. Three blocks from public transit. Within walking distance of restaurants and shopping. Chocolates on the pillows, sherry, robes, and hair dryers. Full breakfast is served in the dining room. Cash, traveller's cheques. Children over twelve welcome. No pets; cat in residence. Smoking outdoors. **In the hosts' own words:** "Relax on the sundeck and enjoy traditional fragrant gardens. We are nestled in a historical neighbourhood and we continually strive to make our B&B a place you'll want to stay."

A Treehouse B&B

Barb and Bob Selvage
2490 West Forty-ninth Avenue
Vancouver, BC V6M 2V3
(604) 266-2962 fax: (604) 266-2960
email: bb@treehousebb.com
web site: www.treehousebb.com

•Room and two suites: One person $100–155; two people $110–165. Queen-sized bed; queen-sized bed, double futon, and single futon; queen-sized bed and single futon. Ensuite and private bathrooms. Additional person $30.

•A multi-level house with contemporary art and sculpture, close to hiking, horseback riding, golf, tennis, swimming pools, and a community centre. Twenty-five minutes' drive from ferries to the islands. Fifteen minutes' drive from downtown. Ten minutes' drive from the University of British Columbia and the airport. Near dining and shopping. One of the suites occupies the entire third floor and has private decks, a four-post queen-sized bed, a single futon, a skylit bathroom with Jacuzzi, and a sitting room with plants. The other suite is on the main floor and has a queen-sized bed, a sitting room with double futon and single futon, and an ensuite bathroom with Jacuzzi. The guest room has a queen-sized bed and a private bath, is decorated with Asian arts and crafts, and opens onto a Japanese courtyard garden. Guest living/dining room. Covered deck with a view of woodlands. Guest room and suites have telephones, TVs, VCRs, fridges, coffeemakers, tea kettles, hair dryers, robes, slippers, toiletries, and chocolates on the pillows. Infants and children over ten welcome. Smoke-free environment. **In the hosts' own words:** "Our B&B provides a unique experience. Discover why our guests return year after year."

Balfour Inn B&B

Muni Nazerali
1064 Balfour Avenue
Vancouver, BC V6H 1X1
(604) 730-9927 fax: (604) 732-4998
email: balfourbb@aol.com
web site: www.balfourbb.com

•North of King Edward Avenue, between Oak and Granville.

•Rooms: Two people $65–120. Ensuite and shared guest bathrooms. Off-season and weekly rates.

•A 1908 mansion surrounded by gardens, fifteen minutes from downtown, ocean beaches, the Vancouver Trade and Convention Centre, B.C. Place, the Queen Elizabeth Gardens, Stanley Park, Gastown, Vancouver General Hospital, and the Ford Centre for the Performing Arts. A few minutes' walk from the VanDusen gardens and synagogues on Oak Street. Near direct routes to the University of British Columbia, the U.S. border, the airport, and ferries to Vancouver Island and the Gulf Islands. One block from transit. Tours arranged, with pick-up from the B&B. Small groups and weddings welcome. Guest sitting room. Parking. Full breakfast. Visa, MasterCard, American Express. No pets. Smoke-free environment. **In the hosts' own words:** "This is a green oasis in the city. Come and share it with us."

Peloquin's Pacific Pad

Janet Peloquin
426 West Twenty-second Avenue
Vancouver, BC V5Y 2G5
(604) 874-4529 fax: (604) 874-6229
email: peloquin@vancouver-bc.com
web site: www.vancouver-bc.com/peloquin/

- Near King Edward Avenue and Cambie Street.
- Two rooms: One person $65–75; two people $85–110. Private bathrooms. Additional person $25. Child $15–20.
- A B&B in a residential neighbourhood, within walking distance of restaurants, shops, parks, and bus routes. A few minutes by car or bus from downtown, the University of British Columbia, General Motors Place, B.C. Place Stadium, and Vancouver General Hospital. Near the airport, ferries, and Highway 99 to the U.S. Host shares knowledge of Vancouver. Guest rooms have private entrances, private bathrooms, and TVs. Guest common area with fridge, toaster, microwave, dishes, and supplies for making coffee and tea. No cooking; the microwave is for warming food. Full breakfast, including homemade preserves, is served in a solarium-like kitchen. Check-in and check-out times are flexible. French and Ukrainian spoken. Children welcome. No pets. Nonsmokers welcome. **In the hosts' own words:** "Have a happy holiday."

Shaughnessy Village B&B Guest House

Jan Floody
1125 West Twelfth Avenue
Vancouver, BC V6H 3Z3
(604) 736-5511 fax: (604) 737-1321
email: info@shaughnessyvillage.com
web site: www.shaughnessyvillage.com

• Between Granville and Oak streets, 5 minutes from downtown.

• Two hundred and forty rooms: One-room studio, one person $39.95–69.95; two-room suite, one person $79.95–98.95. Ensuite and private bathrooms. Additional person $10. Rates include video movies and health club membership. Weekly rates.
Monthly rate $665.

• A resort-style B&B with gardens, a gazebo, a wedding pavilion, a heated swimming pool, Jacuzzis, miniature golf, outdoor chess and checkers, shuffleboard courts, a barbecue, and a soft waterway for toy yacht races. Two blocks from shopping and buses. Five minutes' drive from downtown. On a direct route to the airport. Rooms and suites have Victorian décor, private balconies, microwaves, fridges, TVs, clock radios, ceiling fans, and thermostats for individually controlled heat. Most rooms and suites have views either of Vancouver and False Creek or of trees and Mount Baker. Health club with TV room, reading room, billiard room, exercise room, sauna, aromatherapy steam spa, indoor whirlpool, suntanning bed, and acumassage couch. Licensed restaurant, Internet café, hair salon, full-service and coin laundry, housekeeping service, and secretarial service. On-camera twenty-four-hour front desk security/medicalert response system. Full breakfast is served all day. Visa, MasterCard. **In the hosts' own words:** "Our resort-style complex is designed to accommodate B&B visitors to Vancouver who require affordable, well-equipped, comfortable, furnished facilities. There is lots for the visitor to do in a friendly city-country atmosphere."

Fairview Guest House

Lillian Feist
896 West Thirteenth Avenue
Vancouver, BC V5Z 1P2
(604) 873-0842

- Near Oak Street and West Twelfth Avenue.
- Suites: Shared guest bathrooms. Off-season and weekly rates.
- An alternative to a traditional B&B. A heritage house converted into suites with kitchens. Suites have twin beds and TVs. One block from Vancouver General Hospital. Ten minutes from downtown and Granville Island. Well-behaved pets welcome. **In the hosts' own words**: "Our guest house is perfect for extended stays in Vancouver."

Three Gables B&B

Amandah and Marke
3257 Columbia Street
Vancouver, BC V5Y 3G7
(604) 874-3566
email: info@threegables.com
web site: www.threegables.com

- Five minutes from downtown. Twenty minutes from the Vancouver airport.
- Room and suites.

Room: Two people $95–135. King-sized bed. Private bathroom.
Two suites: Two people $125–170. Queen-sized bed. Ensuite bathrooms.
Additional person $20.
Extended stay rates.

- A new neoclassical-style house with the interior designed by one of the hosts, who is an interior designer. Small back garden. Guest room and suites have TVs, telephones, Jacuzzi tubs, and terry robes. A few steps from restaurants and shopping. Five minutes from downtown. Ten minutes from Kitsilano Beach and Granville Island. Twenty minutes from Stanley Park. Within walking distance of Queen Elizabeth Park. Near public transportation. Street parking. Restaurant reservations and tour bookings can be made by the hosts. Full breakfast, including homemade baked goods, eggs benedict, French toast, fresh fruit, and homemade preserves, is served in the dining room. Reservations recommended. Cancellation deposit required. Cash, Visa. Children welcome. No pets. Smoke-free environment. **In the hosts' own words:** "Welcome to our home. We have incorporated many special features to create a sophisticated, yet welcoming environment. We want you to experience all that Vancouver has to offer. Whether you come for a holiday, business, or a romantic getaway, you'll leave planning to return."

Pillow and Porridge Guest Suites

Dianne Reader Haag
2859 Manitoba Street
Vancouver, BC V5Y 3B3
(604) 879-8977 fax: (604) 879-8966
email: suites@pillow.net
web site: www.pillow.net

• From Cambie Street, turn east onto Twelfth Avenue (city hall) and continue for four blocks. Turn right onto Manitoba Street. The B&B is the third house south of Twelfth Avenue.

• One-bedroom self-contained suite: $85–135 per night, from $1500 per month. Queen-sized bed and sleeping loft with double bed; queen-sized bed and double sofa bed.
Two-bedroom self-contained suite (sleeps four): $130–170 per night, from $2000 per month. King-sized bed, double bed, and twin beds.
Three-bedroom self-contained suite (sleeps six): $195–255 per night, from $3000 per month. Two queen-sized beds and twin beds. Two bathrooms.
Additional person $10. Minimum stay. Breakfast not included.

• Three colourfully painted houses built between 1906 and 1910, on one lot in the city hall area, within walking distance of fine dining and ethnic restaurants, grocery shopping, Queen Elizabeth Park, Granville Island, Science World, and Vancouver General Hospital. Five minutes' drive from downtown. Three blocks from bus and rapid transit routes. Suites are decorated in themes and are self-contained, with bedrooms, bathrooms, living rooms, dining areas, private entrances, kitchen utensils, stoves, microwaves, fridges, telephones, linen, TVs, clock radios, and supplies for making coffee and tea. VCR available. Three of the suites have dishwashers, washers and dryers, and fireplaces. The three-bedroom suite has two sitting areas with TVs, a deck, and a front porch. Minimum stay required. Smoking outdoors.
In the hosts' own words: "Our affordable and charming apartments are perfect for family reunions, temporary relocations, executive transfers, and travellers who prefer to have their very own comfortable home away from home."

Creekside B&B

Donna P. Hawrelko and John C. Boden, Sr.
1515 Palmerston Avenue
West Vancouver, BC V7V 4S9
(604) 926-1861 fax: (604) 926-7545
cel: (604) 328-9400
email: donnajohnboden@bc.sympatico.ca

• From Highway 1, turn south onto Fifteenth Street. Turn right onto Palmerston Avenue.
From Marine Drive in West Vancouver, turn north onto Fifteenth Street. Turn left onto Palmerston Avenue.

• Room and honeymoon suite: $119–169. King-sized bed; queen-sized bed. Ensuite and private bathrooms. Minimum stay two nights.

• A post-and-beam house on a wooded lot with a small stream, a bridge, and five waterfalls. Garden with two-hundred-year-old cedar and spruce trees and four thousand flowering plants. Near transit, parks, hiking, tennis courts, golf, fine dining restaurants, shopping, ocean beaches, and skiing at Grouse Mountain and Mount Seymour. Guest room and honeymoon suite have balconies overlooking the stream and garden, dual showers, TVs, radio alarm clocks, coffeemakers, and fridges with wine, other beverages, and snacks. Robes, toiletries, and half-price coupons for dining, sightseeing, and entertainment. Honeymoon suite is air-conditioned and has a gas fireplace and a two-person marble Jacuzzi tub; at night, stars can be seen through a glass ceiling over the Jacuzzi. Guest room has a brass queen-sized bed and a private bathroom with six-foot marble Jacuzzi tub and skylights. Full breakfast includes cereal, fresh fruit, eggs, Canadian back bacon, English muffins, homemade bread, juice, coffee, and tea. Deposit of half of one night's rate required to hold reservation. Cash, Visa, MasterCard. Not suitable for children under ten. Small pets permitted by arrangement; small poodle in residence. **In the hosts' own words:** "Our heritage house has recently been renovated but retains its charm and serenity."

Beachside B&B

Gordon and Joan Gibbs
4208 Evergreen Avenue
West Vancouver, BC V7V 1H1
(604) 922-7773 fax: (604) 926-8073
toll-free from within Canada and the U.S.: 1-800-563-3311
email: info@beach.bc.ca
beach@uniserve.com
web site: www.beach.bc.ca

• From the Lions Gate Bridge, take Marine Drive west for 7 kilometres. Turn south onto Ferndale Avenue and continue for half a block. Turn left onto Evergreen Avenue. The B&B is at the end of the cul-de-sac.

• Three rooms: In high-season, two people $150–300. Queen-sized bed. Ensuite bathrooms.
Additional person $30. Minimum stay of two nights may apply. Off-season rates.

• A house on the ocean, at the end of a quiet cul-de-sac, with a sandy beach and a view of Vancouver and the Gulf Islands. Twenty minutes from downtown Vancouver, Stanley Park, the Horseshoe Bay ferry terminal, and North Shore attractions. Half a block from a bus route. Sunrises, sunsets, Alaska cruise ships, seals, sea otters, birds, and eagles can be seen from the beach. Near fishing, sailing, wilderness hiking, skiing, golf, parks, trails, tennis courts, antique stores, a convenience store, shopping, and fine dining restaurants. Guest sitting room with fireplace, videos, board games, puzzles, and books. Guest outdoor beachside Jacuzzi and beach patios. Indoor Jacuzzi. Guest rooms have private garden patios, fireplaces, TVs, VCRs, flowers, fruit baskets, fridges, coffee makers, hair dryers, and curling irons. Two of the guest rooms have ocean views. Antique stained glass, old brick, and hanging baskets throughout. One of the hosts is available as a tour guide. Full breakfast, including muffins, scones, fresh-ground coffee, and tea, is served in the dining room, which has a view of the ocean. Off-street parking. Deposit of 50 percent required to hold reservation. Cancellation notice fourteen days. Check-in 5:00 to 6:00 p.m. or by arrangement. Cash, traveller's cheques, Visa, MasterCard. No pets. Smoking on covered patios. **In the hosts' own words:** "We are well-travelled former teachers and can advise guests on local attractions. Relax, make new friends, and enjoy Vancouver's legendary scenery, cultural events, and attractions, in quiet seclusion just minutes from the city centre. We offer an ideal place for getaways and honeymoon retreats."

Union Steamship Company

Rondy and Dorothy Dike
1 Government Road
Snug Cove
Mail: Box 250
Bowen Island, BC V0N 1G0
(604) 947-0707 fax: (604) 947-0708
email: ussc@direct.ca
web site: www.steamship-marina.bc.ca

• Fifteen minutes by ferry from the Horseshoe Bay ferry terminal. The B&B is next to the ferry landing on Bowen Island.

• Cottages, float house, and house.

Two two-bedroom cottages: One or two people $110. Queen-sized bed and two sets of bunk beds with double-width lower bunks.

One-bedroom float house: Two people $90. Queen-sized bed. Private bathroom.

Two-bedroom house: Two people $160. King-sized bed and one twin bed; bunk beds with double-width lower bunk.

Breakfast not included.

Additional beds $10. Discount of 15 percent on stays of five or more nights.

Minimum stay two nights on summer weekends.

• A B&B with a two-bedroom house and two of the original cottages of the Union Steamship Company, in a resort village in Snug Cove on Bowen Island, with views of mountains and Howe Sound. Bald eagles can be seen. Each cottage has two bedrooms, a living room with wood stove, a TV, a kitchen, and a porch. Remodelled float house on a dock has a bedroom, a living room, a kitchen, a TV, and a futon sofa. Two-bedroom Victorian-style house has a view of Snug Cove, stained-glass windows, a claw-foot tub, a living room with fireplace, and a kitchen with wood stove. One block from a bakery, a deli, and a restaurant. A few minutes from public beaches, coves, parks, and hiking and biking trails. Bowen Island's port has boutiques, boardwalks, and turn-of-the-century buildings. Breakfast not included. Credit cards. Children and pets welcome. **In the hosts' own words:** "There's no place in the world like the B.C. coast, and there's no better way to see its scenery and natural sights than seated on the front porch of one of our rustic cottages."

Cedar Hill B&B

Jean and Adolph Olson
1095 West Keith Road
North Vancouver, BC V7P 1Y6
(604) 988-9629 fax: (604) 990-8966
email: cedarhil@imag.net
web site: www.bbcanada.com/162.html

• Near Marine Drive, Capilano Road, and the Lions Gate Bridge. From Highway 1 westbound, take exit 14 and turn left onto Capilano Road. At the first traffic light, turn left onto the road that leads to Highway 1. Before Highway 1, turn right onto West Keith Road.
From Highway 1 eastbound, take exit 14. From the off-ramp, turn left onto West Keith Road.
• Rooms and suite.
Rooms: One person $55; two people $65–75. Queen-sized bed; double bed and one twin bed; double bed. Private and shared guest bathrooms.
Suite: $95. King-sized bed. Bathroom in suite. Adjoining room with double bed for additional $65.
• A B&B at the foot of Grouse Mountain, with cedar trees and a garden, ten minutes from downtown Vancouver. Views of downtown Vancouver and cruise ships entering the harbour. Flowers throughout. Near the Capilano suspension bridge, the Grouse Mountain gondola, a fish hatchery, Stanley Park, ocean beaches, hiking trails, shopping, restaurants, the Royal Hudson steam train to Whistler, and a passenger ferry to downtown Vancouver. Guest rooms have private entrances and TVs. Suite has a private entrance, a patio, and a sitting room with fireplace, TV, VCR, fridge, bar, organ, and piano. Garden. Off-street parking. Suitable for large groups. Children welcome. Smoking outdoors. **In the hosts' own words:** "Make yourselves at home, savour our gourmet breakfast, and enjoy a North Shore treat."

The Hidden Garden B&B

Karin Essinger
230 West Twenty-second Street
North Vancouver, BC V7M 2A1
(604) 987-2872 fax: (604) 987-2897
web site: www.bbchannel.com/bbc/p608065.asp

• Rooms and suite.

Three rooms: In summer, two people $110–150. In winter, two people $95–125. Queen-sized bed and day bed; queen-sized bed; double bed. Ensuite and private bathrooms. Additional person $25.

Self-contained one-bedroom suite: Two people $150. Ensuite bathroom. Additional person $30.

• A B&B with a Japanese-influenced West Coast–style garden that has a pond, a bridge, and a creek. Evergreens, dogwoods, cedars, birches, and alders surround the property. Near winter sports, Grouse Mountain, the Capilano suspension bridge, the Royal Hudson steam train, Stanley Park, and a passenger ferry to downtown Vancouver. Boat trips with views of Vancouver on the hosts' thirty-two-foot cabin cruiser and guided hiking trips on nearby mountains can be arranged by hosts. Afternoon coffee and cake. Guest living room with a fireplace. Guest rooms have TVs and telephones. One of the guest rooms has a fireplace. Another has a view of the garden. The self-contained suite is at ground level and has a fireplace, a sofa bed, a washer and dryer, and a kitchen. Breakfast is served in the garden or delivered to guests' rooms. Self-contained suite is suitable for families. **In the hosts' own words:** "Book early for our guided hiking tours of the local mountains or enjoy a panoramic view of Vancouver from our thirty-two-foot cabin cruiser."

Pacific View B&B

Sylvia and Gerhard Gruner
139 West St. James Road
North Vancouver, BC V7N 2P1
(604) 985-4942 fax: (604) 985-4942

• From Highway 1, take exit 18 to Lonsdale Avenue. Go north on Lonsdale and turn left onto St. James. The B&B is in the first block.

• Two people $70–85. Queen-sized bed. Ensuite and private bathrooms.

• A B&B with a view of the ocean and the city, in a residential neighbourhood, twenty minutes from downtown Vancouver, Stanley Park, and the Horseshoe Bay ferry terminal. Fifteen minutes' drive from Grouse Mountain. Ten minutes' drive from the Royal Hudson steam train, the Capilano River fish hatchery, the Capilano suspension bridge, and a passenger ferry to downtown Vancouver and a rapid transit station. Two minutes' walk from a bus stop. Suites have TVs. Guest living room is on the upper floor and has a balcony with a view. Full breakfast is served in a heated sun room overlooking a garden. German and Polish spoken. No pets; small bird in residence. Nonsmokers welcome. **In the hosts' own words:** "Our house is your home away from home."

Norgate Parkhouse B&B

Vicki Tyndall
1226 Silverwood Crescent
North Vancouver, BC V7P 1J3
(604) 986-5069 fax: (604) 986-8810
email: sarahb@norgateparkhousebandb.bc.ca
web site: www.bandbinn.com/homes/9/

• Fifteen minutes from downtown Vancouver. Take Georgia Street (Highway 99) across the Lions Gate Bridge to North Vancouver and along Marine Drive. Turn right at Tatlow. Turn right onto Silverwood Crescent. The B&B is on the right.

• Three rooms: In summer, one person $75–105, two people $95–115. In winter, one person $65–95, two people $85–105. King-sized bed; queen-sized bed; twin beds. Ensuite and shared guest bathrooms. Minimum stay two nights on holiday weekends.

• A contemporary ranch-style house with a West Coast–style garden. Fifteen minutes from downtown Vancouver and Horseshoe Bay. Ninety minutes from Whistler. Three blocks from a bus route and a B.C. Rail station. Three to five blocks from restaurants and car rentals. Ten minutes from wilderness hiking on Grouse Mountain. Guest rooms have telephones. Two of the guest rooms open onto the back garden. The third guest room has a private enclosed patio. Guest sitting room with fireplace, books, tourist brochures, and TV. Parking. Full breakfast. Deposit required to hold reservation. Check-in times are flexible. Not suitable for small children. Two cats in residence. Smoking outdoors. **In the hosts' own words:** "At our B&B, enjoy a lush, park-like garden setting, delicious breakfasts, stimulating conversation, congenial surroundings, our travel treasures, and a quiet sleep. We are just minutes from the centre of the city."

Laburnum Cottage B&B

Delphine Masterton
1388 Terrace Avenue
North Vancouver, BC V7R 1B4
(604) 988-4877 fax: (604) 988-4877
toll-free: 1-888-207-8901
email: laburnum@home.com
web site: www.vancouver-bc.com/LaburnumCottageBB

• From Vancouver, take Georgia Street (Highway 99) across the Lions Gate Bridge. Turn right onto Marine Drive, left onto Capilano Road, right onto Paisley Road, right onto Philip, right onto Woods, and left onto Terrace.
From the U.S. border, take Highway 15 north. Take Highway 1 west to North Vancouver. Take exit 14 north to Capilano Road. Turn right onto Paisley, right onto Philip, right onto Woods, and left onto Terrace.
From the Horseshoe Bay ferry terminal, take Highway 1 east. Go north on Capilano Road. Turn right onto Paisley, right onto Philip, right onto Woods, and left onto Terrace.
• Rooms and cottages.
Rooms: Queen-sized bed. Private bathrooms.
Self-contained cottage (sleeps five): King-sized bed and children's loft. Private bathroom.
Self-contained cottage (sleeps two): Double bed. Private bathroom.
• A B&B with Victorian antiques and an English garden, on three-quarters of an acre, surrounded by old-growth forest, fifteen minutes from downtown Vancouver and from Horseshoe Bay. Ninety minutes from Whistler. Five minutes from Grouse Mountain. Two blocks from a bus route. Covered porch with an open deck that has a view of the garden and a creek. Cottages have fireplaces, kitchens, TVs, and soaker tubs. Parking. Afternoon tea. Breakfast includes homemade jam, biscuits, and English-style pancakes. Deposit of one night's rate, $15 of which is nonrefundable, required to hold reservation. Cancellation notice seven days. Check-in times are flexible. Visa, MasterCard. Smoking outdoors. **In the hosts' own words:** "We invite you to enjoy restful, peaceful seclusion. Our charming B&B has a Victorian air and beautifully appointed guest rooms. We serve a wide variety of specialties, including English-style pancakes. We hope you will find a few moments to relax on the covered porch overlooking the gardens and the meandering creek."

Poole's B&B

Doreen and Arthur Poole
421 West St. James Road
North Vancouver, BC V7N 2P6
(604) 987-4594 fax: (604) 987-4283
email: rapoole@lightspeed.bc.ca

• From Highway 1, take exit 17 north onto Westview. Turn right onto Queens. Turn left onto Stanley, which leads to St. James.

• Three rooms: One person $50; two people $65. Queen-sized bed; double bed; twin beds. Shared guest bathrooms. Additional person $15. Child 6 to 12 $5; children under 6 free. Crib and cot available.
Off-season and weekly rates.

• A colonial-style house in a residential district, twenty minutes' drive from downtown Vancouver and two blocks from bus stops. Within walking distance of a pub, restaurants, shopping, parks, and an indoor public swimming pool. Ten minutes by car or bus from the Capilano suspension bridge, the Grouse Mountain skyride, and a passenger ferry to downtown Vancouver. Twenty minutes' drive from Stanley Park and ferries to Vancouver Island. Tea or coffee when guests arrive. Guest room with twin beds has a TV. Breakfast is served at a candlelit dining table with flowers from the garden. No pets. No smoking. **In the hosts' own words:** "We are retired and are happy to help you with directions and information about our beautiful city and surrounding areas. We welcome guests to share our quiet, relaxed B&B and to enjoy our sundeck, patio, and private back garden."

A Grand Manor Guest House

Donna Patrick
1617 Grand Boulevard
North Vancouver, BC V7L 3Y2
(604) 988-6082 fax: (604) 988-4596
email: donna@helix.net
web site: www.grandmanor.net

• From Vancouver, go east on Broadway, left onto Rupert Street, right onto First Avenue, left onto Highway 1, and continue over the Second Narrows Bridge to the Lynn Valley turnoff (exit 19). Turn left onto Lynn Valley Road. Lynn Valley Road becomes Grand Boulevard. The B&B is on the right.

• Rooms and suite.
Three rooms: One person $45–70; two people $90–130.
Self-contained suite (sleeps six): Two people $120. Queen-sized bed, queen-sized hide-a-bed, twin beds. Bathroom in suite.
Less $5–10 without breakfast. Additional person $10–20. Minimum two night stay. Weekly and monthly rates available in winter. Massage, reflexology, and Touch for Health sessions $60.

• A newly renovated Edwardian-style house built in 1912 as a private residence for a former Councillor and Reeve of the District of North Vancouver. Five blocks from shopping on Lonsdale Avenue. Twenty minutes' drive from downtown Vancouver and Horseshoe Bay ferry terminal. Ten minutes' drive from the Capilano suspension bridge and skiing at Grouse Mountain. Five minutes' drive from the Lynn Valley Canyon and suspension bridge. One block from a park and tennis courts. Near public transit. Within walking distance of Lions Gate Hospital. Guest rooms have TVs and ocean or mountain views. Antique décor. Suite has two bedrooms, kitchen facilities, TV, porch, parking, and backyard garden with swings. Fax and email services available. Massage, reflexology, and applied kinesiology sessions by reservation. Full breakfast is served from 8:30 to 9:30 a.m. in the dining room, or in guest rooms by arrangement. Deposit of one night's rate required to hold reservation. Deposit less $10 is refunded if reservation is cancelled two weeks before arrival. Check-in 4:00 to 6:00 p.m.; check-out until 11:00 a.m. Cash, traveller's cheques, Visa. Children welcome. No pets. Smoking outdoors. **In the hosts' own words:** "Our heritage home is located in the heart of North Vancouver. It is a place to enjoy new friends in a warm, comfortable, and informal atmosphere."

Sue and Simon's Victorian Guest House

152 East Third Street
North Vancouver, BC V7L 1E6
(604) 985-1523
toll-free: 1-800-776-1811
web site: www.angelfire.com/or2/SuesVictorian/index.html

- Half a block east of Lonsdale Avenue.
- Rooms and apartments.

Three rooms: One person $60–75; two people $70–85. Ensuite and shared guest bathrooms. No showers. Additional person $25. Breakfast not included.
Six apartments: Ensuite bathrooms.
Seventh night free in the off-season. Extended stay rates.

- A 1904 house with original exterior finish, authentically framed double-glazed windows, original staircases, antiques, soaker tubs, and a full-width front veranda. Refurbished 1999. Guest rooms have TVs, VCRs, heaters, fans, telephones (for short local calls), and keyed doors. Six private apartments with TVs, telephones, refurbished bathrooms, and kitchens in a separate building. Four blocks from the harbour and Lonsdale Quay. Near a fitness centre, the Royal Hudson steam train, Grouse Mountain, two suspension bridges, and Stanley Park. Twelve minutes across the harbour by passenger ferry from Gastown, a conference centre, an Imax theatre, downtown Vancouver, and connections to rapid transit, buses, and Alaska cruise ship departures. Off-street parking behind the house and behind 158 East Third. Breakfast is not provided; there is a guest fridge, and there are restaurants and stores nearby. Nonrefundable deposit of first night's rate required to hold reservation. Visa for reservations only. Cancellation notice eight days. Cash, traveller's cheques. Adult oriented. Nonsmoking guests. **In the hosts' own words:** "Years of love and effort have gone into restoring our charming heritage house and apartments in North Vancouver. So many guests have stayed with us. Why? The price and location are right."

Ellison House

Ellison Massey
542 East First Street
North Vancouver, BC V7L 1B9
(604) 990-6730 fax: (604) 990-5876
toll-free from within North America:
1-800-561-3223
email: ellison@b-b.com
web site: www.b-b.com

• On Highway 1, follow the signs to North Vancouver. Take exit 18 and go south on Lonsdale Avenue. Turn left onto East First Street and continue for five blocks.

• Two rooms: One person $40–60; two people $65–95. Queen-sized bed; double bed. Shared bathroom. Weekly rates.

• A B&B in a quiet residential area, five blocks from Lonsdale Quay and a passenger ferry to downtown Vancouver, Gastown, Chinatown, Imax Theatre, and the Alaska cruise ship terminal. Ten minutes' drive from Stanley Park, the Royal Hudson steam train, the Capilano suspension bridge, and the Lynn Canyon suspension bridge. Living room with hardwood floors, TV, and fireplace. Outdoor patio. Guest rooms and living room have a view of the harbour. Breakfast ingredients supplied. Deposit with credit card required to hold reservation. Cancellation notice seven days. Cash, traveller's cheques, Visa, MasterCard, American Express. Cat in residence. No smoking. **In the hosts' own words:** "Come and enjoy our quiet and relaxing home, which is minutes away from the attractions of downtown Vancouver and the attractions and outdoor activities of North and West Vancouver."

Mavis' B&B

Mavis Walkley
1—269 East Keith Road
North Vancouver, BC V7L 1V4
(604) 986-9748

• From Highway 1, take exit 18 to Lonsdale Avenue. Go south on Lonsdale and turn left onto Keith Road. The B&B is between St. Georges and St. Andrews Avenues.

• Two rooms: One person from $55; two people $75–95. Twin beds; queen-sized bed. Private and ensuite bathrooms. Child 2 to 6 $5; child 7 to 12 $10.

• A B&B within walking distance of restaurants, Lonsdale Quay, and a passenger ferry to downtown Vancouver. On bus route to Capilano Canyon and Grouse Mountain. Ten minutes' drive from Stanley Park, the Royal Hudson steam train, and Lynn Canyon. Twenty minutes' drive from the Horseshoe Bay ferry terminal. Guest rooms have TVs. One of the guest rooms has a queen-sized bed, an ensuite bathroom with Jacuzzi tub, and a private patio. Sitting room and family room. Full or Continental breakfast is served in the dining room. Children welcome. No pets; cats in residence. No smoking indoors. **In the hosts' own words:** "Enjoy your stay in an attractive, clean, comfortable house with us as your friendly hosts."

A. D. Paterson House

Moira Rushton
7234 Ladner Trunk Road
Mail: RR 3
Delta, BC V4K 3N3
(604) 952-0952 fax: (604) 952-0022
email: moira_rushton@bc.sympatico.ca
web site: www.bnb.bc.ca

• From Highway 99, take Highway 17 south. Turn left onto Highway 10 (Ladner Trunk Road).

• Three rooms: One person $70–90; two people $90–115. Queen-sized bed, ensuite bathroom; queen-sized bed, private bathroom; two twin beds, private bathroom.
Seasonal rates.

• A 1914 house that was the private residence of a lieutenant governor of British Columbia, with a wrap-around veranda and a view of Mount Baker. The house is on two and a half acres and is surrounded by hundred-year-old 150-foot trees that house bald eagles and other birds of prey. The TV and film industry has used the property for set locations. A few minutes' walk from the Boundary Bay conservation area. Two minutes from the Boundary Bay airport. Fifteen minutes' drive from the Tsawwassen ferry terminal. Twenty minutes' drive from the Vancouver airport. Thirty minutes' drive from downtown Vancouver. Sitting area with fireplace. Breakfast is served on the veranda or in the breakfast room, both of which have views of Mount Baker. No smoking indoors. **In the hosts' own words:** "Enjoy the peace of rural life in a heritage house that has been visited by dignitaries from around the world. Our B&B welcomes you with gorgeous finishings, woodwork, and freshly decorated rooms."

Duck Inn Cottage

Jill and Allen York
4349 River Road West
Ladner, BC V4K 1R9
(604) 946-7521 fax: (604) 946-7521
email: duckinn@dccnet.com
web site: www.bbcanada.com/1671.html

- In Ladner, 20 minutes south of the Vancouver airport.
- Self-contained one-bedroom cottage: Two people $120–150. King-sized bed. Ensuite bathroom. Breakfast ingredients supplied. Extended stay, off-season, and weekly rates.
- A waterfront cottage on pilings at the edge of the Fraser River, with views of the Ladner Reach and the North Shore mountains. Ducks and other marine birds can be seen on the river below. Ten minutes from the Tsawwassen ferry terminal's ferries to Victoria, Nanaimo, and the Gulf Islands. Near the George C. Reifel Migratory Bird Sanctuary. Living and dining area with waterfront views, fireplace, TV, VCR, CD player, telephone, and French doors that lead to a balcony. Sherry and snacks provided. Bathroom with jetted tub. Private twelve-by-twelve-foot floating dock. Canoe, bikes, hammock, and patio with barbecue. Kitchen is stocked with smoked salmon and other breakfast items. Visa, MasterCard, American Express. Smoking on the balcony. **In the hosts' own words:** "At our B&B, enjoy a romantic riverfront escape and explore the waterways of the Fraser delta at your leisure. Let the river lull you to sleep at night and enchant you by day."

Blue Heron Inn B&B

Mladen and Laurie Zuvich
4543 River Road West
Ladner, BC V4K 1R9
(604) 946-2754
web site: www3.bc.sympatico.ca/blue_heron_inn

- In Ladner, on the Fraser River.
- Two suites: $140–190. King-sized bed; queen-sized bed. Ensuite bathrooms.
- A new floating house on the Fraser River, designed as a B&B and moored by the hosts' house, with views of the river and the North Shore mountains. Wildlife can be seen from the guest suites. The suite with the queen-sized bed has a double air-jet Jacuzzi tub, free-standing gas fireplace, and private balcony. The suite with the king-sized bed has a wood-burning stove, a two-person shower, and a private deck with a Japanese soaker tub. Both suites have private entrances, fridges, microwaves, CD players, coffee makers, and river and mountain views. TV and VCR available by request. Bicycles, barbecue, and a two-person kayak available. Twenty-five minutes' drive from downtown Vancouver. Twenty minutes' drive from the Vancouver airport. Ten minutes' drive from the Tsawwassen ferry terminal. Five minutes' drive from the George C. Reifel Migratory Bird Sanctuary. Within walking distance of shops and restaurants. Full breakfast, including seasonal fruit, homemade baked goods, and an entrée, is delivered to guest suites. Visa, MasterCard. Adult oriented. No pets. Smoking outdoors. **In the hosts' own words:** "At our B&B, watch the marine life from your suite or in a kayak built for two—either way it will be an experience to remember."

Moldovanos B&B

John and Anne Moldovanos
6869 Sussex Avenue
Burnaby, BC V5J 3V1
(604) 430-2123 fax: (604) 436-2115
toll-free from within North America:
1-888-430-2123

• Rooms and suite.
Rooms: One person $75–85; two people $85–95. Queen-sized bed; twin beds. Ensuite bathrooms.
Self-contained two-bedroom suite. Monthly rates.
• A B&B within walking distance of rapid transit, buses, a shopping mall, theatres, restaurants, a library, and Central Park. The park has trails, ponds, golf, tennis, and cycling. Near rapid transit to downtown Vancouver, B.C. Place, Science World, Omnimax, a passenger ferry to North Vancouver, and a shuttle bus to the Vancouver airport. Living room with gas fireplace, books, and TV. Air and water filtration system. Breakfast is prepared and served by one of the hosts, who is a restaurateur. Parking on the premises. Visa, MasterCard, American Express. Smoking on a covered porch.

Chambres d'Hôtes Sunflower B&B

Rosina Iantosca
1110 Hamilton Street
New Westminster, BC V3M 2M9
(604) 522-4186 fax: (604) 522-4176
email: yourhosts@sunflower-bnb.com
web site: www.sunflower-bnb.com

• One person $65–70; two people $75–85. Shared guest bathrooms. Additional person $25. Children under 2 free. Group, weekly, and monthly rates. In summer, minimum stay required.
• A B&B twenty minutes by rapid transit from downtown Vancouver and twenty minutes' drive from the Vancouver airport. A few minutes from the Westminster Quay market, a riverboat casino, golf, restaurants, and shops. One block from a bus stop. Thirty minutes' drive from the U.S. border and the Tsawwassen ferry terminal. Guest rooms have individually keyed locks and clock radios. Bathrobes and slippers provided. Guest living room with TV and VCR. Guest sitting room with desk and books. Guest telephones. Local guidebooks, tourist publications, daily newspapers, and magazines. Fax service and email access for a fee. Hosts share their knowledge of the area. Breakfast is served in the dining room, which has a fireplace. Deposit of one night's rate or 30 percent of total rate required to hold reservation. Cancellation notice required. Check-in after 4:30 p.m.; check-out until 11:00 a.m. or by arrangement. Cash or traveller's cheques. French and Italian spoken. Children welcome. No pets. Smoke-free environment. **In the hosts' own words:** "We invite you to enjoy the comfort and tranquillity of our conveniently located character house with tastefully decorated bedrooms and unforgettable gourmet breakfasts."

Henley House B&B

Anne O'Shaughnessy and Ross Hood
1025 Eighth Avenue
New Westminster, BC V3M 2R5
(604) 526-3919 fax: (604) 526-3913
email: henley@istar.ca
web site: www.henleyhouse.com

• Three rooms: One person $60–75; two people $65–80. Queen-sized bed, shared guest bathroom; double bed, shared guest bathroom; queen-sized bed, ensuite bathroom. Additional person $10. Cot available.
Weekly rates.

• A 1925 Craftsman-style house with antiques, quilts, embroidered linen, art, and flowers. Five minutes' from golf, restaurants, the New Westminster Quay, and a riverboat casino. One block from tennis courts. Twenty minutes by rapid transit from downtown Vancouver. French doors that lead to a deck, bird feeders, flower beds, and a year-round hot tub. Robes and slippers provided. TV room. Living room. Guest telephones, TVs, books, and videos. Guest bathrooms have hair dryers and toiletries. Breakfast, including fruit dishes, homemade muffins or scones, and a hot entrée, is served in a formal wainscoted dining room that has crystal, silver, bone china, and hand-woven linen. Morning coffee or tea is served by the fireplace or on the deck. Cancellation notice three days. Cash, cheques, Visa, MasterCard. Children over ten welcome. No pets; dog in residence. Smoking on the balcony. **In the hosts' own words:** "Friendly hosts and a welcoming heritage house bring our guests back time and again. We bet you'll be among them."

Tall Cedars B&B

Dwyla and Ed Beglaw
720 Robinson Street
Coquitlam, BC V3J 4G1
(604) 936-6016 fax: (604) 936-6016
cel: (604) 813-6019
email: tallcedars_bnb@telus.net
web site: www.bbcanada.com/2490.html

• In Coquitlam, bordering on North Burnaby. From Seattle, take the Bellingham-Lynden route to the Aldergrove border crossing. Take Highway 1 west to exit 37 (Cariboo). Phone or email for further directions.

• Three rooms: One person or two people $45–75. Queen-sized bed; double bed; twin beds. Private and shared bathrooms. Weekly rates.

• A B&B with tall fir and cedar trees and a lighted, covered balcony with flowers. Near three golf courses and Rocky Point Park, where there are eagles and rare swallows. Near a boat ramp with hiking and rollerblading trails around the inlet. In the area are lakes, hiking trails, and wildlife viewing. Three minutes' drive from Como Lake. Ten minutes by bus from Simon Fraser University. Near two shopping centres and restaurants. Bus connection to rapid transit to downtown Vancouver. Guest rooms have TVs and ceiling fans. Flower garden. Breakfast. Smoking on the covered balcony. **In the hosts' own words:** "A wonderful alternative to hotels and motels, our B&B offers you comfort and warm country hospitality right in the city and delicious breakfasts. We make every effort to make you feel comfortable and at home, and we truly enjoy hosting guests from around the world."

Woodside B&B

Helen A. Wood
100 College Park Way
Port Moody, BC V3H 1S4
(604) 939-3718
email: woodside@intergate.ca
web site: www.bbcanada.com/woodside

- Two rooms and one honeymoon suite: One person $45–60; two people $65–85. Queen-sized bed; double bed; twin beds.
- A B&B on a quiet, tree-lined residential street, across the street from a large park with forest trails and a swimming pool. Near Burnaby and Simon Fraser University. A bus that stops in front of the B&B connects to rapid transit and a commuter train that reaches downtown Vancouver in twenty minutes. Five minutes' drive from cafés, movie theatres, and malls. Sitting room with grand piano and fireplace. Dining room with antique mahogany table and buffet and adjacent patio that looks out onto a flower garden and trees. Honeymoon suite has a view of the forest, a pine queen-sized bed, pine dressers, a TV, a VCR, a telephone, and a bathroom with soaker tub and shower. One of the guest rooms has a double antique brass bed, a TV, a VCR, and a telephone. Rooms and suite have flowers from the garden, duvets, and antiques. Directions and information on places to see in the Vancouver area can be provided by hosts. Full, three-course breakfast is served in the dining room or on the patio. Cat and dog in residence. Smoking on the patio. **In the hosts' own words:** "Enjoy your stay in our attractive, clean, comfortable house, with us as your friendly hosts. Once you have visited us you'll want to return."

Riverside B&B

Wilma and Alan Wilson
21868—132nd Avenue
Maple Ridge, BC V4R 2T1
(604) 463-3167 fax: (604) 463-7351
email: wwilson@uniserve.com
web site: www.bbcanada.com/1458.html

• Fifty-five minutes from Vancouver. Five minutes from downtown Maple Ridge. From Vancouver, take Highway 7 (Lougheed). Turn left onto 216th Street. Turn right onto 132nd Avenue.

• Two suites: One person $55; two people $75. Two double beds; double bed and double sofa bed. Ensuite bathrooms. Additional person $20.

• A hand-built log house with antiques, on two acres along the South Alouette River. Near hiking in Golden Ears Park, boating, swimming, and golf courses. Walking, biking, and horseback riding trails from the B&B. Across the street from an equestrian centre and restaurant. Veranda with a view of the river and wildlife. One of the suites is upstairs and has two antique brass double beds, a sitting area with loveseat, armchair, desk, and TV, and a balcony with a view of the river. The other suite has a view of the river, a private wheelchair-accessible entrance, an antique brass double bed, a double sofa bed, a loveseat, a dining table, a TV, and access to the veranda. Full breakfast, including a hot entrée, juice, fruit, homemade muffins, scones, and rolls, is served in the suites, in the dining room, or on the veranda. Cash, cheques, Visa. No pets; dog in residence. Smoking on the veranda. **In the hosts' own words:** "We look forward to welcoming you and ensuring that you have a pleasant stay in beautiful Maple Ridge."

The Counting Sheep Inn

Virginia C. Edwards
8715 Eagle Road, RR 3
Mission, BC V2V 4J1
(604) 820-5148 fax: (604) 820-5149
email: vcesheep@uniserve.com
web site: www.countingsheep.com

• Sixty minutes from Vancouver. Five minutes from Mission, off Highway 7 (Lougheed). Fifteen minutes from the U.S. border.

• Three suites: $115–130. King-sized bed; queen-sized bed; twin beds. Ensuite and private bathrooms. Additional person $20.
Off-season rates. Knitting and spinning classes available with advance notice. Winter packages.

• A country inn on a six-acre working sheep farm, bordering on Hatzic Lake and a wetland preserve with trumpeter swans. Stalls and pastures for guests' horses. Flower and vegetable gardens. Apple picking in season. Children can attend lambs' births in spring and help with farm chores such as collecting eggs from the hens. Wool and gift shop on the property. Guest rooms have sitting areas, fireplaces, private gardens, TVs, VCRs, duvets, and robes. One of the bathrooms has a double-jetted Jacuzzi. Some of the guest rooms have sofa beds. Guest rooms are separate from the hosts' living quarters. In the area are birdwatching, golf, horseback riding, swimming, skiing, fishing, boating, hiking trails, stores, and restaurants. Bicycles available for exploring neighbouring farms and antique stores. Picnic baskets and dinners can be arranged with advance notice. Breakfast, including homemade baked goods, preserves, and farm-fresh eggs, is served in the guest suites, in the garden, or on the veranda. Kosher and vegetarian diets accommodated. Children welcome. Smoking outdoors. **In the hosts' own words:** "Our country inn offers an escape from the bustle of the city. Relax by the fire with a book or sit in our garden and watch the sheep grazing in our fields. Experience elegant accommodations while enjoying country life at its best."

Fence Post Lane B&B

Fran and Martin Perdue
8575 Gaglardi Street
Mission, BC V4S 1B2
(604) 820-7009 fax: (604) 820-4974
toll-free from within North America:
1-877-833-7009
email: mperdue@direct.ca
web site: www.bbcanada.com/906.html

• Eight kilometres west of Mission. From Mission, take Highway 7 (Lougheed). Turn right onto Chester Street, left onto Silverdale Avenue, and right onto Gaglardi Street.

• One person $45–50; two people $60–75. Queen-sized bed; double bed. Private bathrooms.

• A new thirty-six-hundred-square-foot ranch-style house in the country, on landscaped acreage with a creek and a bridge. Eight minutes from restaurants, shops, golf, Mission Raceway, and Westminster Abbey. Forty-five minutes from Harrison Hot Springs. Twenty minutes from Abbotsford and the U.S. border. One hour from Vancouver. Hiking in Mission, Whonnock Lake, Hayward Lake, and Rolly Lake. Entertainment room and patios. Full breakfast with homemade baked goods. Diets are accommodated. Cat in residence. No smoking. **In the hosts' own words:** "Come and enjoy our country hospitality—it's quiet and you'll love it."

Shalynne-by-the-Lake B&B

Marlene and David Johnston
29487 Silver Crescent, RR 2
Mission, BC V2V 4H9
(604) 826-3161

• From the junction of highways 11 and 7 in Mission, take Highway 7 west for 7 kilometres and turn right onto Hayward Street. Take the first left onto Silver Crescent.

• Two rooms: In winter, $40–55. In summer, $55–70. Queen-sized bed; double bed and one twin bed. Two shared guest bathrooms. Additional person $20. Roll-away bed available.

• An all-cedar house on a lake, an hour from Vancouver and ten minutes from Mission City and a commuter train that reaches downtown Vancouver in seventy minutes. Hot tub and private beach with beach chairs. Swimming, fishing, canoeing, sailing, paddle-boating, biking, and hiking. Water skiing is available by arrangement, as are picnic lunches for biking and hiking on local trails. Guests can have fires on the beach. Living room with stone fireplace, TV, VCR, books, and a view of the lake. Guests can play board games and cards at the kitchen table, by a second stone fireplace. Portable fireplace on patio. Full or Continental breakfast is served in the dining room, which has a view of the lake, or on the patio. Cash, Visa, traveller's cheques. Children over five welcome. No pets. Smoking outdoors. **In the hosts' own words:** "Enjoy outstanding hospitality in a wonderful setting. Be our special guests. Come as strangers, leave as friends."

DeGraff Haus B&B Inn

Susan Morgan
13085 DeGraff Road
Mission, BC V2V 4J1
(604) 820-8585 fax: (604) 820-8567
email: degraff-haus@telus.net
web site: www.degraff-haus.com

- Fifteen minutes east of Mission.
- Three rooms: Two people $60–90. King-sized bed; queen-sized bed; double bed. Ensuite and private bathrooms. Additional person rates.
- A B&B on five acres with one-half to three-quarters of an acre of ponds and water fowl including Australian black swans. Guest rooms have air-conditioning and may have a balcony, a fireplace, a table, a Jacuzzi, a sitting area, and/or a private ground-level deck. Loft with balcony. Guest living room, dining room, bar, hot tub, and games room. Pickup and drop-off for guests travelling by air or train. Hosts assist in trip planning and vehicle and camper rentals. RV parking. Full or European-style breakfast, including sausage, cheese, marmalade, and homemade bread, is served in the dining room or on one of the covered decks, which have views of the mountains. Fine dining, including a four-course meal, is available for a fee, with advance notice. Reservations recommended. Visa, MasterCard, American Express. Adult oriented. No smoking indoors. **In the hosts' own words:** "At our B&B, enjoy fresh country air, a view of the mountains, and the sounds of the forest."

Harrison Mills Country House

Fred and Betty Block
828 Kennedy Road
Mail: Box 59
Harrison Mills, BC V0M 1L0
(604) 796-0385 fax: (604) 796-2214
toll-free from within Canada and the U.S.: 1-800-551-2511
web site: www.bbcanada.com/2035.html

• Ninety minutes east of Vancouver. Thirty minutes from Mission. Take Highway 7 (Lougheed) east through Mission. (Alternatively, take Highway 1 to the Abbotsford-Mission turnoff (Highway 11), go north to Highway 7 (Lougheed), and turn right.) Take Highway 7 (Lougheed) east to School Road, just past the Harrison Bridge. The B&B is a yellow farmhouse.

• Four rooms: Two people $130–160. Queen-sized bed. Ensuite bathrooms. Additional person $20.

• A Victorian farmhouse on a seventeen-acre Christmas-tree farm in the Fraser Valley, ninety minutes from Vancouver. Antiques and views of mountains and rivers. Guest rooms have antiques, terry robes, and views of surrounding farms. Coffee and tea are set at guest room doors in the morning. Library with books, magazines, games, and puzzles. Family room with pool table, TV, and fireplace. Movies in a sixteen-seat theatre. Indoor hot tub and sauna. Near skiing at Hemlock Valley and boating and swimming at Kilby Park. Two minutes from a new golf course. Fishing for cutthroat trout and coho and spring salmon in the Harrison River. Eleven hundred bald eagles winter in the area; some can be seen in the trees around the house. Near Harrison Mills, a historical sawmill town with a turn-of-the-century heritage store and museum. Fifteen minutes' drive from hot springs pool at Harrison Hot Springs. Small weddings and reunions accommodated. Full breakfast, including fresh fruit, cereal, baked goods, and a hot entrée, is served in the dining room. No pets; English setter in residence. Smoking outdoors. **In the hosts' own words:** "Enjoy a brisk walk around our acreage, meander along country roads, or pick some luscious blackberries. Our home is your home, and we encourage you to relax and live on country time for a while."

Historic Fenn Lodge

Diane Brady and Gary Bruce
15500 Morris Valley Road
Mail: Box 67
Harrison Mills, BC V0M 1L0
(604) 796-9798 fax: (604) 796-9274
toll-free from within Canada and the U.S.: 1-888-990-3399
email: info@fennlodge.com
web sites: www.fennlodge.com

• Ninety minutes from Vancouver. Three hours from Seattle. Thirty minutes from Mission.

• Seven rooms: Ensuite and shared guest bathrooms. Additional person $30.

• An eight-thousand-square-foot Victorian house built in 1903, on ninety acres with forest trails that lead to a half mile of riverfront, a labyrinth, and a two-hundred-foot waterfall. Sixty-by-twenty-foot swimming pool with patio. Covered porch with tables and chairs. Guest library/sitting room and guest living room with fireplace are on the main floor. The suite, which accommodates up to six people, is on the ground floor and has a fireplace and doors that lead to the pool. Hammocks, swings, benches, picnic tables, and garden furniture. Twenty minutes from Harrison Hot Springs and skiing at Hemlock Valley. Fifteen minutes from Weaver Creek spawning channels, Agassiz-Harrison Historical Museum, and an agricultural research station. Ten minutes from Kilby historical store and farm. Five minutes from Sand Piper Gold Course. Near hiking, biking, downhill and cross-country skiing, canoeing, kayaking, birdwatching, horseback riding, hang-gliding, paragliding, and year-round fishing for steelhead, sturgeon, trout, and salmon; guides and gear available. Lunch and dinner by arrangement, for an extra fee. Full breakfast. Reservations recommended. Cash, traveller's cheques, Visa, MasterCard, Interac. Phone for information on children and pets. Smoking outdoors. **In the hosts' own words:** "We extend a warm invitation to relax and revitalise at our B&B. We offer an ideal setting for a workshop, retreat, or reunion. The Chehalis River curls around the property, providing deep fishing pools and pleasant paths for strolling. Share a healthy and delicious breakfast with us, and then set out on your day's adventure or just relax and enjoy the B&B."

Harrison Heritage House and Kottage

Robert and Sonja Reyerse
312 Lillooet Avenue
Mail: Box 475
Harrison Hot Springs, BC V0M 1K0
(604) 796-9552
toll-free from within North America: 1-800-331-8099
web site: www.bbharrison.com

• From Vancouver, go east on Highway 1 for 90 minutes. Take exit 135 (Agassiz-Harrison). At the four-way stop in Harrison, turn right and continue for one block. The B&B is on the right.
• Suites and cottage.
Three suites: $85–155. Queen-sized bed; twin beds. Ensuite bathrooms.
Two-bedroom self-contained cottage: $135. Queen-sized bed; bunk bed with twin-sized upper bunk and double lower bunk.
• A house and a cottage on the banks of the Miami River, on one acre, surrounded by mountains. One block from Harrison Lake and a beach. Riverside lounge chairs, swing, and picnic tables. Canoe available. Guest suites have private entrances, sitting areas, TVs, and supplies for making coffee and tea. One of the suites has a two-person Jacuzzi. Another suite has a double Jacuzzi and a wood-burning fireplace. Breakfast. Visa, MasterCard. Dutch spoken. Cottage suitable for families. No pets. No smoking indoors. **In the hosts' own words:** "Our B&B offers a country setting in the heart of Harrison village. Come and enjoy the tranquil setting—perfect for quiet getaways and romantic weekends. We are steps away from the natural beauty and fabulous beaches of Harrison Lake."

Little House on the Lake

Arla and Wayne Swift
6305 Rockwell Drive
Mail: Box 492
Harrison Hot Springs, BC V0M 1K0
(604) 796-2186 fax: (604) 796-3251
toll-free from within Canada and the U.S.: 1-800-939-1116
email: lilhouse@uniserve.com
web site: www.littlehouseonthelake.com

• Ninety minutes from Vancouver. From Highway 1, turn north onto Highway 9. At the four-way stop in Harrison Hot Springs, turn right and continue for 3 kilometres to the B&B.

• Four rooms: One person $140–170; two people $155–185. Queen-sized bed. Ensuite bathrooms. Extended stay rate for two nights or more, $10 less per night.

• A hand-hewn log lodge with a private beach on the shore of Harrison Lake. Guest rooms have fireplaces, sitting areas, balconies, skylights, CD players, small TVs with VCRs, and flowers. Lake, mountain, and forest views. Hand-carved mahogany four-post or iron and brass beds with down comforters (alternatives to down available). Guest living room with stone fireplace, billiards, games table, upright grand piano, TV, VCR, conversation area, and washroom with utility sink for artists to use. Guest fridge with soda and juice. Books, videos, and CDs. Hot tub with a view of the lake. Robes provided. Afternoon tea and evening snack. Dock and canoe. Roof-top and lower decks with views. In the area are skiing, swimming, windsurfing, sailing, kayaking, hiking, mountain biking, golf, art and music festivals, and country fairs. Near fine dining restaurants. Morning coffee and muffins delivered to guest rooms. Full breakfast is served in a library/dining room with a view of the lake. Reservations recommended. Visa, MasterCard. Young people over sixteen welcome. No pets; German shepherd, hamsters, and squirrels in residence. Nonsmoking establishment. **In the hosts' own words:** "At our B&B, a warm welcome in a beautiful setting awaits you with an invitation to retreat, relax, and renew. Permission to do absolutely nothing is gladly given."

White Heather Guest House

Glad and Chuck Bury
12571 Ninety-eighth Avenue
Surrey, BC V3V 2K6
(604) 581-9797

• Ten minutes from Highway 1. Twenty-five minutes from the U.S. border.
• Two rooms: One person $50–60; two people $60–70. Queen-sized bed; double bed. Ensuite half bathroom and shared guest bathroom. Children's rates negotiable.
• A house with mountain views, in a quiet suburb close to rapid transit, near the highway to downtown Vancouver. Guest rooms, breakfast room, TV, and living rooms are on the main floor. Patio, deck, and guest TV room. Hosts share their knowledge of the area and Vancouver Island. Pickup and drop-off for guests arriving by air, ferry, train, or rapid transit. Full English breakfast with homemade bread is served in a sun room that has a view of the mountains on the North Shore. Children welcome. No pets. No smoking. **In the hosts' own words:** "We are well travelled and enjoy sharing our home with you."

B&B on the Ridge

Dale and Mary Fennell
5741—146th Street
Surrey, BC V3S 2Z5
(604) 591-6065 fax: (604) 591-6059
toll-free from within North America: 1-888-697-4111
email: stay@bbridgesurrey.com
web site: www.bbridgesurrey.com

• From Highway 1, take exit 66 or exit 53 onto Highway 15 (Pacific). Turn right onto Highway 10 (Fifty-sixth Avenue). Turn right onto 146th Street.
From Vancouver, take Highway 99. Take exit 16 onto Highway 10. Turn left onto 146th Street.
From the Victoria ferry, take exit 17 onto Highway 10. Turn left onto 146th Street.
From the U.S., take Highway 5. Take exit 275 (truck crossing) onto Highway 15 (Pacific). Turn left onto Highway 10 (Fifty-sixth Avenue). Turn right onto 146th Street.

• Rooms and suite.
Three rooms: One person $50–75; two people $55–90. Queen-sized bed; queen-sized bed and day bed; twin bed. Ensuite and private bathrooms. Additional person $10. Two cots, pull-out couch, and crib available. Off-season rates.
Honeymoon suite: $80–90. June to September or by request.

• A B&B on half an acre in a quiet country setting, with eight skylights, antiques, ceiling-to-floor windows, and a wrap-around deck. Ten minutes' drive from beaches, shopping, eight golf courses including a country club that holds a PGA Open golf tournament, rapid transit to downtown Vancouver, a race track, antique shops, restaurants, and the U.S. border. Twenty-five minutes from ferries and the Vancouver airport. Thirty-five to forty-five minutes from downtown Vancouver. One hour from skiing and snowboarding at Grouse, Seymour, and Cypress. Near shopping. Guest rooms have TVs and bathrooms with towels, shower dispensers, hair dryers, and toiletries. Honeymoon suite has a private deck, a TV, and an ensuite bathroom with skylight, Jacuzzi tub, and shower. Guest living room with TV, VCR, books, tourist information, a small fridge, and facilities for making tea and coffee. Full breakfast is served in the dining room or on the deck. **In the hosts' own words:** "We offer a warm welcome with a relaxed and tranquil atmosphere. Our light is always on and our door is always open."

Dorrington B&B

Pat Gray
13851—19A Avenue
White Rock, BC V4A 9M2
(604) 535-4408 fax: (604) 535-4409
email: grayp@direct.ca
web site: www.dorrington.com

• In Surrey, go south on Highway 99A (which is south of Highway 99) to exit 10. Take Crescent Beach Road. Turn left onto 140th Street. Turn right onto 19A Avenue.

• Three rooms: One person $85–105; two people $100–120. Queen-sized bed; double bed. Ensuite bathrooms. Off-season rates.
Minimum stay two nights.

• A B&B on half an acre of gardens, with an outdoor tennis court and hot tub, five minutes from White Rock's beach promenade, cafés, specialty shops, art galleries, antiques, and restaurants. Thirty minutes from ferries to Victoria and the Gulf Islands. Sitting room with twelve-foot ceilings, a river rock fireplace, and a view of the gardens. Guest rooms are decorated in themes. Robes, slippers, and scented soap. Tennis rackets and balls. Local restaurant menus and restaurant recommendations are provided by the hosts. Full breakfast is served indoors or on the patio. Deposit of one night's rate required to hold reservation. Cancellation notice seven days. Check-in 2:00 to 9:00 p.m.; check-out until 11:00 a.m. Visa. Adult oriented. No pets; miniature dachshund in residence. No smoking. **In the hosts' own words:** "Our B&B offers luxury and elegance in a peaceful setting."

Sparrow's Nest B&B

Aldric and Joanna Hovenkamp
21646 Murray's Crescent
Langley, BC V3A 8N2
(604) 514-3261 fax: (604) 514-3267
toll-free: 1-877-514-3261
email: sparrowsnestbb@home.com

• Forty minutes from downtown Vancouver. Five minutes from downtown Langley.

• Three rooms: One person $55–65; two people $65–85. King-sized bed; queen-sized bed; twin beds. Ensuite and shared guest bathrooms. Additional person $20. Cot available.

• A new, four-storey, Heritage-style house in a quiet residential area, with a mix of new, antique, and reproduction furniture. A few minutes from golf courses, a skating rink, a swimming pool, and antique stores. Fifteen minutes from the U.S. border. Guest sitting/reading room in a loft. Individually keyed doors. Morning coffee is served in another sitting room on the main floor. Full breakfast, including a hot entrée, is served in a country-style kitchen which has nine-foot ceilings and a gas fireplace, or in a nook which has a view of the garden. Check-in time is flexible. Dutch spoken. Cash, Visa. Suitable for families and wedding parties. No pets. Smoking on a covered porch. **In the hosts' own words:** "We offer a quiet, relaxing atmosphere with warm hospitality and views of beautiful sunsets from the front porch, minutes away from the restaurants and entertainment of the city."

Traveller's Joy B&B

Sylvia and Alan Schwertner
59 Wagonwheel Crescent
Langley, BC V2Z 2R1
(604) 533-2696 fax: (604) 533-3480
toll-free from within North America:
1-888-550-6611
web site: www.bbcanada.com/
travellersjoy

• From Highway 1, take exit 66 south to 232nd Street. Follow the signs and turn left to stay on 232nd Street. Turn left onto Fifty-sixth Avenue, right onto Clovermeadow and Wagonwheel Crescent.

• Two rooms: One person $40; two people $60–70. Queen-sized bed and sofa bed; queen-sized bed. Ensuite and private bathrooms. Weekly and off-season rates.

• A B&B in a quiet residential area, ten minutes' drive from Fort Langley, downtown, the U.S. border, parks, and restaurants. One hour from Vancouver. Five minutes from Highway 1. A few minutes from golf, cycling and walking trails, beaches, a race track, the Langley airport and flight museum, equestrian centres, horseback riding trails, farms, parks, beaches, a winery, antiques stores, and historic sites. Guest living room with fireplace, TV, books, and games. One acre garden. Guest rooms have private balconies. Full breakfast with seasonal garden produce. Cash, cheques, traveller's cheques. Not equipped for children under three. Pets by arrangement; cat in residence. Smoking outdoors. **In the hosts' own words:** "We invite you to enjoy our friendly, informal hospitality. We are happy to provide you with information on local, Vancouver, and Fraser Valley attractions and to direct you to a variety of day trip options."

Everett House B&B

Cindy and David Sahlstrom
1990 Everett Road
Abbotsford, BC V2S 7S3
(604) 859-2944 fax: (604) 859-9180
email: EverettBB@bc.sympatico.ca
web site: www.vancouver-bc.com/EverettHouseBB

• From Highway 1, take exit 92. Go north on Sumas Way for two blocks. Turn right onto Marshall and continue for about six blocks. Turn right onto Everett Road. The B&B is the first house on the left.

• Two suites: Two people $75–125. King-sized bed; queen-sized bed. Ensuite and private bathrooms. Additional person $15.

• A Victorian house in the central Fraser Valley, with a view of Sumas Prairie and Mount Baker. Suites have claw-foot tubs, private decks, double-head showers, and Victorian décor. Beds have Battenburg lace linen. In the area are shopping, golf, horseback riding, hiking, fishing, skating, and swimming. Forty minutes from skiing at Mount Baker. Guest hot tub in the garden. Home theatre and movies. Full breakfast is served in guest rooms, in the dining room, or outdoors. Cash, Visa, MasterCard. Smoking outdoors. **In the hosts' own words:** "Our B&B is an ideal retreat from the world or a romantic getaway. We specialize in wedding nights. When you are our guest, we want you to feel special."

The Olde Manse

Yoko and Dick Goold
4314 Wright Street
Abbotsford, BC V2S 7Y8
(604) 853-7984 fax: (604) 853-3753
web site: www.faximum.com/clayburn
www.oldemanse-clayburn.com

- In the town of Clayburn, off Highway 11 between Abbotsford and Mission.
- Three rooms: One person $60; two people $65. Queen-sized bed and sofa bed, ensuite bathroom; double bed, shared guest bathroom; twin beds, shared guest bathroom. Additional person $20.
- A 1912 house built originally for ministers of the village church, with a garden and a patio. Near hiking, cycling, and trail riding. Clayburn has a general store, a tea shop, a brick church, an old schoolhouse, and turn-of-the-century buildings. Two of the guest rooms have French doors that lead to a balcony that overlooks the garden. Guest sitting room on the main floor with fireplace, grand piano, and French doors that lead to the patio and garden. Bicycles available. Full breakfast is served in guests' rooms, in the dining room, or on the patio. Traveller's cheques, Visa, MasterCard. Children welcome.

Glacier View B&B

Beryl and Mike Murrell
40531 Thunderbird Ridge
Mail: Box 3786
Garibaldi Highlands, BC V0N 1T0
(604) 898-1630 fax: (604) 898-1630
email: glacierv@mountain-inter.net
web site: www.bbcanada.com/1574.html

• In Squamish (halfway between Vancouver and Whistler).
• Two rooms: One person $65; two people $80. Double bed; queen-sized bed. Private and shared bathrooms. Additional person $15. Fold-up bed available.
• A modern house in the Garibaldi Highlands area of Squamish, with views of the Coast Mountains. Near trail walks, valley and alpine hiking, rock climbing, golf, fishing, river rafting, and, in winter, eagle viewing. Guest sitting room with private entrance, TV, and small fridge. Full breakfast is served in the dining room or on the deck. Wheelchair accessible. Children welcome by arrangement. Small pets may be accommodated; dog and cat in residence. Smoking on the deck. **In the hosts' own words:** "From our B&B high in the Garibaldi Highlands, enjoy warm hospitality and spectacular Coast Mountain views while you share a delicious full breakfast with us."

Brew Creek Lodge

Didier and Shelley Toutain
1 Brew Creek Road
Whistler, BC V0N 1B1
(604) 932-7210 fax: (604) 932-7223

• Fifteen minutes south of Whistler Village. At the lodge's signpost on Highway 99, turn west onto Brew Creek Road and continue for 1 kilometre.

• Rooms, guest houses, and a cabin.
Six rooms in a lodge: One person or two people $85. Ensuite bathrooms. Additional person $25.
Two-storey guest house (sleeps thirteen): One to six people $450. Two private bathrooms. Additional person $75.
Three-storey guest house (sleeps eight): One to six people $450. Two private bathrooms. Additional person $75.
Cabin: One to four people $200. Private bathroom.
Breakfast not included; Continental breakfast provided for a fee.

• A lodge, a two-storey guest house, a three-storey guest house, a meeting house, and a cabin on two landscaped acres in a wilderness setting, fifteen minutes south of Whistler. Lodge has six guest rooms, a dining area, and a sitting area with a stone fireplace. Two-storey guest house, which accommodates up to thirteen people, has a kitchen, a dining room, a living room, a Jacuzzi, and a suite with king-sized bed, fireplace, bathroom, and private entrance. Three-storey guest house, which accommodates up to eight people, has a kitchen, a dining room, a dry sauna, a Jacuzzi, and a living room that has a stone fireplace and opens onto a deck. Log meeting house, built over Brew Creek, has a stone fireplace and a view of the surrounding forest and mountains and accommodates meetings of up to thirty people. On the grounds are a six-person guest outdoor hot tub, a volleyball court, and a natural swimming pond. Near hiking and biking trails, tennis, golf, horseback riding, and river rafting.

Golden Dreams B&B

Ann and Terry Spence
6412 Easy Street
Whistler, BC V0N 1B6
(604) 932-2667 fax: (604) 932-7055
toll-free: 1-800-668-7055
email: goldendreams@whistlerweb.net
web site: www.virutalcities.com/bc/goldendreams.htm

• From Vancouver, take Highway 99 for 111 kilometres to Whistler. At the traffic light at Lorimer, turn left. Go down the hill past the school and turn right onto Balsam Way. Take the first left onto Easy Street. The B&B is the fourth house on the left; enter through the separate arched guest entrance.

• Rooms: In winter, one person or two people $95–125. In summer, one person or two people $75–95. Queen-sized bed; two double beds. Private and shared guest bathrooms. Additional person $25. Child over 5 $10.

• A B&B with mountain views, one mile from ski lifts, restaurants, and village shops. Bike rentals at the B&B. Adjacent to the Valley Trail, which leads to several golf courses, Rainbow Beach, and a sports centre. Guest rooms are decorated in Victorian, Asian, and Aztec themes and have down comforters, sherry decanters, and sinks. Guest living room with fireplace and mountain view. Guest kitchen. Outdoor hot tub. Breakfast includes homemade bread, waffles, homemade preserves, and cappuccino. Vegetarian diets are accommodated. Visa, MasterCard. Children welcome. No smoking indoors. **In the hosts' own words:** "We invite you to be surrounded by nature's beauty and enjoy a wholesome breakfast at our B&B."

Alta Vista Chalet B&B Inn

Tim and Yvonne Manville
3229 Archibald Way
Whistler, BC V0N 1B3
(604) 932-4900 fax: (604) 932-4933
toll-free: 1-888-768-2970
email: avcb_b@direct.ca
web site: www.altavistachalet.com

• Two kilometres north of Whistler South (Creekside). Turn left onto Hillcrest Drive, immediately right onto Alpine Crescent, and left onto Archibald Way.

• Eight rooms: In summer, one person from $79, two people from $89. In winter, one person from $120, two people from $135. Queen-sized bed; twin beds. Ensuite bathrooms. Additional person $20–25. Child 3 to 10 $10.

• A B&B on a treed lot beside the Valley Trail, with a view of Alta Lake, two kilometres from the ski centres of Whistler Village and Whistler South. Fifteen minutes' walk along the Valley Trail from Whistler Village. Near a beach, swimming, picnic tables, barbecues, and canoe, kayak, and windsurfer rentals. Two of the guest rooms are larger than the other six, have TVs, and can accommodate up to four people; one of these rooms has a fireplace. Antiques. Guest living room opens onto a deck with Jacuzzi. Adjoining games room with TV, VCR, and guest fridge. Sauna. Afternoon tea. Breakfast is served in the dining room. Off-street parking and ski storage. No smoking.

The Inn at Clifftop Lane

Sulee and Alan Sailer
2828 Clifftop Lane
Whistler, BC V0N 1B2
(604) 938-1229 fax: (604) 938-9880
toll-free: 1-888-281-2929
email: cliffinn@direct.ca
web site: www.whistler.net/cliffinn

• One kilometre from Whistler Creekside and 4 kilometres from Whistler Village. Approaching from Vancouver, turn right at the Bayshores sign and right onto Cheakamus Way. At the end of Cheakamus Way, bear right onto Clifftop Lane.

• Five rooms: In winter, two people $140–185. In summer, two people $125. Twin beds side by side with king-sized bedding (or twin beds); queen-sized bed; double bed and pull-out sofa bed. Ensuite bathrooms. Additional person $30.
Ski and golf packages.

• A West Coast–style house of log pier and beam construction, with mountain and forest views. Guest rooms have French or Asian antiques, down duvets with cotton linen, TVs, VCRs, radios, and ensuite bathrooms with Jacuzzi tubs, hair dryers, robes, and toiletries. Selection of videos. Guest sitting room and dining area with stone floors, Asian carpets, two fireplaces, art, books, phone, and long distance phone line. Guest patio and gazebo with covered hot tub. Guest entrance. Daily housekeeping. Dinner is available for a fee on occasion. Parking. Ski and equipment storage. Full breakfast includes fresh juice and fruit, homemade bread and pastry, and a hot entrée. Deposit of one night's rate required to hold reservation. Cancellation notice thirty days. Check-in after 3:00 p.m.; check-out until 10:30 a.m. Smoking outdoors. **In the hosts' own words:** "Our inn blends the best qualities of a small European hotel and the traditional hospitality of a B&B; enjoy our quiet location, well-decorated rooms, and warm and comfortable surroundings. We welcome your visit."

Edelweiss Pension

Jacques and Ursula Morel
7162 Nancy Green Drive
Mail: Box 850
Whistler, BC V0N 1B0
(604) 932-3641 fax: (604) 938-1746
toll-free from within North America: 1-800-665-2003
email: jacquesm@idmail.com
web site: www.whistleronline.com/edelweiss

• From Highway 99, at the second intersection north of Whistler Village, turn right onto Nancy Green Drive. Cross the bridge and continue for 200 metres. The B&B is on the left.

• Eight rooms: In summer, one person $79–119, two people $89–129. In winter, one person $119–139, two people $129–149. Queen-sized bed; twin bed. Private bathrooms.

• A German-style B&B with views of Blackcomb and Whistler mountains. Fifteen minutes' walk from Whistler Village, Lost Lake Park, and cross-country ski trails. Near public transit. Guest rooms have down comforters. Some guest rooms have a balcony, a sofa, and/or a fireplace. Guest living room with fireplace. Hot tub. Sauna. Garden and patio. Parking. Bicycle storage. Full breakfast. **In the hosts' own words:** "We offer one of the best breakfasts in the valley—twelve different menus from twelve different countries."

Edgewater Lodge

Jay Symons
8841 Highway 99
Mail: Box 369
Whistler, BC VON 1B0
(604) 932-0688 fax: (604) 932-0686
email: jays@direct.ca
web site: www.whistler.net/resort/edgewater

• Three kilometres north of Whistler Village, at the intersection of Highway 99 and Alpine Way.

• Twelve rooms: Two people $105–255. King-sized bed; twin beds. Additional pull-out twin and/or queen-sized bed in each room. Additional person $25–35.
Retreat packages.
Lunch and dinner available.

• A lodge on a lake, with views of Whistler and Blackcomb mountains, on forty-five acres of forested land on Green Lake, beside the Nicklaus North golf course, the River of Golden Dreams, the Valley Trail, and Wedge Park. A few minutes from Whistler Village. Guest rooms and licensed guest lounge/dining room have views of the lake and of Whistler and Blackcomb mountains. Spa and horseback riding on the property. Canoeing and kayaking on the lake. Five minutes' walk from a recreation centre with a pool, a spa, exercise equipment, ice skating, racquetball, tennis, and conference room facilities. Art classes, cooking classes, float-plane tours, biking, hiking, golf, sailing, swimming, summer and winter skiing, cross-country skiing, parapenting, rock climbing, and horseback riding can be organized by lodge staff. Six of the guest rooms have living rooms with queen-sized sofa beds and private decks. The lounge/dining room has seating for up to forty-five guests; and additional seating is available outdoors in the summer. Lakeside patio and grass area. Meeting space in a nearby private meeting facility, which has audio-visual equipment and accommodates up to twelve people, or in the lounge, which accommodates up to twenty-five people. Itineraries for groups, including inviting experts to teach sessions, can be organized by lodge staff. Breakfast includes fruit salad, yogurt, homemade granola, and homemade croissants. Other meals available. Diets are accommodated at all meals.

Idylwood Inn B&B Chalet

Lily Antunes
8725 Idylwood Place
Mail: Box 797
Whistler, BC V0N 1B0
(604) 932-4582 fax: (604) 932-4556
toll-free from within North America: 1-877-932-4582
email: idylwood@whistlerhome.com
web site: www.whistlerhome.com

• From Whistler Village, take Highway 99 north for 3.5 kilometres. At Alpine Meadows, turn left onto Alpine Way. Take the fourth left, onto Idylwood Place.

• Rooms and suite.

Three rooms in a separate part of the house from the hosts' living quarters: In summer, two people $95–125. In winter, two people $125–155. King-sized bed; queen-sized bed; twin beds. Ensuite and shared guest bathrooms.

Self-contained suite: In summer, two people from $150. In winter, two people from $275.

The entire house: In summer, from $395. In winter, from $495. For guests renting the suite or the entire house, breakfast is available for an additional fee.

Summer and winter adventure packages.

• A B&B on a quiet cul-de-sac a few minutes' drive from Whistler Village, with a view of Blackcomb and Whistler mountains. Five minutes from Whistler village, shopping, and ski lifts. Within walking distance of a sports complex, a children's water park, tennis courts, a playground, the Valley Trail, the Nicklaus North golf course, and Green and Lost lakes. Outdoor hot tub, barbecues, decks, and yard. Guest living room with wood-burning and propane fireplaces. Loft with TV, VCR, and videos. Guest rooms have down duvets. The room with a king-sized bed has an ensuite bathroom with Jacuzzi. Suite has an ensuite bathroom with steam shower. Laundry and storage facilities. Guest room rates include breakfast. For guests renting the suite or the entire house, breakfast is available for a fee. Full or Continental breakfast. Smoking outdoors. **In the hosts' own words:** "Our B&B is suitable for honeymooners, families, and small groups. Stay in the lap of luxury in our casually elegant and spacious B&B and soak up the spectacular mountain view from our outdoor hot tub."

Home Comforts B&B

Gayle and Don Wildfong
1410 Poplar Street
Mail: Box 261
Pemberton, BC V0N 2L0
(604) 894-6424 fax: (604) 894-6212

• Three rooms: One person $55–75; two people $75–95. Queen-sized bed and sofa bed, ensuite bathroom; queen-sized bed, shared guest bathroom; twin beds, shared guest bathroom. Additional person $20. Crib and roll-away cot available.
Extended stay rates.

• A B&B with mountain views, close to seven golf courses including Big Sky, the Chateau, and Nicklaus North. Near fishing, hiking, tennis, horseback riding, overnight trips, and trail rides. Twenty-five minutes' drive from skiing at Whistler and Blackcomb mountains. In the area are snowmobiling, cross-country skiing, kayaking, canoeing, river rafting, whitewater jet boat trips, and adventure tours. Near the Pemberton airport, train station, and bus depot. The guest room with an ensuite bathroom has a Jacuzzi bath. Another guest room has a private balcony. Living room with books, TV, VCR, and fireplace. Air conditioning. Full breakfast, which includes farm-fresh eggs, or continental breakfast. Children welcome. Smoking outside on a covered deck. **In the hosts' own words:** "Come visit us and enjoy the breathtaking beauty. This is a four-season resort area with something for everyone. A photographer's paradise."

The Pemberton Valley Vineyard and Inn

Heather and Patrick Bradner
1427 Collins Road
Mail: Box 817
Pemberton, BC V0N 2L0
(604) 894-5857 fax: (604) 894-1187
email: bradner@whistlerweb.com
web site: www.whistlerwine.com

• In the Pemberton Valley, 34 kilometres north of Whistler. Cross the railway tracks and turn right at the Bank of Nova Scotia. Continue for 1 kilometre and turn right onto Collins Road. The B&B is the fourth house on the left, set back 250 metres from the road.

• Three rooms: $95–109. King-sized bed; queen-sized bed. Private bathrooms. Additional person $15. Extended stay rates. Group rates.

• A log house on a seven-acre farm and vineyard, with a view of Mount Currie. Guest rooms have mountain views, separate entrances, decks, and fireplaces. Outdoor hot tub. Mountain bikes available for guest use. Breakfast includes eggs from the farm. Reservations recommended. No pets. No smoking. **In the hosts' own words:** "Come and enjoy the ambience, stargaze from the secluded hot tub, and savour a gourmet breakfast. We offer a private, relaxing, and very peaceful setting."

The Log House B&B Inn

Donna and Saad Hasan
1357 Elmwood Drive
Mail: Box 699
Pemberton, BC V0N 2L0
(604) 894-6000 fax: (604) 894-6000
toll-free: 1-800-894-6002
email: loghouseinfo@loghouseinn.com
web site: www.loghouseinn.com

• Two and a half hours from Vancouver. Twenty-five minutes north of Whistler. From Vancouver, take Highway 99 to Pemberton. At the Petro Canada gas station, turn left. At the three-way stop, turn left. At the next stop sign, turn right onto Aster Street. Turn right onto Dogwood Street. The B&B is on the corner of Dogwood and Elmwood.

• Seven rooms: One person $85–95; two people $95–160. King-sized bed; queen-sized bed; double bed; queen-sized bed and one twin bed. Ensuite and shared guest bathrooms. Additional person $35.

• A five-thousand-square-foot cedar log house with a wrap-around deck and a view of Mount Currie. Outdoor hot tub and lounge chairs on the deck. Reading loft and guest living area with wood stove. Guest rooms have TVs, robes, and handmade patchwork quilts. Some guest rooms have fridges. Near golf, gliding, hiking, biking, snowmobiling, rafting, fishing, and cross-country skiing. Full breakfast, including local farm produce, is served in the dining area. Afternoon tea. Special-occasion dinners and packed lunches are available for a fee. Diets are accommodated by arrangement. Reservations recommended. Cash, traveller's cheques, Visa, MasterCard, Interac. Children welcome by arrangement. No pets. No smoking. **In the hosts' own words:** "Enjoy our peaceful getaway in a superb setting, with a spectacular view of Mount Currie. Quality, service, hospitality, our large guest living area, and breakfasts of local farm produce and fresh homemade bread make it hard to leave and easy to come back."

Marina House B&B

Sue Bailey
546 Marine Drive
Mail: Box 1696
Gibsons, BC V0N 1V0
(604) 886-7888
toll-free: 1-888-568-6688
email: marinahouse@sunshine.net
web site: www.wcbbia.com/pages/marinahouse.html

• Four kilometres from the Langdale ferry terminal.
Seventy-seven kilometres from the Earls Cove ferry terminal.

• Three rooms: One person $80; two people $90. Queen-sized bed, ensuite bathroom; twin beds (or twin beds side by side with king-sized bedding), private bathroom. Additional person $20. Cots available.

• A house on the ocean, with moorage and beach access, a short walk from Gibsons Landing and Molly's Reach. A base for cross country skiing, hiking, trout fishing, golf, canoeing, and sailing day trips. A few minutes' walk from restaurants, a pub, a bookstore, antique shops, art galleries, pottery and jewelry shops, a government dock, and kayak and canoe rentals. Pebble beach. Near a sandy beach for swimming. Guest rooms are on the top floor and have ocean views of Shoal Channel and Lions Bay. Guest entrance. Sitting room with TV and books. Covered porch. Breakfast includes homemade baked goods and local products. Cancellation notice seven days. Visa, MasterCard. Not suitable for children under twelve. No smoking indoors. **In the hosts' own words:** "You're always welcome in our warm and cozy heritage house."

Oceanview Cottage B&B

Dianne and Bert Verzyl
1927 Grandview Road
Mail: RR 5
Gibsons, BC V0N 1V5
(604) 886-7943 fax: (604) 886-4311
toll-free from within North America: 1-800-231-9122
email: oceanview@dccnet.com
web site: www.vancouver-bc.com/oceanview

• From the Langdale ferry terminal, take Highway 101. Turn left onto Lower Road, left onto Pine Road, and right onto Grandview Road. The B&B is 9 kilometres from the ferry terminal.

• Rooms and cottage.

Two rooms: One person $75; two people $85–120. Queen-sized bed; twin beds. Ensuite bathrooms.

Self-contained cottage (sleeps six): Two people $115. Queen-sized bed, two sofa beds, and cot. Private bathroom. Additional person $20. Child under 12 $10.

• A B&B on three acres, with a view of the Strait of Georgia and Vancouver Island. Guest rooms have sliding doors that lead to a guest deck. Self-contained cottage has a bedroom, a four-piece bathroom with soaker tub, a kitchen, a TV, a fireplace, skylights, and a deck with tables and chairs. Afternoon coffee or tea is served. Near shopping and restaurants. Full breakfast is served in the dining room or the sun room. Cash, traveller's cheques, Visa, MasterCard. French and Dutch spoken. No pets. No smoking. **In the hosts' own words:** "Relax at our B&B and enjoy the Sunshine Coast's spectacular ocean and mountain views and beautiful sunsets."

Bonniebrook Lodge B&B

Karen and Philippe Lacoste
Mail: RR 5, 1532 Oceanbeach Esplanade
Gibsons, BC V0N 1V0
(604) 886-2887 fax: (604) 886-8853
toll-free: 1-877-290-9916
email: info@bonniebrook.com
web site: www.bonniebrook.com

• Take the ferry from Horseshoe Bay to Langdale. From the Langdale ferry terminal, take Highway 101. Turn left onto Pratt Road and continue to the bottom. Turn right onto Gower Point Road. The B&B is at the foot of the road.

• Seven suites: Two people $140–180. Queen-sized bed and double sofa bed.
Ensuite bathrooms.
Additional person $30.

• A 1920s oceanside lodge with a restaurant on the main floor. Four suites are in the main lodge and have ocean views. Three suites are in a new building beside the lodge. All suites have TVs, VCRs, CD players, small fridges, coffee makers, hair dryers, fireplaces, two-person Jacuzzi tubs, and oversized showers. Two of the suites have separate bedrooms. Terry robes. Fans. Full breakfast, including omelettes, hashed brown potatoes, homemade baked goods, fresh fruit, toast, homemade jam, juice, and coffee or tea, is delivered to guests' rooms between 8:30 and 10:00 a.m. For guests leaving early, a Continental breakfast tray is provided. Cancellation notice five days. Check-in after 2:00 p.m.; check-out until noon. Cash, credit cards, Interac. No pets. No smoking in the guest rooms. **In the hosts' own words:** "We invite you to relax and enjoy our romantic Inn."

Country Cottage B&B

Philip and Loragene Gaulin
1183 Roberts Creek Road
Mail: Box 183
Roberts Creek, BC V0N 2W0
(604) 885-7448

• From the Horseshoe Bay ferry terminal (30 minutes from Vancouver), take the Sunshine Coast ferry (40 minutes). Go north on Highway 101 (Sunshine Coast) for 25 minutes. Past the golf course, turn left onto Roberts Creek Road.

• Cottage and lodge.

Self-contained cottage: One person $99; two people $125. Queen-sized bed. Private bathroom.

Self-contained lodge (sleeps six): One person $105; two people $145. Three queen-sized beds. Private bathrooms. Additional person $50.

• A farmhouse, a cottage, and a lodge, five minutes' walk from Roberts Creek, a beach, golf, parks, shops, galleries, and fine dining at a French restaurant or a bistro café. Hosts help guests plan and book day trips for hiking, boating, kayaking, scuba diving, fly fishing, horseback riding, mountain biking, and backcountry skiing. The self-contained cottage is decorated in English country cottage style and has a wrought-iron queen-sized bed, a kitchen, antiques, a wood stove, and a bathroom with shower. The self-contained lodge has views of an acre of cedars and a grassy pasture and is decorated in mountain lodge style, with a river rock fireplace, fly-fishing memorabilia, Navaho rugs, and arts and crafts furniture. It has a kitchen, a campfire circle, two lofts with queen-sized beds, and a bathroom with shower. Separate cottage connected to the lodge by a walkway has a queen-sized bed and a private bathroom with shower. The lodge accommodates up to six people and is rented to one group at a time. English country gardens, sheep, and chickens. One of the hosts is a spinner, weaver, and angler. The other host is a wood worker, a backcountry skiier, and an antique car, vintage truck, and motorcycle restorer and enthusiast. Tea is served to guests' rooms at 4:00 p.m. or when guests arrive. Full breakfast, cooked on an antique wood-burning stove, is brought to guests' rooms between 9:00 and 9:30 a.m. Adults only. No pets; Irish wolfhound and cats in residence. Nonsmokers. **In the hosts' own words:** "Imagine yourself stepping into the pages of a Rosamunde Pilcher novel. Enjoy the romance, privacy, and attention to detail and service of a bygone era in our idyllic country setting. Once you're here, you'll never want to leave."

Shoreline Place B&B

Liane and Andrew Hansen
6550 Gale Avenue North
Mail: RR 2 Shoreline Site C–6
Sechelt, BC V0N 3A0
(604) 740-0767 fax: (604) 740-0767
web site: www.bigpacific.com/guests/shoreline

• From the Langdale ferry terminal, take Highway 101 to Sechelt. At the traffic lights in Sechelt, turn right onto Wharf. Turn right onto Trail, which bends to the right and becomes Reef. Turn left onto Shoal, right onto Fairway, and left onto Gale. Follow Gale along to Shoreline. The B&B is a corner house on the side of the road closer to the water. Distance from the traffic light in Sechelt is 4.5 kilometres.

• Two-bedroom self-contained suite: One person $50–120; two people $80–120. Queen-sized bed, twin beds, and a twin roll-away. Ensuite bathroom. Off-season, weekly, and group rates.

• A Victorian-style B&B built by the hosts, with views of the ocean, five minutes' drive from downtown. Two minutes from golf. Thousand-square-foot self-contained suite is at garden level and has views of the ocean. Kayaks and canoes for rent in the area. Swimming, fishing, crabbing, and beachcombing in the inlet. Near hiking and biking at Kinnikinnick Park. Covered outdoor hot tub with ocean and mountain views. Fireplace. Yard with swing set. Breakfast is served in guest suite or in the garden. No pets indoors. Smoke-free environment. **In the hosts' own words:** "Our B&B offers a perfect romantic getaway or family vacation spot. We invite you to feel at home and enjoy peace and serenity in the spacious and comfortable suite."

Heron House on the Shores

Bruce and Jean Scholton
6490 North Gale Avenue
Mail: C–16 The Shores RR 2
Sechelt, BC V0N 3A0
(604) 885-5429 fax: (604) 885-5429
web site: www.bigpacific.com/guests/heronhouse

• Take Highway 1 to the Horseshoe Bay ferry terminal in West Vancouver.
Take the Langdale ferry (40 minutes). Go north on Highway 101 for 25 kilometres to Sechelt. Turn onto Trail Avenue and continue for 3 kilometres.
Turn onto North Gale Avenue.

• Two rooms: Two people $95–135. Queen-sized bed; double canopied bed.
Ensuite and shared guest bathrooms.
Golf packages.

• A B&B on the ocean, with a quiet sandy beach for swimming and a view of the Sechelt Inlet mountains. Herons, eagles, geese, ducks, and loons can be seen. Three blocks from an old-growth forest park with walking trails. One kilometre from an 18-hole golf course. Three kilometres from restaurants and shops downtown. Canoe available. Near kayak rentals. Golf discounts and excursions by boat to Skookumchuk Narrows and Princess Louisa Inlet can be arranged by the hosts. One of the guest rooms has wicker chairs and table, a TV, two eight-foot windows with a view of Sechelt Inlet, and a five-piece ensuite bathroom with soaker tub. Games room with TV, pool table, shuffleboard, and patio doors that lead to a deck and garden. Porches and decks with chairs and a view of the ocean. English-style breakfast is served in an Asian-style dining room or on the patio. No pets. No smoking indoors. **In the hosts' own words:** "Enjoy our warm welcome, relax and unwind in our beachfront house, and enjoy the lovely mountain views."

Four Winds Beach House and Spa

David Fedor and Brenda Wilkinson
5482 Hill Road
Mail: RR 2 Black's Site C–33
Sechelt, BC V0N 3A0
(604) 885-3144 fax: (604) 885-3182
toll-free from within North America: 1-800-543-2989
email: four_winds@sunshine.net
web site: www.sunshine.net/fourwinds

• From Langdale, take the Sunshine Coast Highway (101) to Sechelt. Five kilometres past Sechelt, turn left onto Hill Road, a cul-de-sac. Keep left and continue to the end of the road.
From Earls Cove, on Highway 101, watch for Hill Road on the right, 1 kilometre past the second entrance to Redrooffs Road and 5 kilometres before Sechelt.

• One person $110–130; two people $125–145. Queen-sized bed; twin beds.
Ensuite and private bathrooms.
Golf packages.

• A B&B on a rocky point jutting out into the ocean. Guest living room with a stone fireplace is surrounded by water on three sides. Guest rooms have window seats that are six metres from the water. Winter storms. Heavy quilts and wool mattress covers. One of the hosts is a registered massage therapist and takes advance bookings. Fifteen minutes from golf, kayaking, guided mountain biking and hiking, and mountain bike rentals. Pickup and drop-off for guests travelling by bus from Vancouver and Powell River. Waterfront guest deck with hot tub. Breakfast is served on the deck or in the dining room; seals and a resident heron are often seen during breakfast. Visa, MasterCard. No children. No pets. No smoking.
In the hosts' own words: "Celebrate a special occasion or plan a healthy weekend retreat at our B&B."

Burchill's B&B by the Sea

Jack and Millie Burchill
5402 Donley Drive
Mail: RR 2 Donley Site C–17
Halfmoon Bay, BC V0N 1Y0
(604) 883-2400
web site: www.bbcanada.com/478.html

- Off Highway 101, 24 kilometres north of Sechelt.
- Self-contained cottage: One person or two people $90. Double bed and two double bunk beds. Private bathroom. Breakfast ingredients supplied. Additional person $40. Child $25.
- A self-contained cottage a few steps from the ocean, with a view of Malaspina Strait and Texada Island. Cottage accommodates eight people and has a master bedroom with double bed, two bedrooms with double bunk beds, a kitchen, a deck, and a living room with fireplace. Rowboats available. Swimming in the ocean and in a saltwater swimming pool. Breakfast supplies, including homemade bread, muffins, and jam, are provided in the cottage kitchen. Children welcome. No pets. No smoking. **In the hosts' own words:** "There is always a lot to see and do on the Sunshine Coast, or you can just relax at the beach or on the deck by our pool."

Seawind B&B

Donna and John Stevenson
9207 Regal Road
Mail: RR 2 Curran Site C–17
Halfmoon Bay, BC V0N 1Y0
(604) 885-4282 fax: (604) 885-4272
toll-free from within North America:
1-888-999-5993
email: seawind@sunshine.net
web site: www.SeawindBandB.com

• From the Langdale ferry terminal, take Highway 101 to Sechelt. Fifteen kilometres past Sechelt, turn left onto Curran. At the second intersection, turn left onto Regal Road.
From Earls Cove, take Highway 101 for 40 kilometres to Curran Road.

• Two rooms: One person $80; two people $90. Queen-sized bed. Ensuite bathrooms. Additional person $25.

• A contemporary West Coast–style house among Douglas fir and cedar trees, with a view of Halfmoon Bay and Georgia Strait. Guest rooms have ocean views, covered decks, and private entrances. Guest sitting room with games, books, TV, VCR, sink, fridge, and microwave. Hot tub. Personal training available for a fee in a fitness studio. Near fishing, sea kayaking, cycling, swimming, golf, birdwatching, and summer and winter scuba diving. Multi-course breakfast is served in the dining room, which has a view of Halfmoon Bay and Georgia Strait. Visa or MasterCard required to guarantee a reservation. Cancellation notice seven days. Cash, Visa, MasterCard. Adult oriented. No pets. No smoking. **In the hosts' own words:** "Enjoy our warm hospitality and the spectacular view or improve your fitness."

Beacon B&B

Roger and Shirley Randall
3750 Marine Avenue
Powell River, BC V8A 2H8
(604) 485-5563 fax: (604) 485-9450
toll-free: 1-877-485-5563
email: beacon@aisl.bc.ca
web site: www.vancouver-bc.com/beaconbb

• On Marine Avenue, 2.2 kilometres south of the Comox ferry (the Westview ferry terminal). Thirty kilometres north of the Sechelt ferry (the Saltery Bay ferry terminal). Take Highway 101 and watch for the B&B's sign.

• Two rooms and one suite: One person $75–125; two people $85–125. Queen-sized bed; queen-sized bed and one twin bed; queen-sized bed, one twin bed, and queen-sized murphy bed. Ensuite and private bathrooms. Additional person $20.

• A modern house on the ocean with a view of the Strait of Georgia and snowcapped mountains on Vancouver Island. Half a block from beach access. Thirty minutes from an eighteen-hole golf course, hiking trails, lakes, canoe rentals, a canoe route, and a diving area. Five minutes' drive from fishing. Suite has a sitting room with queen-sized bed that swings up into a cabinet when not in use. Advance bookings for charters, diving, and sightseeing at Desolation Sound can be arranged by hosts. Indoor hot tub with ocean view. Massages available from your hostess for a fee. Full breakfast is served between 7:00 and 9:00 a.m. Suite is wheelchair accessible. Cash, traveller's cheques, Visa, MasterCard. Adult oriented; children over twelve by arrangement. Cat in residence. Smoking outdoors. **In the hosts' own words:** "If you are trying to get away from all the hustle and bustle of city life, you will truly enjoy our modern house and waterfront setting."

Ocean Beach Lodge

Barbara and Roger Canzian
Mail: RR 3 C–9
12297 Scotch Fir Point Road
Powell River, BC V8A 5C1
(604) 487-9299 fax: (604) 487-9299
email: canzian@prcn.org
web site: www.prcn.org/oceanbeachlodge

• From Powell River's Westview ferry terminal, go 17 kilometres south. Turn right onto Loubert Road.
From the Saltery Bay ferry terminal, go 10 kilometres north. Turn right onto Roberts Road.

• Rooms: One person $65–80; two people $75–90. Queen-sized bed; twin beds. Ensuite bathrooms. Additional person $15. Extended stay rates.

• A quiet lodge on the ocean, with a sheltered beach and an acre of lawn and garden. Guest rooms are decorated in themes and have private entrances, ocean views, and facilities for making tea, instant coffee, and hot chocolate. One of the guest rooms has a view of a garden and a swimming pool. Guest living room and dining area with fireplace and view. Two decks with views of the ocean. Outdoor swimming pool with deck. Sauna. Kayak and canoe. Small boat ramp. Full breakfast. German, French, and Italian spoken. Cash, Visa, traveller's cheques. Some restrictions on small children and pets may apply. Smoking outdoors. **In the hosts' own words:** "Discover and enjoy our lodge-style B&B. We offer West Coast comfort with European detail and flair. Each piece of antique furniture and art has its own story that we will be glad to share with you."

Chrysalis Retreat B&B

Bronwyn Punch
31278 Douglas Street
Mail: Box 50
Yale, BC V0K 2S0
(604) 863-0055

• Fifteen minutes north of Hope on Highway 1. Two hours from Vancouver. One block from Highway 1, on the Fraser River.

• Two-bedroom cottage (sleeps six): In summer, two people $105. In winter, one person $65, two people $85. Double beds and double hide-a-bed. Additional person $15.
Sauna, massages, hydrotherapy, and spa packages.

• A cottage with an English-style garden, a quarter acre of fenced yard, and an outdoor hot tub. Host is a registered massage therapist and hydrotherapist. In the area are whitewater river rafting, hiking, historical attractions, gold panning, and Hell's Gate cable car and suspension bridge. Cottage has a kitchen with fridge, stove, dishes, and some dry goods, and a living room with wood stove and books. Sauna available for a fee. Snacks and drinks. Lunch and dinner, delivered to the cottage or packed for picnics, are available for a fee. Full breakfast, including fresh fruit, baked goods, homemade jam, bacon or sausages, and a choice of pancakes, crêpes, quiche, or eggs, is delivered to the cottage. Children welcome. Pets welcome by arrangement. No smoking indoors. **In the hosts' own words:** "Come visit our heritage cottage. We offer our guests a range of services. Our B&B is a perfect place for a weekend getaway or a full vacation for relaxation, recreation, and revitalization."

Elephant Cottage B&B

Pat and Annie Wheeldon
291 Hillcrest Road
Mail: Box 805
Lillooet, BC V0K 1V0
(250) 256-7139

• Rooms and suite.

Two rooms: In summer, one person $45, two people $65. In winter, one person $40, two people $55. Double bed; twin beds. Shared bathroom.

Basement suite: In summer, one person $75, two people $85. In winter, one person $60, two people $75. Queen-sized bed. Ensuite bathroom.

• A B&B with fruit trees, weeping willows, and a garden. Near swimming and fishing lakes, winter activities, an indoor recreation centre, historical sites, and a museum. Barbecue facilities and patios. Air conditioning. Basement suite has satellite TV, a coffee maker, a sitting area, and a door with a lock. Snacks. A tour of the area is offered by the hosts. Full breakfast includes fruit, bacon, ham, eggs, and waffles. Cash, traveller's cheques. Children welcome. Smoking on the patio. **In the hosts' own words:** "Our B&B is your home away from home. Come and sit under the trees and watch many varieties of birds in the summer. Enjoy the fresh taste of seasonal fruit and our beautiful mountain view."

Running Waters

Rose and Rick Isbister
44 Miller Road
Merritt, BC V1K 1N6
(250) 378-4476

• From Merritt, go west on Highway 8 for 11 kilometres towards Spences Bridge. Turn right at the Sunshine Valley/Miller Road intersection and continue for 1 kilometre. The B&B is on the right.

• Four rooms: One person $40–50; two people $50–60. Queen-sized bed; twin bed. Ensuite bathrooms. Extra beds available. Children under 8 free. Additional person $12.

• A new house on ten acres with ponds, fountains, a creek, and views of mountains and valleys. Hawks can be seen on the property. Twelve minutes from downtown. Near sport fishing, lakes, the Kane Valley, and cycling, hiking, and cross-country ski trails. In the area are an annual four-day country/western music festival, First Nations traditional ceremonial dances, and stock car races. Hosts share their knowledge of the area. Three of the guest rooms have private balconies and are air-conditioned and decorated in themes. The other guest room is wheelchair accessible and has linoleum instead of carpet, for guests with allergies. Guest sitting room with satellite TV. Dinner and trail lunches available for a fee. Full or Continental breakfast. Diets are accommodated. Check-out until 11:00 a.m. Cash, traveller's cheques, Visa. Smoking on balconies and outdoors. **In the hosts' own words:** "Relax on a private balcony to the sound of running water and watch for hawks gliding over the fields. We have often enjoyed staying at B&Bs and would very much like the opportunity to offer our hospitality and share our home with you."

Ben Brae Chalet

Maggie Deane
3907 Summers Creek Road
Missezula Lake, BC
Mail: Box 293
Princeton, BC V0X 1W0
In BC, for reservations, dial 0, ask for radio operator, ask for Princeton channel YS Ben Brae Chalet N69-3505
Outside BC, for reservations, dial the operator, ask for British Columbia, Canada, operator, ask for radio operator, ask for Princeton channel YS Ben Brae Chalet N69-3505

• From Princeton, take Highway 5A north for 9 kilometres. Turn right onto Summers Creek Road (a gravel road) and continue for 29 kilometres to the Village of Missezula Lake.
• Four rooms: One person $35; two people $70. Queen-sized bed; one twin bed. Shared guest bathroom. Packed lunch and dinner $20 per person.
• A B&B in a village surrounded by tree-covered hills, at 3200 feet elevation. Five minutes' walk from a five mile long mountain lake. Boating, fishing, swimming, hiking, outdoor ice skating, and snowmobiling. Boat-launching ramp. Wildlife often visit the village. Wildflowers. Walking trails and mountain lakes. Reiki and oil massage by appointment. Canoe rentals, canoeing lessons, and guided hiking and snowmobiling tours can be arranged by the hosts. Two of the guest rooms have balconies. Living room with gas fireplace. Full breakfast. Packed lunch and candlelit dinner available. Smoking outside. **In the hosts' own words:** "We extend warmth and friendly hospitality to make your stay pleasant and enjoyable."

Osprey Lake Lodge B&B

Vivian Paterson
401 Bankier Place
Mail: RR 1 Site 10 C–5
Princeton, BC V0X 1W0
(250) 295-6866 fax: (250) 295-6832
toll-free: 1-877-295-6866
email: ospreylakelodge@nethop.net

• Forty-two kilometres northeast of Princeton on the Princeton-Summerland Road. Turn right onto Link Lake Road. The B&B, which has a blue roof, is the third house on the left.
• Three rooms: One person $65; two people $85. Double beds. Private and shared guest bathrooms. Additional person $25. Child $10.
• A B&B across the road from a beach and a boat launch and adjacent to the Trans Canada Trail. Hiking trails, fishing, ice fishing, swimming, cross-country skiing, and snowmobiling from the B&B. Guest rooms are furnished with antiques. Living room with fireplace, satellite TV, and books. Handmade slippers for guest use. Deck with telescope for night sky and wildlife viewing. Binoculars available. Lunch and dinner by arrangement. Full breakfast. Well-behaved pets welcome. **In the hosts' own words:** "At our B&B, enjoy friendly hospitality, delicious meals, miles of hiking, fishing in beautiful Osprey Lake, and the spectacular scenery along the Trans Canada Trail—don't forget your camera."

Login B&B

Helen Falkenberg
RR 1 Site 27 C–1 Highway 3 West
Keremeos, BC V0X 1N0
(250) 499-2781 or (250) 499-2664
email: loginbnb@keremeos.com
web site: www.keremeos.com/LOGINBNB

- On Highway 3, 5 kilometres west of Keremeos. Four hours east of Vancouver.
- Three rooms: One person $55; three or four people $90. Queen-sized bed.
Shared guest bathrooms. Roll-away beds and queen-sized sofa beds available.
Discount of 10 percent on reservations made 48 hours in advance.
Group and family rates.
- A log house in the country, three minutes' walk from downtown, with a view of the Similkameen River. Hiking trails from the B&B. Swimming in the river. Ten minutes' drive from Ashnola River, Fairview wilderness area, Cathedral Lakes Park, fruit farms, and local vineyard tasting rooms. Thirty minutes' drive from Penticton. Forty-five minutes from downhill and cross-country skiing and the U.S. border. Guest rooms are in a self-contained guest house separate from the hosts' house. The guest house has a living room with fireplace, a kitchen, a video/satellite room, laundry facilities, and a wrap-around deck with barbecue. The guest rooms have air conditioning and views. Full breakfast includes fresh fruit, home-made bread/cereals, and egg dishes. Visa, MasterCard. Horses and leashed pets welcome. No smoking.

Arosa Guest Ranch

Marianne and Retus Arpagaus
Mail: RR 1
Bridesville, BC V0H 1B0
(250) 495-5043 fax: (250) 495-5027
email: arosaranch@img.net

• From Osoyoos, go 23 kilometres east on Highway 3. From Rock Creek, go 27 kilometres west on Highway 3.

• Four rooms: One person $50; two people $65. King-sized bed. Ensuite bathrooms. Children under 12 free. Sauna $12 per person.

• A five-thousand-square-foot custom-built log house on 160 acres, 1020 metres (3350 feet) above sea level. Fishing in a stocked lake, swimming, hiking, and horseback riding on the property. Near a pocket desert, beaches, gold panning, river rafting, golf, skiing, the U.S. border, and the annual Ironman Canada triathlon. A base for day trips to historical sites and wildlife viewing. Guest living room. Sauna available for a fee. Campground on the property with RV and tent sites. Breakfast. Cash, traveller's cheques. German spoken. **In the hosts' own words:** "We invite you to watch the sun rise and set over the mountains while being treated to traditional Swiss hospitality."

Mountain Valley Ranch

Franz and Janet Bergendahl
RR 1, Johnstone Creek Road West
Rock Creek, BC V0H 1Y0
(250) 446-2805 fax: (250) 446-2805

• From Osoyoos, go east on Highway 3 for 40 kilometres. Take the turnoff for Conkle Lake Provincial Park and continue for 1.2 kilometres.

• Three self-contained suites: One person \$50; two people \$70. Queen-sized bed and one twin bed. Additional person \$20. Children under 7 free. Weekly rates.

• A guest log house at eleven-hundred-metre elevation, with a veranda and a view of forest, hills, and wildflowers. Birds and wildlife can be seen. Authentic log barn and outbuildings. Barn and bale for guests' horses. Suites have kitchens. Near cross-country skiing, tobogganing, and trails for hiking and horseback riding. Fire pit and barbecue. Swimming, fishing, gold panning, river floating, and mountain biking on crown land adjacent to the B&B, in Kettle River Provincial Park, which is fifteen minutes away, and in Conkle Lake Provincial Park, which is thirty-five minutes away. Breakfast includes farm-fresh eggs, fruit, and homemade baked goods. **In the hosts' own words:** "We love to serve you."

Lindale Farm Guest House

Roger and Linda Lebert
10932—337th Avenue
Mail: Box 1056
Oliver, BC V0H 1T0
(250) 498-4196 fax: (250) 498-4197
web site: www.bbcanada.com/2433.html

• From Highway 97 (between Osoyoos and Penticton), turn west onto 350th, left onto 3b Road, and left onto 337th.

• Rooms and suite.

Two rooms: One person $60; two people $80. Queen-sized bed; twin beds. Private and shared bathrooms.

Suite: One person $80; two people $100. Queen-sized bed. Ensuite bathroom.

Discount of 10 percent on stays of three or more days.

• A French-style guest house in a quiet vineyard setting, a few minutes' drive from Oliver, wineries, and golf courses. Guest rooms and suite have sitting areas. Patio with a view of a nine-acre vineyard, Mount Baldy, and surrounding hills. Front veranda with a view of a golf course, hills, and neighbouring orchards. Sitting room with TV and fireplace. Air conditioning. Near wine tastings, water sports, skiing, and the Kettle Valley Trail for hiking and biking. Thirty-seven kilometres from Mount Baldy. Farm-style breakfast is served in the dining room. Off-street parking. Reservations required. No pets. No smoking indoors. **In the hosts' own words:** "We invite you to enjoy our B&B, in a quiet location in the hub of wine country, with fruit trees and a lovely landscaped garden."

Bear's Den B&B

Ross Arnot and Ed Schneider
189 Linden Avenue
Mail: Box 172
Kaleden, BC V0H 1K0
(250) 497-6721 fax: (250) 497-6453
email: bearsden@vip.net
web sites: www.moriah.com/bearsden
www.wcbbia.com/pages/bearsden.html
www.bearsdenbb.com

• Ten minutes south of Penticton. From Highway 97, turn east onto Lakehill Road. Just past the fire hall, turn right onto Linden Avenue. Past the elementary school, turn left onto Cypress, an access road. The B&B is a coral-coloured house.

• Rooms and suite.
Two rooms: In summer (May to October), two people $85. In winter (November to April), two people $55. Queen-sized bed, private bathroom; twin beds (or twin beds side by side with king-sized bedding), ensuite bathroom.
Suite: In summer, two people $100. In winter, two people $85. Queen-sized bed. Ensuite bathroom.

• A modern three-bedroom house with a pond and views of orchards, vineyards, lakes, mountains, and the city of Penticton. Rose garden and vegetable garden. Near hiking, cycling, beaches, swimming, boating, golf, winery tours, fine dining, and shopping. Ten minutes' drive from Penticton. Guest suite has a canopied bed, a sitting area, a soaker tub, and views of lakes, orchards, and the city of Penticton. The guest room with a queen-sized bed has a window seat and a view of a garden and pond. The room with twin beds has sleigh-style beds, a soaker tub, and garden views. Air-conditioning. Hot tub, deck, and two living rooms with books and videos. Hosts share their knowledge of the area and help plan day trips. Full breakfast includes juice, fruit, baked goods, and an entrée. Deposit of one night's rate required to hold reservation. Cancellation notice seven days. Check-in 4:00 to 6:00 p.m. Cash, cheques, Visa. Small dogs welcome by arrangement; dogs in residence. No smoking indoors. **In the hosts' own words:** "You'll feel like you've found your own Garden of Eden, as the peacefulness and tranquillity of our B&B envelop you. Why not stay several days and savour all that the valley of heaven has to offer?"

Twin Poplar B&B

Edna Reid
192 Lakehill Road
Mail: Box 471
Kaleden, BC V0H 1K0
(250) 497-8833 fax: (250) 497-8833
email: twinpoplar@img.net

• From Penticton, go south on Highway 97 for 10 kilometres.

• Rooms and suite.

Two rooms: One person or two people $75–85. Queen-sized bed; twin beds. Ensuite bathrooms.

Suite: One person or two people $85–95. Queen-sized bed. Ensuite bathroom.

• A B&B decorated with local art, a few minutes from Apex ski resort, golf courses, cottage wineries, and restaurants. Suite has a double Jacuzzi, a private balcony, and a view of Skaha Lake. Sixty-five minutes from the U.S. border. Living room with TV and fireplace. Air-conditioning. Perennial gardens and decks. Breakfast. Cash, traveller's cheques, Visa. No pets. Nonsmoking. **In the hosts' own words:** "Enjoy our elegant air-conditioned house with a lakeview suite."

Riordan House B&B

John and Donna Ortiz
689 Winnipeg Street
Penticton, BC V2A 5N1
(250) 493-5997 fax: (250) 493-5997
email: jeortiz@img.net
web sites: www.icontext.com/riordan
www.bbcanada.com/2590.html

• Two blocks from downtown, at the corner of Winnipeg and Eckhardt.

• Four rooms: Two people $50–85. Queen-sized bed; double bed. Additional person $15.

• A 1920 arts and crafts house beneath vines of English ivy and Virginia creeper, with munioned windows, gables, and a bay window. Known locally as "the house that rum built." Within walking distance of the Kettle Valley Railway section of the Cross Canada Trail, a beach, galleries, and restaurants. Near estate wineries, amusement parks, fishing, parks, golf, sporting events, waterskiing, and downhill and cross-country skiing. Guest rooms have sitting areas, antique furnishings, air conditioning, TVs, VCRs, robes, slippers, glasses of lemon water when guests arrive, and treats on the pillows. One of the guest rooms has a fireplace and two bay windows. Antique shop on the property. Library. Veranda and gardens with wisteria and tamarax trees. Bicycles. Fax services. Pickup from airport or bus. Picnic lunches available. Full or Continental breakfast, including homemade bread and fruit dishes, is served in the dining room. Visa, MasterCard, American Express, Diner's Club. Children over thirteen welcome. No pets; small dog in residence. No smoking. **In the hosts' own words:** "We are in the heart of wine country."

Paradise Cove B&B

Ruth Buchanan
3129 Hayman Road
Mail: RR1 S2 C31
Naramata, BC V0H 1N0
(250) 496-5896 fax: (250) 496-5896
email: buchanan@vip.net
web site: pcove@bctravel.com

• From Westminster and Main in Penticton, take Naramata Road and continue for 13 kilometres. Turn left onto DeBeck Road (firehall on the corner) and continue for 1 kilometre. Turn right onto Hayman Road.
• Rooms and suite.
Two rooms: In summer, two people from $85. In winter (November to March), two people from $75. Queen-sized bed. Ensuite bathrooms.
Self-contained suite: In summer, two people from $125. In winter (November to March), two people from $115. Queen-sized bed and sofa bed. Bathroom in suite.
Additional person $15.
• A modern two-storey house above Manitou Beach, among orchards and vineyards, with a view of Okanagan Lake. Three hundred metres from the lake. Twenty minutes from downtown Penticton. Near swimming, hiking along the historical Kettle Valley Railway, five wineries, a wharf, two fine dining restaurants, and a pub. Forty-five minutes from skiing at Apex. Self-contained suite has a queen-sized bed, a sofa bed, a five-person hot tub, a fireplace, laundry facilities, and a kitchen. Suite and guest rooms have lake views, private decks, telephones, TVs, fridges, and beverages. Suite and one of the guest rooms have private entrances. Full breakfast is served in the dining room or on the deck. One of the guest rooms is wheelchair accessible. Cash, Visa, MasterCard. Adult oriented. No pets. No smoking indoors. **In the hosts' own words:** "Our B&B offers idyllic surroundings with a lake view, friendliness, and comfort."

Lavender Lane Guest House

Dick and Anne Leechman
3005 Upper Debeck Road
Mail: S11 C–81 RR 1
Naramata, BC V0H 1N0
(250) 496-5740 fax: (250) 496-5741
email: Leechman@telus.net
web site: www.bctravel.com/lavenderlane/

• In Penticton, go east onto Westminster Street and continue to the end of Westminster. Follow the signs for Naramata onto Front Street, which becomes Vancouver Street and then Naramata Road. Go 13 kilometres onto Naramata Road. Turn right onto Arawana Road (Arawana trail rides on the corner) and continue for 2 kilometres to Upper Debeck Road. The B&B is on the corner on the left.

• Rooms and suite.

Two rooms: In summer, two people $85. In winter, two people from $70. Ensuite bathrooms.

Suite: In summer, two people $115. In winter, two people $90.

• A B&B in the hills, among orchards and vineyards, with views of Lake Okanagan. European antiques. Near swimming, wineries, and fine dining. Hiking, biking, and horseback riding at the Kettle Valley Trail. All-terrain bike rentals available at the B&B. Ten minutes' drive from golf, shopping, and beaches in Penticton. Guest rooms and suite have TVs and VCRs. One of the rooms has a Jacuzzi tub. Full breakfast is served in the dining room or on the balcony, which has a view of the lake, or Continental breakfast is served in guest rooms. Smoke-free environment. **In the hosts' own words:** "Our exquisitely decorated B&B is a perfect blend of comfort and elegance. Relax, rejuvenate, and enjoy our gourmet breakfasts and special hospitality for an ideal getaway. After a day of activity, watch the sunset from our balcony, surrounded by scents of roses and lavender."

Heidi's B&B

Heidi and Lyle
4510 Gartrell Road
Mail: RR 4 Site 86 C–16
Summerland, BC V0H 1Z0
(250) 494-4335 fax: (250) 494-4428

- Four hundred kilometres from Vancouver. Forty-five minutes south of Kelowna. Fifteen minutes north of Penticton. Half an hour south of the Coquihalla Connector at Peachland. Five minutes from Summerland.
- Room: One person $50; two people $60. After one night, one person $40, two people $50. Queen-sized bed. Private bathroom.
- A B&B on a five-acre hobby farm with a cherry orchard, birds, dogs, cats, horses, llamas, and wildlife. East-facing patio with a view of Okanagan Lake and mountains. West-facing patio with a view of Giant's Head Mountain. Fifteen minutes' drive from golf courses, swimming beaches, boat and sailboat launches and rentals, the historical Kettle Valley Railway, and winery and vineyard tours. Forty-five minutes' drive from trail rides, hiking, and Apex Alpine and Crystal Mountain ski areas. Living room. Full breakfast is served on the patio, weather permitting. Patio dinners available by arrangement. Reservations required. German spoken. Pets and horses welcome. No smoking. **In the hosts' own words:** "There is so much to say about our place that we just don't know where to begin. Please pay us a visit and we'll share it with you."

Make Thyme B&B

Phyllis and Marvin O'Connell
5115 Pineridge Road
Mail: RR 1 Site 3 C–23
Peachland, BC V0H 1X0
(250) 767-9204
email: makethymebandb@telus.net

• Forty minutes from Penticton, 35 minutes from Kelowna, and 10 minutes from the Coquihalla Connector. From Highway 97 in Peachland, go west up Princeton Avenue for 4 kilometres to Pineridge Road.

• Three rooms: One person $50–60; two people $65–75. Queen-sized bed; twin beds. Shared guest bathroom. Extended-stay rates.

• A B&B on one acre, with views of Okanagan Lake and the surrounding mountains from the deck. Eight minutes from golf, swimming, fishing, hiking, orchards, and wine tours. One hour from skiing at Apex and Big White. Thirty minutes from skiing at Crystal Mountain. Guest rooms with herbal-themed decoration. Large-screen TV and videos. Sitting room with books. Refreshments any time. Air conditioning. Parking for cars and RVs. Full breakfast includes farm-fresh eggs and herbs and seasonal fresh fruit. Cash, traveller's cheques. Children welcome. Smoke-free environment. **In the hosts' own words:** "Our guests feel completely at home. Enjoy our gourmet breakfasts, wander through the herb gardens, and soak up the sunshine and views from our large deck. This retreat is the perfect recipe for relaxation."

Casa Del Sol B&B and Bale

Reinhard and Ute Senne
3485 Fenton Road
Westbank, BC V4T 1V8
toll-free: 1-800-261-4255
(250) 768-3392 fax: (250) 768-3392
cel: (250) 470-2046
email: CasadelSol@telus.net
web site: www.kanadanews.de/casadelsol.htm

• Five minutes from the Coquihalla Connector. From the Kelowna airport, go south on Highway 97 for 22 kilometres to Westbank. Exit right onto Glenrosa Road and go 3 kilometres uphill to Fenton Road. The B&B is across from a firehall.

• Room and suites.
Room: One person $75; two people $85. Queen-sized bed. Ensuite bathroom.
Suite: One person $85; two people $95. Queen-sized bed. Ensuite bathroom.
Self-contained suite: One person $95; two people $110. Queen-sized bed and futon. Ensuite bathroom.
Additional person $20. Horse $20.

• A contemporary, newly renovated B&B on six and a half acres with a view of Lake Okanagan, Kelowna, and Westbank. Surrounded by rolling hills. Guest rooms and suites have private entrances, patios, verandas, satellite TV, and views of Lake Okanagan, mountains, or the cities. Suite has a Jacuzzi and table and chairs. Self-contained suite has a fireplace. Garden and outdoor swimming pool. Five minutes from shopping and movie theatres. Ten minutes from horseback riding, hiking, mountain biking, and cross-country skiing. Fifteen to twenty minutes from downhill skiing, water sports, and floatplane tours. Hay for horses provided. Full breakfast is served from 7:00 to 9:00 p.m. on the veranda or in the dining room, which has eight-foot windows, a waterfall, and a fireplace. Greek, Italian, etc. dinners available for a fee on Friday, Saturday, and Sunday. Deposit of one night's rate required to hold reservation. Check-in from 4:00 to 9:00 p.m. or by arrangement; check-out until 11:00 a.m. Cash, traveller's cheques, Visa, MasterCard. Adult oriented. No pets. Smoking outdoors. **In the hosts' own words:** "Our garden offers lots of space to relax and unwind and an outdoor swimming pool. We pamper both guests and horses."

Sunnybank B&B

Elvy and Ron Marsh
2479 Reece Road
Westbank, BC V4T 1N1
(250) 768-5110

• From Kelowna, take Highway , go eleven kilometres south on Highway 97 (across the bridge) to Westbank. Turn right onto Old Okanagan Highway. Continue to Reece Road and turn left. From the Coquihalla Connector (Highway 97C) go six minutes north on Highway 97 and turn left onto Elliot Road. Continue for two kilometres, turn right onto Reece Road.

• Two rooms: One person $55–75; two people $75–85. Queen-sized bed, ensuite bathroom; twin beds and sofa bed, private bathroom. Additional person $20. Extended stay rates.

• A quiet modern house 300 feet from the road, on an acre of flower and herb gardens, with a view of Okanagan Lake, orchards, and vineyards. Designed as a B&B by one of the hosts. Three minutes from shoping centres, golf, a waterslide park, and a public pool. Ten minutes from Mission Hill and Quails Gate and Hainle wineries. Fifteen minutes from beaches and skiing at Crystal Mountain. Guest living room with TV, VCR, books, stereo, piano, hide-a-bed, fridge, coffee maker, dishes, and a table for board games or cards. French doors that lead to a covered patio and deck are used as a private entrance for guests. Full breakfast, including local fresh fruit and berries, beverages, homemade bread and muffins, preserves, and an entrée, is served on the upper deck or in the dining room. Diets are accommodated. Off-street parking. Reservations are recommended, and necessary on holidays—July 1 and first Mondays of August and September. Cash, traveller's cheques. Swedish spoken. Adult oriented. No pets. No smoking. **In the hosts' own words:** "We are happy to give information and directions to the four-season playground that surrounds us. Our house is dust-free and we welcome you to sunshine and relaxation. Flower sniffing and birdwatching are free."

Augusta View B&B

Kurt and Edith Grube
998 Augusta Court
Kelowna, BC V1Y 7T9
(250) 763-0969 fax: (250) 763-0969
toll-free from within Canada and north western U.S.: 1-800-801-2992

• Rooms and suite.

Two rooms: One person $69; two people $79. Queen-sized bed; queen-sized bed and one twin bed. Ensuite bathrooms.

Suite: Two people $95. Queen-sized bed, one twin bed, and double hide-a-bed. Ensuite bathroom.

Additional person $20. Child under 12 $10. Off-season rates.

• A quiet, centrally located B&B with a garden, fruit trees, and a view of a golf and country club. Five minutes' drive from shopping, restaurants, golf, and wineries. An hour from Penticton, Vernon, and three ski hills. Near cross-country skiing, horseback riding, and boating, fishing, and lake cruises on Okanagan Lake. Air-conditioned rooms have views of the city, lake, mountains, and golf course. Guest sitting room with antiques, TV, VCR, telephone, library, wood stove, and fridge. Suite has a TV and a private entrance through the garden. Two of the guest rooms share an entrance through the guest sitting room. Guest patio with wicker furniture leads to the garden. Guest garden gazebo with a view of the mountains. Full breakfast is served on the deck, weather permitting. German spoken. No pets. No smoking.

In the hosts' own words: "Experience a peaceful retreat in our spacious house, decorated with antiques and an artist's touch. You'll enjoy our warm hospitality."

Bluebird Beach House B&B

Bernie Breitkreuz and Bettina Voigt-Breitkreuz
3980 Bluebird Road
Kelowna, BC V1W 1X6
(250) 764-8992 fax: (250) 764-8992
web site: www.bbcanada.com/571.html

• From Highway 97, turn east onto Gordon. Turn right onto Lexington and continue straight onto Bluebird.

• Three rooms: One person $95; two people $95–140. Queen-sized bed; two double beds. Ensuite bathrooms. Additional person $20. Extended stay rates. In summer, minimum stay two nights.

• A custom-built two-storey modern house on Okanagan Lake, with a thirty-metre private beach and a dock, ten minutes from downtown. Near golf courses, hiking trails, boat rentals, and a boat launch. Guest rooms have southwest lake views, private balconies facing the lake, sitting areas, TVs, and fridges. Patio, backyard, and sandy beach. Swimming. Kitchen facilities and barbecue in the cabana are available for guests to prepare meals. Walking along Bluebird Beach Bay and Mission Creek. Within walking distance of shopping, fine dining restaurants, wineries, and a bus stop. Full breakfast is served at a beach cabana on the lake. Parking. Check-in 3:00 to 6:00 p.m. or by arrangement. Reservations recommended. Deposit required to hold reservation. Cancellation notice fourteen days. Cash, traveller's cheques, Visa. German spoken. Children over ten welcome. No pets. Smoking outdoors. **In the hosts' own words:** "At our B&B, relax on a beach chair at the beach and enjoy the ambience. At sunset, sip a glass of local wine on the dock, and later sleep well with the soothing sound of the waves. We are world travellers and truly enjoy having guests."

The Cedars Inn

David and Jane
278 Beach Avenue
Kelowna, BC V1Y 5R8
(250) 763-1208 fax: (250) 763-1109
toll-free: 1-800-822-7100
email: info@cedarsinnokanagan.com
web site: www.cedarsinnokanagan.com

- Five minutes from downtown and city park.
- Three rooms: Two people $125–175. Queen-sized bed. Ensuite bathrooms. On holiday weekends, minimum stay two nights. Off-season mid-week rates. Golf and ski packages.
- A house with gardens, built between 1906 and 1908, on a landscaped quarter acre surrounded by a cedar hedge. Cobblestone terrace with swimming pool and hot tub. Guest sitting areas; two with with original stone fireplaces and a reading room. Guest rooms have sitting areas. TVs, VCRs, and videos available for in-room use. Wine and appetizers are served late afternoon. Golf and ski packages, beach picnics, private dinners, and esthetician services can be arranged by the hosts. Bicycles available. Within walking distance of a public beach. Near award-winning wineries; wine tours available. Full breakfast is served in the formal dining room, in guests' rooms, or on the terrace. Diets are accommodated. Cancellation notice three days. Check-in 3:00 to 6:00 p.m.; check-out until 11:00 a.m. or by arrangement. Cash, traveller's cheques, Visa, MasterCard. Adult oriented. No pets; cat in residence. Smoking outdoors. **In the hosts' own words:** "We welcome guests to experience a much loved heritage house and our exceptional service. Let us suggest how we can customize your stay to celebrate a special occasion."

The Schroth Farm

Fred and Helen Schroth
3282 East Vernon Road
Vernon, BC V1B 3H5
(250) 545-0010 fax: (250) 260-3757

- One kilometre east of Vernon.
- Room and suite: One person $30; two people $55. Double bed; queen-sized bed, double bed, and three twin beds. Private bathrooms. Additional person $15. Child $10.
- A farmhouse with a patio and views of cattle grazing on nearby pastures, miniature goats, a minature horse, and mountains in the distance. Near sandy beaches for swimming, golf courses, trail riding, a water slide, wineries, and skiing at Silver Star. Guest room is on the upper floor and has a TV and a fridge. Three-room suite is on the lower floor, sleeps eight, and has a private entrance and a living room with TV, VCR, and kitchen facilities. Shaded lawn with barbecue, picnic table, and swing. German spoken. Children welcome. Smoking outdoors. **In the hosts' own words:** "We have travelled to many parts of the world, and we enjoy guests from all parts of the world."

Harbour Lights B&B

Joyce and Doug Stewart
135 Joharon Road
Vernon, BC V1H 1C1
(250) 549-5117 fax: (250) 549-5162
email: harbourlights@telus.net
web site: www.bbexpo.com/harbourlights

• Ten minutes from downtown Vernon. From downtown go west on Thirtieth Avenue and continue on Bella Vista Road (winding road). Turn right onto Fleming and right onto Joharon.

• Three rooms: Two people $75–80. Queen-sized bed; queen-sized bed and futon. Ensuite bathrooms. Additional person $20.

• A custom-built house on two hillside acres in a quiet area, with views of mountains and Lake Okanagan from a deck and all guest rooms. The deck also has a view of a lawn and flower gardens. Ring-necked pheasants and quail can be seen on the property. Five minutes' walk from a sandy swimming beach on Lake Okanagan. Fifteen minutes' drive from golf, fishing, boating, and trail rides. Forty-five minutes' drive from downhill and cross-country skiing at Silver Star. A base for exploring the Okanagan Valley. Guest TV room with VCR. Guest sitting room with reading material. Guest small fridge, ice, and water cooler. Guest rooms have sitting areas. Two of the guest rooms have patio doors that open onto the lawn. Central air-conditioning. Lawn chairs. Guests are welcome to join the hosts for a glass of B.C. wine or lemonade and an appetizer before deciding where to dine. Full breakfast includes seasonal fresh fruit, juice, homemade bread, scones or muffins, preserves, and a hot entrée. Check-in after 4:00 p.m.; check-out until 11:00 a.m. Visa. Adult oriented. No pets. Nonsmoking. **In the hosts' own words:** "Come and visit our B&B, designed for your comfort and privacy. We'd love to share the tranquillity, the lake views, and the opportunity to enjoy life at a slower pace. We have a background in business, marketing, and agriculture, and our interests include travel, wine, cooking, sailing, and good books."

The Tuck Inn

Bill and Irene Tullett
3101 Pleasant Valley Road
Vernon, BC V1T 4L2
(250) 545-3252 fax: (250) 549-3254
web site: www.bbcanada.com/3196.html

• In Vernon, turn east from Highway 97 onto Thirtieth Avenue and continue for 1 kilometre to Pleasant Valley Road.

• Four rooms: One person $40–45; two people $65–75. Double bed; queen-sized bed; queen-sized bed and one twin bed. Additional person $15–20. Crib available.

Ski, golf, honeymoon, and anniversary packages.

• A house built in 1906 that has its original interior doors, casings, and mouldings. Victorian antiques. Sitting room with books and TV. Twenty-two kilometres from downhill and cross-country skiing at Silver Star. Ten minutes' drive from beaches at Kalamalka Lake and Okanagan Lake. Five minutes' walk from downtown Vernon's art galleries, museum, theatres, and playhouse. Fifteen minutes' drive from the historical O'Keefe Ranch. Ten minutes' drive from golf courses. Lunch available for a fee in the B&B's Victorian-style tea room restaurant, which has a nine-foot ceiling and a circular fireplace. Breakfast is served from 7:30 to 9:00 a.m. in the tea room restaurant. Deposit of 50 percent of total payment required to hold reservation. Cancellation notice seven days. Check-in 3:00 to 7:00 p.m.; check-out until noon. Visa, MasterCard. Children welcome. No pets; cat in residence. No smoking indoors. **In the hosts' own words:** "The décor of our large heritage house lets you step back in time to the Victorian era. Our specialty breakfast is a sumptuous delight."

Castle on the Mountain B&B

Eskil and Sharon Larson
8227 Silver Star Road
Vernon, BC V1B 3M8
(250) 542-4593 fax: (250) 542-2206
toll-free from within North America: 1-800-667-2229
email: castle.eskila@telus.net
web sites: www.bbcanada.com/2040.html

• Ten kilometres east of Highway 97, on Forty-eighth Avenue, which becomes Silver Star Road.

• Rooms, suites, and apartment.

Rooms: One person \$70–165; two people \$80–185. Queen-sized bed; queen-sized bed and double futon; twin beds (or twin beds side by side with king-sized bedding). Ensuite and private bathrooms.

Additional person \$35. Child \$15–30.

Two honeymoon suites: King-sized bed; queen-sized bed.

Special occasion packages.

Self-contained one-bedroom apartment: Twin beds (or twin beds side by side with king-sized bedding) and double futon.

• A Tudor-style house on the way to Silver Star Mountain, with views of the city of Vernon and Okanagan and Kalamalka lakes. In the area are swimming, horseback riding, snowmobiling, and winery tours. Ten minutes from beaches, skating, and downhill and cross-country skiing. Hiking from the B&B. Toboggan slide and walking trails on the property. Guest sitting room with fireplace, books, games, puzzles, TV, and videos. Guest kitchen for light snacks. Outdoor hot tub. Patio with barbecue. Playground and picnic area with fire pit. The honeymoon suite is six-hundred-square-feet and has a king-sized bed, a covered balcony with a view, an open balcony, a gas fireplace, a stereo, a TV, and a Jacuzzi. The suite with a queen-sized bed has a private entrance, a gas fireplace, an in-room Jacuzzi, a TV, a VCR, a wet bar, a balcony, and a view. The apartment has a covered balcony with a view, a courtyard, a kitchen, a gas fireplace, a TV, and a stereo and is suitable for longer stays. The house was designed and built by the hosts, who are artists and specialize in custom-design picture framing; guests can visit their gallery and studio. Covered parking. Full breakfast with fresh fruit is served between 7:30 and 9:00 a.m. For guests staying in the honeymoon suite, breakfast is served in the suite. Credit cards, traveller's cheques. Suitable for families. No pets. Smoking outdoors. **In the hosts' own words:** "Our home is your castle. The view, the privacy, the space, the outdoors, and the artwork create a special feeling that you must experience."

Father's Country Inn

David and Brenda
Tod Mountain Road
Mail: Box 152
Heffley Creek, BC V0E 1Z0
(250) 578-7308 fax: (250) 578-7334
toll-free: 1-800-578-7322
email: mmfathers@telus.net
web site: www.dconover.com

• From Kamloops, take Highway 5 (Yellowhead) north for 20 kilometres. Take the Sun Peaks exit and follow the B&B's signs.

• Rooms: One person $45–65; two people $65–95. Queen-sized bed. Private bathrooms. During ski season (November to April), rates subject to change.

• A B&B in the mountains near the Sun Peaks ski area, with a view of valleys and mountains. Indoor swimming pool in a room with a fireplace, a hot tub, a woodstove, and tropical plants. Nature walks from the B&B through meadows and by streams and fields with cows. Sitting rooms, one with a fireplace. Heated ski room with lockers, drying racks, and benches. A few minutes' drive from downhill and cross-country skiing, golf, mountain biking, hiking, lakes, fishing, and trail rides. Guest rooms have four-post queen-sized beds. Some of the guest rooms have fireplaces and Jacuzzi tubs. Full breakfast includes homemade bread and preserves. Evening meal available for a fee on request. Reservations recommended. In summer, cancellation notice three days, with $25 nonrefundable. In winter, cancellation notice fourteen days, with $35 nonrefundable. Check-in after 3:30 p.m.; check-out until 10:30 a.m. Visa, MasterCard. Adult oriented. No pets. Smoking outdoors. **In the hosts' own words:** "Our B&B is named in honour of David Conover, Sr., who was an author and photographer and who discovered Marilyn Monroe. Rare photos of her are displayed throughout our house."

Macqueen's Manor B&B

Jack and Pat Macqueen
1049 Laurel Place
Kamloops, BC V1S 1R1
(250) 372-9383 fax: (250) 372-9384
toll-free from within North America:
1-800-677-5338
web site: www.bbcanada.com/3809.html

- Take exit 367 and turn south onto Pacific Way. Turn left onto Hugh Allen, left onto Gloaming Drive, and left onto Laurel Place.
- Three rooms: One person $50; two people $65–75. King-sized bed, ensuite bathroom; queen-sized bed and hide-a-bed, private bathroom; queen-sized bed, ensuite bathroom. Additional person $15.
- A seven-year-old house in the Aberdeen Hills area of Kamloops, with a view of the city, within walking distance of shopping, restaurants, and a golf course. Across the highway from several hundred acres of hiking and mountain biking trails in Mount Dufferin Park, the largest municipal park in North America. Two decks with views. Guest rooms have TVs, magazines, coffee supplies and facilities, and fruit baskets. Guest rooms are decorated with antiques and are distinguished by their colour schemes. Guest room with a queen-sized bed has a sitting room with a hide-a-bed. Laundry facilities available. Breakfast includes homemade jam and baked goods. Two dogs in residence. Smoking outdoors. **In the hosts' own words:** "Guests enjoy the beautiful views from our decks and our wholesome breakfasts. We pride ourselves on providing the little extras that make guests' stays pleasant and that make our B&B a home away from home."

Reimer's B&B

Ray and Cookie Reimer
1630 Slater Avenue
Kamloops, BC V2B 4K4
(250) 376-0111 fax: (250) 554-2717

- Cross the Overlander Bridge to the North Shore and take Fortune Drive, which becomes Tranquille Road. Turn left onto Singh Road, continue for one block, and turn right onto Slater. The B&B is the fourth house on the right.
- Three rooms: One person $35; two people $60–65. Queen-sized waterbed; queen-sized bed; double bed. Shared and private bathrooms. Open May 15 to December 15. Tent space available.
- A B&B with an outdoor pool on a landscaped, fenced lot, in a quiet area. One of the guest rooms is downstairs and has a private entrance, a queen-sized waterbed, and a private bathroom with shower. The other guest rooms are upstairs. Patio and deck. Tea or coffee served any time. Ten minutes from golf, tennis courts, and a bike path at McArthur Park. Ten minutes from the airport and downtown. Near a shopping mall, a theatre, and restaurants. An hour from Sun Peaks and Harper Mountain ski areas. Varied breakfast menu includes homemade jam and preserved fruit. Check-in any time; check-out until 11:00 a.m. Cash, traveller's cheques. Adult oriented. Guests with alternative lifestyles welcome. Well-behaved pets welcome; dog in residence. Smoking outdoors. **In the hosts' own words:** "We'll make your breakfast any way you like. Our guests say our hospitality is second to none."

Highridge B&B

Guido and Marjorie Ponne
1221 Highridge Drive
Kamloops, BC V2C 5G5
(250) 573-5914 fax: (250) 573-5916
toll-free from within North America:
1-877-573-5914
email: hridgebb@mail.ocis.net
web site: www.highridgebb.com

• From downtown Kamloops, go east on Highway 1 for 10 minutes. Take the Barnhartvale/Dallas Road exit. Turn right onto Todd Road and left onto Highridge Drive.
• Two rooms: One person $45; two people $55. Queen-sized bed; double bed. Shared guest bathroom. Additional person $15.
• A B&B on a hill with views of mountains, valleys, and pine trees. Near golf courses, horseback riding, waterslides, and a wildlife park. Guest rooms are in a downstairs suite. Guest living room with fireplace, TV, VCR, radio, books, and private entrance. Upper and lower decks. Picnic table. Brochures, maps, and travel information. Full breakfast. Traveller's cheques, Visa, MasterCard. Two cats and a rabbit in residence. Smoking outdoors. **In the hosts' own words:** "Our B&B is a getaway to relax and enjoy. Savour a hearty breakfast before beginning another day of touring. Happy travelling."

Sevinth Heaven B&B

Anne Sevin
7007 Paul Lake Road
Kamloops, BC V2H 1N9
(250) 573-7533 fax: (250) 573-5337
email: asevin@direct.ca
web site: www.bbexpo.com/bc/Sevinth.htm

• Three rooms: One person $40–55; two people $50–65. Queen-sized bed, ensuite bathroom; queen-sized bed, shared bathroom; double bed, shared bathroom. Additional person $20. Weekly rates.
• A hillside house across the road from private frontage and a dock on a lake where there is swimming and trout fishing. Near hiking and biking trails. Fifteen minutes' drive from Kamloops. Ten minutes' drive from downhill skiing at Harper Mountain. Forty-five minutes' drive from downhill skiing at Sun Peaks. Near golf, horseback riding, shopping, and restaurants. Backyard with a view of Paul Lake. Laundry. Living room with fireplace, TV, and a view of the lake. Full or light breakfast. Dinner available for a fee, by arrangement. Reservations recommended. Cancellation notice fourteen days, with 20 percent nonrefundable. Cash, traveller's cheques, money orders. Most pets welcome by arrangement; dog in residence. No smoking indoors. **In the hosts' own words:** "Our B&B is a great half-way stop for travelling between Jasper and Vancouver. You'll feel like you're in heaven here. Our hillside home provides privacy indoors and out, with a breathtaking panoramic view of Paul Lake."

The Inn at the Ninth Hole

Michael and Carla Van der Kraats
5091 Twentieth Avenue SE
Salmon Arm, BC V1E 1X6
(250) 833-0185 fax: (250) 833-0113
toll-free from within Canada and the U.S.: 1-800-221-5955
email: ninthhol@shuswap.net
web site: www.shuswap.net/mall/ninthhol

• From Highway 1, take Highway 97B south for 3 kilometres. Turn right onto Twentieth Avenue SE. The B&B is the last house on the right.

• Three rooms: Two people $89.95–125. King-sized bed; queen-sized bed. Ensuite bathrooms.

• A colonial-style house with a view of the greens of a golf and country club, ten minutes from Salmon Arm. Guest rooms have sitting areas, fireplaces, TVs, VCRs, and ensuite bathrooms with jetted tubs. Air conditioning. In the area are hiking, riding stables, cross-country skiing, boating, shopping, and eighteen-hole and nine-hole golf courses. Full breakfast. Reservations recommended. Cancellation notice seven days. Visa, MasterCard, American Express. No pets. No smoking. **In the hosts' own words:** "Our B&B is a place for all seasons. Come and enjoy a relaxing time in peaceful surroundings."

Stone Castle B&B

Lawrence and Sherrin Davis
3325 Allen Frontage Road
Mail: Box 2113
Revelstoke, BC V0E 2S0
(250) 837-5266 fax: (250) 837-5266
toll-free from within North America: 1-800-313-6613
email: stcastle@revelstoke.net
web site: www.pixsell.bc.ca/bb4216.htm

• Off Highway 1, 5 kilometres west of Revelstoke (6 hours from either Vancouver or Calgary).

• Rooms and suite.

Two rooms: One person $45-55; two people $70; four people $120 for the two rooms. Queen-sized bed and one twin bed, private bathroom; queen-sized bed, shared bathroom.

Suite: One person $75; two people $90. Queen-sized bed and one twin day bed. Ensuite bathroom. Additional person $15.

Golf discounts.

• A stone house near Boulder Mountain, five minutes' walk from two fine dining restaurants. Ten minutes from Revelstoke, a tour of Revelstoke Dam, golf, hiking, summer evening outdoor entertainment, a train museum, and alpine meadows in Revelstoke National Park. In the area are downhill and heli-skiing, cross-country ski trails, and snowmobiling. Drying room for snow gear. Guest living room with TV, VCR, books, and videos. Suite has a sun room. Full breakfast. Reservations recommended. Cash, traveller's cheques. No pets; cat in residence. Smoking outdoors. **In the hosts' own words:** "We offer a warm welcome and a relaxed atmosphere."

Four Seasons Manor B&B

Susan Akhurst and Robert Restall
815 MacKenzie Avenue
Mail: Box 2628
Revelstoke, BC V0E 2S0
(250) 837-2616 fax: (250) 837-2616
toll-free: 1-877-837-2616
email: fourseasonsmanor@cablelan.net
web site: www.revelstokecc.bc.ca/vacation/4seasonsbb.htm

• Three suites: In summer (May 15 to September 15), two people $90–125. In winter (September 15 to May 15), two people $75–100. Queen-sized bed; queen-sized bed and queen-sized sofa bed. Ensuite bathrooms. Additional person $20.

• A 1905 Edwardian house in a quiet, residential neighbourhood, with views of mountains and the Columbia River. Period furniture, wrap-around veranda, and enclosed hot tub. Five minutes' walk from downtown. Fifteen minutes' drive from snowmobiling, snowshoeing, and downhill, cross-country, cat, and helicopter skiing. Pickup and drop-off to and from downhill and cross-country skiing and snowmobiling. Suites have sitting areas, mountain views, and antiques. One of the suites has a Battenburg lace down comforter and pillows. Two of the suites have claw-foot tubs with showers. Tea room, sitting room, TV room, and games room. Pool table, ping pong, darts, antique square grand piano, guitar, stereo, TV, VCR, and videos. Choice of beverages served when guests arrive. Robes. Trailer parking. Drying room for clothing. Storage for gear. Full breakfast, including homemade baked goods and jam, is served from 6:30 a.m. in the dining room which has a fireplace, or on a second-floor balcony. Vegetarian diets are accommodated. Personal cheques, traveller's cheques, Visa, MasterCard. Deposit of one night's rate required to hold reservation. Cancellation notice seventy-two hours, with $20 nonrefundable. Adult oriented. **In the hosts' own words:** "Each of the rooms in our heritage house is unique and has been furnished with the style of the house in mind. Breakfasts vary from day to day and are always sure to delight the senses and the palate."

Mulvehill Creek Wilderness Inn

Cornelia and René J. Hueppi
4200 Highway 23 South, Box 1220
Revelstoke, BC V0E 2S0
cel: (250) 837-8649 fax: (250) 837-8649
toll-free: 1-877-837-8649
toll-free fax: 1-877-837-8649
email: BCBBG@mulvehillcreek.com
web site: www.mulvehillcreek.com

• From Highway 1 at Revelstoke, go south on Highway 23 for 19 kilometres. Turn left onto a private road and continue for 1.5 kilometres to the lake.

• Rooms and suites.
Six rooms: One person from $75; two people from $85. King-sized bed; queen-sized bed; twin bed. Ensuite bathrooms.
Suite: $125. King-sized bed and queen-sized bed. Ensuite bathroom.
Honeymoon suite: $195. King-sized bed. Ensuite bathroom.
Extended-stay rates.
Adventure packages.

• A new cedar house on fifty-six acres of a wooded peninsula on Upper Arrow Lake, with a heated outdoor pool and a hot tub in landscaped gardens. Flower and herb gardens, a sand and gravel shore with firepits and picnic areas, a fish pond with fountain, trails, a creek, a hundred-metre waterfall, a playground, fishing, cross-country skiing, snowshoeing, an eight-hundred-metre toboggan run, birdwatching, wildlife viewing, a trampoline, and canoes. Floatplane flights available for a fee. Three- and seven-night adventure packages including whitewater rafting, horseback riding, cycling, or golf can be arranged by the hosts. Fifteen minutes' drive from shopping, museums, and fine dining. Ten to thirty minutes' drive from national parks, hot springs, alpine meadows, hiking, climbing, downhill skiing at Powder Springs, and cross-country skiing at McPhearson. Living room with stone fireplace. TV, VCR, books, CDs, and billiards. Honeymoon suite has a Jacuzzi, a deck, a stereo, a loveseat, and a fireplace. Most guest rooms have thermostats for individually controlled temperature and fans. Pickup and drop-off for guests travelling by bus or air. Beverages and snacks. Candlelit dinners available for a fee. Swiss-style breakfast, including seasonal fresh fruit and vegetables from the B&B's organic garden, homemade bread and baked goods, and farm-fresh eggs, is served in the dining room or on the deck. Reservations recommended. Cancellation notice fourteen days. Traveller's cheques, Visa, MasterCard, American Express, Interac. German, French, Italian, and Spanish spoken. Suitable for small seminars. **In the hosts' own words:** "Be enchanted by nature's beauty, the amenities of our house, the delicious meals, and the endless possibilities, whether relaxing or looking for adventures. Meet other guests from around the world. Come as a visitor, stay as a guest, leave as a friend."

Wooly Acres B&B

Chris and Jim
1030 Bo Hill Place
Mail: RR 1 Box 1739
Clearwater, BC V0E 1N0
(250) 674-3508 fax: (250) 674-2316
email: wlyacres@mail.wellsgray.net
web site: www.bbcanada.com/woolyacres

• Five kilometres from Highway 5. Turn onto Clearwater Valley Road (tourist information centre on corner) and continue for 3.5 kilometres. Turn right onto Greer Road and continue for 1 kilometre. Turn right onto Bo Hill Place and continue for 500 metres to the gate. The B&B has signs on Greer Road and Bo Hill Place.

• Three rooms: One person $40–60; two people $60–75. Queen-sized bed and twin beds; queen-sized bed and one twin bed; double bed and one twin bed. Ensuite and shared guest bathrooms. Additional person $15.

• A quiet house in the country on ten acres surrounded by mountains. Farm atmosphere. Five to ten minutes' drive from Yellowhead Highway 5, restaurants, shopping, and a nine-hole golf course. Thirty-five minutes from an eighteen-hole golf course, Wells Gray Provincial Park, hiking, and sightseeing. Near snowshoeing and cross-country skiing. Two guest sitting rooms, one of which has a gas fireplace and a view. Large yard with gardens, fire pit, and picnic table. Parking area. Guest deck on the upper floor. Full breakfast, including fresh muesli, farm-fresh eggs, berries in season, homemade whole-grain bread and muffins, jam, and jelly, is served in the dining room. Children by arrangement. No pets; sheep on the property and dogs and cats in residence (although not in the guests' quarters). No smoking in or near the house. **In the hosts' own words:** "When visiting Clearwater, enjoy country comfort at our B&B and sleep like a lamb. The sheep have names—ask for an introduction to them."

Trophy Mountain Buffalo Ranch B&B

Joe Fischer
Clearwater Valley Road
Mail: Box 1768
Clearwater, BC V0E 1N0
(250) 674-3095 fax: (250) 674-3131
email: buffranch@hotmail.com

• Between Jasper and Kamloops, on Highway 5. In Clearwater, turn onto Wells Gray Park Road (tourist information centre on corner) and continue for 20 kilometres.

• Six rooms: One person $35–55; two people $50–60. Queen-sized bed and one twin bed; queen-sized bed; double bed; bunk beds. Ensuite and private bathrooms. Additional person $15–25. Children under 6 free.

• A restored 1926 log house in a quiet, rural setting. Hiking, biking, and cross-country skiing on the property. Guest entrance. Near Wells Gray Provincial Park, Trophy Mountain hiking area, Helmcken Falls, canoeing, river rafting, hiking, cross-country and downhill skiing, and a shopping centre. Hosts keep bison and horses as a hobby. Hosts are outdoor adventure guides and can provide information about the area and its outdoor activities. Guided horseback rides available for a fee. Off-street parking. Visa, MasterCard. Pets welcome outdoors. Smoking outdoors.

Abigail's Garden and Guest House

Abigail and Richard Rutley
Mail: Box 576
Clearwater, BC V0E 1N0
(250) 674-2514

• On Clearwater Valley Road, 19.5 kilometres from Highway 5 (Yellowhead).
• Two rooms: Two people $80–100. Queen-sized bed. Private and shared bathrooms. Additional person $20.
Teepee: $30 per person.
Cabin: $30 per person. Child 6 to 12 $20.
• A white pine timber house near Wells Gray Provincial Park, well-marked hiking trails, whitewater rafting, horseback riding, Helmcken Falls, golf, and lake fishing. Fifteen minutes from downtown. Forty-five minutes from Clearwater Lake and boat tours. Living room, library with fireplace, and balcony. Bagged lunch available for a fee. Dinner available for a fee with advance notice. Breakfast includes farm-fresh eggs, homemade baked goods, seasonal fruit and jam, garden produce, fresh-ground organic coffee, mountain water, and garden herb tea. For guests staying in the room or suite, breakfast is served before 9:30 a.m. by a wood stove. One of the guest rooms has wheelchair access. For reservations, payment is required thirty days in advance. No pets; dog in residence. No smoking. **In the hosts' own words:** "Enjoy beautiful sunsets, great wilderness, and an abundance of wildlife at our back door."

The Gallery B&B

Len and Donalda Grassie
1433 Sixth Avenue
Mail: Box 988
Valemount, BC V0E 2Z0
(250) 566-0061 fax: (250) 566-4543
toll-free from within North America: 1-877-566-0061
web site: www.monday.com/thegallery

• From Highway 5, turn onto Fifth Avenue (the main entrance to the village centre) and continue for one block. Turn right onto Fir and continue for one block. The B&B's driveway is at the end of the road.

• Three rooms: One person $45; two people $65. Queen-sized bed; twin beds (or twin beds side by side with king-sized bedding). Ensuite and private bathrooms.
Off-season rates.

• A B&B decorated with paintings, sculptures, and art by one of the hosts. Near stores, golf, hiking, and a bird sanctuary. One block from restaurants. Twenty minutes' drive from Mount Robson. In the area are snowmobiling, heliskiing, mountain lake fly-in fishing, and all-terrain vehicle, helicopter, and canoe tours. Living room with TV, VCR, and videos. Paved off-street parking with plug-ins and space for snowmobile trailers. Full breakfast includes hotcakes, fresh or frozen fruit, whipped cream, and homemade jam and marmalade. Diets are accommodated if possible. Cash, traveller's cheques, Visa, MasterCard, American Express. Not suitable for children under twelve, although exceptions are sometimes made. No pets. No smoking. **In the hosts' own words:** "We love to make our guests feel welcome and very special. We make strangers into friends."

Mountain Reach B&B

Terry and Chris Hurst
3840 Bryan Road
Mail: Box 1107
Valemount, BC V0E 2Z0
(250) 566-4052 fax: (250) 566-4056
email: relax@mountainreach.com
web site: www.mountainreach.com

• Four hundred metres off Highway 5, 4.5 kilometres north of Valemount. Eleven kilometres south of Tête Jaune Cache (junction of Yellowhead Highways 5 and 16).

• Three rooms: One person $50–55; two people $65–75. Queen-sized bed; double bed. Ensuite bathrooms. Additional person $15. Roll-away cots available.

• A log-sided bungalow on a wooded lot with views of the McLennan River, the Fraser Valley, and the Premier range and Canoe Mountains. Deck, barbecue, tables, and chairs. Living room with stone fireplace, books, games, and views. Gift shop with local arts and crafts. Dining room with view. Backyard with fire pit and games area. Guest rooms have satellite TVs. Laundry facilities. Near a wildlife sanctuary, salmon spawning in August, hiking, golf, fishing, horseback riding, rafting, canoeing, snowmobiling, and cross-country and heli-skiing. Fifteen minutes' drive from Mount Robson Provincial Park. Seventy minutes' drive from Jasper National Park. Pickup and drop-off for guests travelling by bus or train. Full breakfast includes Japanese, herbal, and black teas, Bridgehead coffee, and juice. Visa, MasterCard. Japanese spoken. Children welcome. Pets welcome outside or in guest quarters, by arrangement; dog in residence, though not in guest quarters or common area. Nonsmoking environment. **In the hosts' own words:** "Enjoy a restful retreat in our secluded country B&B and share your love of nature with us."

Brady's B&B

Alan and Mavis Brady
9060 Buffalo Road
Mail: Box 519
Valemount, BC V0E 2Z0
(250) 566-9906
email: brady@valemount.com
web site: www.bbcanada.com/4136.html

• From Valemount, go north on Highway 5 for 7 kilometres. Turn left onto Blackman Road and continue for 5 kilometres. Turn left onto Buffalo Road. Turn right at the B&B's sign.

• Two rooms and one semi-private loft: Two people $60. Queen-sized bed; two double beds. Shared guest bathroom and shared guest half bathroom.

• A log house built by its owners, on wooded acreage with a view of the McLennan River, Mica Mountain, and the Premier Range. Wildlife on the property. Guest rooms have down comforters. Upstairs on a mezzanine, a semi-private loft with no door or wall on one side has two double beds. Living room with fireplace. Deck and backyard with swimming pool. In the area are hiking, climbing, fishing, boating, river rafting, trail riding, cross-country skiing, heli-skiing, and snowmobiling. Full breakfast is served in the kitchen, which has a view of a field and mountains. No smoking indoors. **In the hosts' own words:** "Our home is quiet and comfortable, with spectacular views. Bring your camera; wildlife is just outside the door."

Rainbow Retreat B&B

Keith and Helen Burchnall
11944 Essen Road, Highway 16W
Mail: Box 138
Valemount, BC V0E 2Z0
(250) 566-9747
web site: www.bbcanada.com

• Twenty kilometres north of Valemount. Half a kilometre west of the junction of Highways 5 and 16 (the Yellowhead highways). The B&B has signs on the highway and a large sign at the driveway.

• Two rooms: One person $65–70; two people $70–75. Queen-sized bed. Shared guest bathroom. Crib and highchair available. Infants free.

• A post-and-beam log house in an old-growth forest on the western slope of the Rockies, with a view of the Cariboo Mountains. Ten minutes' walk from the Fraser River. Thirty minutes' walk from Lost Lake. Fifteen minutes' drive from Mount Robson, a world heritage site. An hour from Jasper. A stopover point between Vancouver and Edmonton. Stained glass, original art, sitting/dining room, and stone fireplace. From a deck and a covered porch, hawks, hummingbirds, woodpeckers, and swallows can be seen among the forest trees and wildflowers. Deer, elk, and bears often visit. One of the hosts is an experienced outdoorsperson and shares his knowledge of the history of the area. He is also a pianist and composer and plays for guests on a concert grand piano. Breakfast and dinner are served on fine china and with silver cutlery, in a licensed dining room. Diets are accommodated. Cash, traveller's cheques. Smoking outdoors. **In the hosts' own words:** "Your visit to our B&B will be memorable. Be prepared to stay a while to enjoy scenic wonders, exciting activities, artists, and artisans in this easily accessible and undiscovered destination."

Sunflower Inn B&B

Kathleen Smythe
159 Alpine Road
Christina Lake, BC V0H 1E1
(250) 447-6201 fax: (250) 447-6592
email: suninnbb@sunshinecable.com
web site: www.christinalake.com/suninnbb

• From Christina Lake village (28 kilometres east of Grand Forks; 70 kilometres west of Castlegar and Rossland), take Highway 3 east for 8 kilometres. Take the Alpine-Texas turnoff to East Lake Drive. At the Y junction, take the left fork onto Alpine Road. The B&B is on the left, at the corner.

• Three rooms: One person $65–125; two people $70–150. Queen-sized bed and double sofa bed; queen-sized bed. Shared guest bathroom. Additional person $15–20.
Golf packages. Health retreats.

• A log house on a lake, with a covered deck, a guest entrance, a private beach, and a dock. Near swimming, canoeing, kayaking, hiking, nature trails, birdwatching, mountain biking, golf, snowshoeing, and skating. Canoe available. Forty-five minutes from Red Mountain ski area. Five to twenty minutes from cross-country skiing. Guest fridge. One of the hosts is a registered nurse and healing touch practitioner and offers craniosacral and somatoemotional release therapy. Full or Continental breakfast is served on the deck, weather permitting, between 9:00 and 11:00 a.m. Diets are accommodated. Visa, MasterCard. Children by arrangement. No pets; dog, who mostly stays outside, in residence. Smoke-free environment. **In the hosts' own words:** "Enjoy our beautiful lakeside log house, nutritious breakfasts, and all-season recreation."

Mistaya Country Inn

Sue and George Iverson
Mail: Box 28
Silverton, BC V0G 2B0
(250) 358-7787 fax: (250) 358-7787
email: mistayaresort@netidea.com
web site: bctravel.net/mistaya

• One kilometre from Highway 6. Ten kilometres south of Silverton. Fifteen kilometres south of New Denver. Ninety kilometres north of Nelson.

• Five rooms: One person $45–50; two people $60–65. Double bed; queen-sized bed; twin beds. Shared guest bathrooms. Additional person $15.
Riding lessons, trail rides, and three-day pack trips.

• A lodge with walking trails on ninety acres in the Slocan Valley, between Valhalla and Kokanee Glacier parks. Guest sitting room with fireplace. Teepee accommodation, firepits, picnic area, and barbecues. Additional meals available for a fee. Near ghost towns and old mining trails in the Selkirk Mountains. Fifteen minutes' drive from Slocan Lake, canoeing, hiking, golf, and cross-country skiing. Full breakfast. Visa, MasterCard. No pets. Smoking on the porch.

Inn the Garden B&B

Lynda Stevens and Jerry Van Veen
408 Victoria Street
Nelson, BC V1L 4K5
(250) 352-3226 fax: (250) 352-3284
toll-free from within North America: 1-800-596-2337
web site: www.innthegarden.com

• In downtown Nelson, one block south of Baker Street, between Stanley and Ward streets.

• Rooms, suite, and guest house.
Five rooms: One person $70–90; two people $80–100. Queen-sized bed; double bed. Ensuite, private, and shared guest bathrooms. Additional person $20.
Two-bedroom suite: One person $100; two people $130. Two queen-sized beds and one double futon. Additional person $25.
Self-contained three-bedroom guest house: Two people $165; four people $195; six people $225. Queen-sized bed, double bed, and twin beds.
Ski and golf packages.

• Two restored Victorian houses with plants, wicker, and antiques. Two minutes' walk from shopping, restaurants, and theatre. Lake and mountain views. Terraced front garden. The suite is on the third floor of the main house and has two bedrooms and a private entrance. The main house has a guest entrance, a guest living room, and a refreshment area. The self-contained guest house has a living room, a dining room, a kitchen, a gas fireplace, and a backyard with a picnic table and chairs. The guest house is suitable for groups. In the area are historical walking tours, hiking, golf, fishing, canoeing, and downhill and cross-country skiing. Full, varied breakfast is served in an old-fashioned dining room. Off-street parking. Storage for bikes, skis, and golf equipment. Check-in 4:00 to 8:00 p.m. Visa, MasterCard, American Express. Adult oriented main house; children welcome in the cottage. No pets. No smoking. **In the hosts' own words:** "Our B&B offers you a comfortable and convenient stay in the heart of historical Nelson."

Emory House B&B

Janeen Mather and Mark Giffin
811 Vernon Street
Nelson, BC V1L 4G3
(250) 352-7007 fax: (250) 352-7007
email: emorybnb@kootenay.net
web site: www.bbcanada.com/189.html

• In downtown Nelson, one block north of Baker Street, between Hall and Cedar streets.
• Four rooms: One person $60–80; two people $70–90. Queen-sized bed; twin beds. Ensuite and shared guest bathrooms. Additional person $15. Off-season and corporate rates. Golf and ski packages.
• A restored arts and crafts–style house with fireplaces, antiques, and original woodwork and floors, near a guided and self-guided walking tour route. Two minutes' walk from shops, cafés, a theatre, and an aquatic centre. Guest living room on the main floor with a tiled fireplace, games, reading material, and information on the area. Guest TV room with lake and mountain views. Backyard with lawn chairs. Air conditioning and fans. Refreshments served when guests arrive. Off-street parking. Ski and bike storage. Full breakfast includes homemade baked goods, homemade preserves, and a choice between two hot entrées such as eggs Florentine with herbed hashed brown potatoes and buttermilk huckleberry pancakes. Check-in 4:00 to 7:00 p.m. Visa, MasterCard. Children over nine welcome. No pets; two cats in residence. No smoking indoors. **In the hosts' own words:** "Our B&B is a home away from home with lots of extras. Come and enjoy our spacious heritage house and all that Nelson has to offer. Discover why our guests return again and again."

Taghum Beach B&B

Willa and Harold Horsfall
3289 Granite Road
Mail: RR 2 Site 21 C–19
Nelson, BC V1L 5P5
(250) 352-0362

• From Nelson, go south on Highway 3 for 7 kilometres. At the Taghum Bridge, turn left onto Granite Road and continue for 1 kilometre.
• Three rooms: One person $60; two people $75. Queen-sized bed; twin beds. Shared guest bathroom. Additional person $15. Cots available.
• A B&B on a landscaped acreage with a private sandy swimming beach and a dock. Ten minutes' drive from Nelson. Thirty minutes' drive from downhill and cross-country skiing. Ten minutes' drive from golf, curling, a fitness centre, restaurants, and shops. Canoe, horseshoe pit, badminton net, picnic tables, lawn chairs, garden, and wildlife viewing on the property. Sports equipment storage. Outdoor hot tub. Decks with views of the garden and the beach. Guest living room with TV, VCR, videos, board games, books, and fridge. Guest rooms have views of the garden and river. Duvets, quilts, bathrobes, and slippers. In-floor heating. Off-street parking. Hosts share their knowledge of the area. Full breakfast, including homemade bread and garden preserves, is served in the dining room or on the deck. Visa, MasterCard. Children welcome by arrangement. No pets; two dogs and a cat in residence. No smoking indoors. **In the hosts' own words:** "You'll want to return to our B&B to experience again our friendship and hospitality and the comfort and serenity of these peaceful surroundings."

Willow Point Lodge

Anni Mühlegg
2211 Taylor Drive
Mail: RR 1 Site 21 C–31
Nelson, BC V1L 5P4
(250) 825-9411 fax: (250) 825-3432
toll-free: 1-800-949-2211
email: willowpl@uniserve.com
web site: www.pixsell.bc.ca/bb/4193.htm

- From Nelson, take Highway 3A north for 6.5 kilometres. Turn left onto Taylor Drive.
- Rooms and suites.

Four rooms: One person $60–135; two people $75–150. Queen-sized bed; double bed; twin beds. Private bathrooms. Additional person $15.
Two honeymoon suites: $150.

- A lodge built in 1920, on acreage with large gardens and a view of Kootenay Lake and the Selkirk mountains. Garden hot tub, gazebo, hiking trails, creek, and waterfalls. Near sandy beaches, golf, fishing, and boating. Thirty minutes from Ainsworth Hot Springs and Whitewater ski area. Large stone fireplaces. Period furnishings, balconies, and canopied beds. Ten minutes from downtown. No cars or houses can be seen from the property. No outdoor shoes in the lodge. No TVs. Full breakfast, including seasonal fruits and homemade baked goods, is served on the veranda which has a view of the lake and mountains or in the dining room by a fireplace. Nonsmoking house. **In the hosts' own words:** "Come stay a while in our comfortable, elegant, eclectic retreat and reconnect with yourselves and nature. Guests return year after year."

Trafalgar Mountain B&B

Barbara Neelands
RR2 S3 C6
Kaslo, BC V0G 1M0
(250) 353-7151

• Ten kilometres north of Ainsworth Hot Springs. Ten kilometres south of Kaslo.
• Two rooms: One person $35–45; two people $45–55. Queen-sized bed, ensuite bathroom; double bed, shared bathroom. Child 6 to 12 $10.
Tour of the area included for guests staying three or more days.
• A log house with heavy beams and a spiral staircase, in a rural setting, near Fletcher Falls and a beach on Kootenay Lake. Main-floor guest room has a queen-sized bed and an ensuite bathroom. Upstairs guest room has a shared bathroom with an old-fashioned bathtub and an antique dresser sink. Nine kilometres by four-wheel-drive vehicle from the trailheads of Woodbury Creek and Cody Caves. Fifteen minutes' drive from restaurants, Kaslo's historical Moyie Sternwheeler, and Ainsworth Hot Springs and hot mineral water caves. Full breakfast includes fruit from the garden in season. Dog in residence. **In the hosts' own words:** "Huckleberry pancakes are a specialty of ours."

Wedgwood Manor

Joan Huiberts and John Edwards
16002 Crawford Creek Road
Mail: Box 135
Crawford Bay, BC V0B 1E0
(250) 227-9233 fax: (250) 227-9233
toll-free from within Canada, Washington, Montana, and Idaho: 1-800-862-0022
web site: www.bctravel.net/wedgwood

• In Crawford Bay (80 kilometres north of Creston), on Highway 3A.

• Six rooms: One person \$79; two people \$79–110. Queen-sized bed; queen-sized bed and one twin bed; double bed. Ensuite bathrooms. Additional person \$20. Open April 15 to October 15.
Golf packages and Ainsworth Hot Springs packages.

• A house built at the turn of the century by the Wedgwood china family, on fifty acres at the foot of the Purcell Mountains. Across the road from Kokanee Springs golf course. A few minutes from beaches, fishing, and boating on Kootenay Lake. Hiking, walking, and biking from the B&B. Landscaped grounds and gardens. Library and sitting room. Guest rooms have Victorian furniture. Some of the guest rooms have Jacuzzis and some have fireplaces. One of the rooms is a honeymoon suite. One is wheelchair accessible. Tea and snacks served any time. Visa, MasterCard. Smoking on the veranda. **In the hosts' own words:** "Relax in the library, sip tea by the parlour fireplace, stroll the garden paths. Our goal is to make you welcome in the most restful and beautiful surroundings."

Singing Pines B&B

Sandra and Robert Dirom
5180 Kennedy Road
Mail: Box A-9 SS 3 Site 15 C–9
Cranbrook, BC V1C 6H3
(250) 426-5959 fax: (250) 426-5959
toll-free from within North America:
1-800-863-4969
email: singingpines@cyberlink.bc.ca
web site: www.bbcanada.com/singingpines

• From Cranbrook, go north on Highway 95A for 4 kilometres. Turn right onto Kennedy Road and continue for 700 metres. Look for the B&Bs sign.

• Three rooms: One person $70–80; two people $80–100. Queen-sized bed and extra-long twin beds; two queen-sized beds. Ensuite bathrooms. Additional person $20. Open April to October and in winter by arrangement.

• A quiet landscaped house on ten forested acres, with views of the Rocky and Purcell mountains. Guest rooms are on the main floor and have TVs, VCRs, fridges, phones, thermostats for individually controlled heat, pine sleigh-style beds, robes, hairdryers, and toiletries. Two of the guest rooms have patio doors that lead to a deck. Guest living room with satellite TV, VCR, stone fireplace, piano, and books. Sun room with fireplace, microwave, fridge, bar, and sink. Hot and cold beverages. Guest hot tub on a deck with a view of the Rocky Mountains. Firepit and picnic tables. Patio with a barbecue and a view of the Purcell Mountains. Wildlife viewing. Birdwatching. Three to twenty-five kilometres from three championship golf courses and two par-three golf courses. Fifteen minutes from the heritage town of Fort Steele. Twenty-five minutes from downhill and cross-country skiing at Kimberley. Ten minutes from cross-country skiing at Cranbrook. Sixty minutes from skiing at Fernie. Five minutes from the Canadian Museum of Rail Travel. Full breakfast is served in the sun room. Deposit of one night's rate required to hold reservation. Cancellation notice seven days. Cash, traveller's cheques, Visa, MasterCard, American Express. Children over eleven welcome. No pets; dog in residence and wildlife in the area. Smoking on the deck. **In the hosts' own words:** "At our B&B, pamper yourself with style, country comfort, and fine food in a cordial, homey atmosphere, while enjoying the beauty of the natural setting."

House Alpenglow

Merna and Darrell Abel
3 Alpenglow Court
Kimberley, BC V1A 3E3
(250) 427-0273 fax: (250) 427-0276
toll-free: 1-877-ALPENGLOW (257-3645)
email: alpenglo@rockies.net
web site: kimberleybc.net/alpenglow

• Take Gerry Sorensen Way towards the ski and recreation area. Take the first left onto Norton Avenue and continue for 150 metres. Turn right onto Alpenglow Court.

• Four rooms: One person $70–80; two people $85–95. King-sized bed and twin bed; king-sized bed; two queen-sized beds and futon bed; two queen-sized beds. Ensuite and shared guest bathrooms. Ski and golf packages available.

• A new Bavarian-style house in a quiet area, adjacent to a golf course and a resort. Across the street from a restaurant and a few minutes from shopping and restaurants downtown. An hour's drive from Fairmont Hot Springs. Twenty minutes' drive from the Cranbrook airport. Adjacent to a nature park with mapped hiking and cross-country ski trails. Near mountain hiking, fly-fishing, rafting, and wildlife viewing. Hot tub. Lower floor is wheelchair accessible. Breakfast, including coffee, tea, juice, fruit, croissants, cinnamon buns, Bavarian sausage, cheese, homemade bread, and jam, is served between 7:30 and 10:00 a.m. Cash, cheques. Children welcome. No pets. Smoke-free. **In the hosts' own words:** "Our B&B is designed for the comfort of our guests while they enjoy Kimberley, the Bavarian city of the Rockies. We offer a great location, a warm wood interior, a great Bavarian-style breakfast, a unique experience—a great place to stay and enjoy."

Wasa Lakeside B&B

James and Mary Swansburg
4704 Spruce Road
Mail: Box 122
Wasa Lake, BC V0B 2K0
(250) 422-3688 fax: (250) 422-3551
toll free: 1-888-422-3636
email: info@wasalakeresort.com
web site: www.wasalakeresort.com

• Thirty-two kilometres north of Cranbrook, on the northwest side of Wasa Lake. From Highway 93/95, turn east at the north exit onto Wasa Lake Park Drive and continue for one block. Turn south onto Poplar Road and continue for three blocks. Turn east onto Spruce Road and continue for 100 metres. The B&B is a peach and white house on the side of the road closer to the lake.

• Three rooms: One person $100–175; two people $125–200. King-sized bed; queen-sized bed; twin beds. Private bathrooms. Additional person $45. Romance, golf, ski, honeymoon, and adventure-travel packages.

• A newly renovated B&B on the shore of Wasa Lake, with a private sandy beach and a dock. Sailboat, pedal boat, waterski boat, canoe, outdoor hot tub, two warm-water beach showers, beachside kitchen, barbecue, fire pit, bicycles, beach toys, swing set, trampoline, and volleyball and basketball equipment. Near hot springs, golf, bird watching, gold panning, fishing and ice fishing, skating, snowmobiling, and cross-country and downhill skiing. Waterskiing and Hobie-cat sailing lessons and equipment rentals available for a fee. Two of the guest rooms have fireplaces. Guest bathrooms have a steam shower, a Jacuzzi tub, and/or a standard tub. Glassed-in veranda with fireplace, air hockey, and table soccer. Media room with TV, VCR, videos, CD player, and slide projector. Full breakfast is served on a beachside patio or in a formal dining room. Credit card required to hold reservation. Cancellation notice thirty days. Check-in between 4:00 and 8:00 p.m.; check-out until 11:00 a.m. Cash, traveller's cheques, Visa, MasterCard. Children welcome. No smoking indoors. **In the hosts' own words:** "Wasa Lake is an undiscovered jewel in the Rocky Mountains. Small, shallow, and clean, it is the warmest lake in the region and is surrounded by a recreational paradise. Stay on our sandy beach with its awesome views and enjoy the comforts of home."

Emerald Grove Estate B&B Inn

Lorraine Klassen and Glenda Lindsay
1265 Sunridge Road
Mail: Box 627
Windermere, BC V0B 2L0
(250) 342-4431 fax: (250) 342-7220
toll-free from within North America: 1-888-835-3959
email: emerald@adventurevalley.com
web site: www.discoveryweb.com/emeraldgroveestate

• Off Highway 93/95, fifteen minutes south of Radium Hot Springs and fifteen minutes north of Fairmont Hot Springs.

• Three rooms: Two people $98–132. Queen-sized bed, twin day bed, and double sofa bed.
Ensuite bathrooms.
Honeymoon suite: Queen-sized bed. Ensuite bathroom.
Additional person $20. Children under 6 free. Child 7 to 16, $1 per year of age.
Golf discounts and ski packages. Off-season rates.

• A house designed as a B&B, on three acres, a few minutes from golf, miniature golf, swimming, fishing, parasailing, boating, hiking, and horseback riding. Ten minutes from shops, a museum, a theatre, and restaurants. Near Radium Hot Springs, Fairmont Hot Springs, Panorama Mountain Village, and beaches on Lake Windermere. Honeymoon suite has a canopied bed, a down duvet, a sofa, a window seat, robes, and a double Jacuzzi tub. Guest rooms have tables and chairs and TVs. Balcony and decks. Guest living room with fireplace on the main floor. On the property are a gazebo, a barbecue, picnic tables, a waterfall, a fish pond, benches, and a large backyard with flower beds, bocci, croquet, and a lawn area that accommodates weddings, staff parties, and reunions. Hot tub. Tray with tea and coffee is delivered to the guest rooms and the suite before breakfast. Full three-course breakfast, including fruit, homemade baked goods, and a hot entrée, is served in the dining room. One of the guest rooms is on the main floor and is wheelchair accessible. Cancellation notice twenty-one days. Check-in after 3:00 p.m.; check-out until 11:00 a.m. Reservations recommended. Deposit of one night's rate required to hold reservation. Cash, traveller's cheques, Visa, MasterCard, Diners Club/enRoute, American Express. No smoking indoors. **In the hosts' own words:** "Our B&B offers comfort, luxury, warmth, and hospitality in a location of great natural beauty. We look forward to having you as our guests."

Windermere Creek B&B Cabins

Scott and Astrid MacDonald
1658 Windermere Loop Road
Mail: Box 409
Windermere, BC V0B 2L0
(250) 342-0356 fax: (250) 342-0356
toll-free: 1-800-946-3942
web site: www.bbexpo.com/bc/windcreek.htm

• From Windermere, take Highway 93/95 south for 1 kilometre to the south end of Windermere Loop Road. Turn left and follow the loop road past Windermere Valley golf course. The B&B is the third house on the right, 1.5 kilometres past the golf course entrance.

• Suite and cabins.
Suite: $80. Queen-sized bed. Private bathroom.
Five log cabins: $85–95. Queen-sized bed. Private bathrooms.
Romance and ski packages.

• A B&B on 107 forested acres with lawns, an orchard, walking trails, a heated pool, creekside hammocks, lookout benches, picnic areas, and beaver ponds. One of the log cabins is an 1887 homestead. Two were built in 1996, and two were built in 2000. Cabins have Jacuzzi tubs. The four newer cabins have kitchens. The suite in the main house has a sun room and a deck. Near swimming and golf at Radium Hot Springs and Fairmont Hot Springs. Five minutes' drive from Windermere's public beach and art shops. Ninety minutes from Lake Louise and Banff. Full buffet breakfast. Not suitable for children under twelve. Smoking outdoors. **In the hosts' own words:** "We offer private dream cabins in the Rockies with our own forest at your doorstep."

Delphine Lodge

Jill and Sebastian Bell
Main Avenue
Wilmer, BC
Mail: Box 2797
Invermere, BC V0A 1K0
(250) 342-6851 fax: (250) 342-6845
toll-free: 1-877-342-6869
email: delphine@rockies.net

• Follow signs from route 93/95 at Invermere turn off. In Wilmer (5 kilometres north of Invermere), on the corner of Main and Wells streets.

• Five rooms in a lodge separate from the hosts' house: One person $55–75; two people $65–80. King-sized bed; double bed; twin beds; double bed and one twin bed. Private and shared guest bathrooms. Additional person $20. Child under 11 $10.

• A restored lodge built in 1899, with an English-style garden in a small village in the Windermere Valley. Views of the Rocky Mountains. Guest rooms have handmade quilts. Antique furniture and oil paintings throughout. Hiking, mountain biking, and cross-country skiing from the lodge. Five kilometres from Lake Windermere. Fifteen kilometres from Panorama ski resort and Grey Wolf golf course. Birdwatching in the area. Full breakfast includes baked goods, eggs, and fruit. Visa, MasterCard, Interac. Pets by arrangement; dogs and a cat in residence. No smoking. **In the hosts' own words:** "Our B&B is the perfect place to relax, whether sitting in our beautiful garden in summer or cozied up to a crackling fire in winter."

Wells Landing B&B

Ron and Jan van Vugt
4040 Sanborn Road
Mail: Box 89
Parson, BC V0A 1L0
(250) 348-2273 fax: (250) 348-2008
email: wellsldg@rockies.net
web site: www.rockies.net/~wellslan/

• From Golden, go south on Highway 95 for 35 kilometres. At Parson, cross the Columbia River to the west side of the valley. Go south on Sanborn Road for 3 kilometres. The B&B is at the end of the road.

• Three rooms: One person $65; two people $98. Additional person $25.

• A log house on thirty acres, with rock and flower gardens, at an historical riverboat landing on the Columbia River. The acreage is bordered by the river, forests, wetlands, and mountains. An abandoned logging road parallel to the river is suitable for walking and mountain biking. Over two hundred species of birds travel through the valley; a great blue heron rookery can be seen from the B&B's living room. Guest rooms have views. One of the guest rooms has a private entrance. Hot tub and music area on the main floor. Gazebo with a view of the river. Canoeing, fishing, hiking, birdwatching, mountain biking, and photography on the property. An hour's drive from whitewater rafting, mountaineering, natural hot springs, and hang-gliding. Near Banff, Yoho, Kootenay, and Glacier national parks. Breakfast includes homemade baked goods, a fruit plate, a hot entrée, fruit smoothies, and edible flower and herb garnishes. Cancellation notice twenty-four hours. Visa, MasterCard. Cats and a dog in residence. Nonsmoking house. **In the hosts' own words:** "Enjoy our beautiful house, spectacular view, and terrific breakfasts."

McLaren Lodge

George and Lou McLaren
1509 Lafontaine Road
Mail: Box 2586
Golden, BC V0A 1H0
(250) 344-6133 fax: (250) 344-7650
toll-free from within North America:
1-800-668-9119
email: wetnwild@redshift.bc.ca
web site: canadianrockies.net/wetnwild

• Off Highway 1, on the eastern limits of Golden (45 minutes west of Lake Louise).

• Ten rooms: One person $65; two people $75. Queen-sized bed; twin beds. Ensuite bathrooms.
Guided flatwater kayaking trips. Guided whitewater rafting trips. Guided heli-fishing in mountain lakes.

• A log house between the Purcell and Rocky mountain ranges, with views of the Columbia and Kicking Horse valleys. Sitting room with books, wood stove, and TV. Decks and garden gazebo. Near hiking, horseback riding, golf, scenic water tours, hang-gliding, and parasailing. Guided whitewater rafting trips leave daily from the lodge. Full breakfast. Adult oriented. No pets. No smoking. **In the hosts' own words:** "We invite you to stay a while and enjoy the mountain beauty."

H. G. Parson House B&B

André and Ruth Kowalski
815 Twelfth Street South
Mail: Box 1196
Golden, BC V0A 1H0
(250) 344-5001 fax: (250) 344-2782
email: hgparsonhousebb@redshift.bc.ca
web site: www.pixsell.bc.ca/bcbbd/4/4000406.htm

- One block off Highway 95.
- Three rooms: One person $72–77; two people $82–87. Extra-long twin beds (or extra-long twin beds side by side with king-sized bedding); queen-sized bed; queen-sized bed and one extra-long twin bed. Ensuite bathrooms and private bathroom with shower. Additional person $15.
- An 1893 house, in a quiet residential area, that was originally the home of H. G. Parson, a merchant and MLA for the Golden area. Antiques. Guest rooms are decorated in themes. Two of the guest rooms have ensuite bathrooms with Jacuzzi tubs; the other guest room has a private bathroom with shower. Within walking distance of shopping and restaurants. Near golf, whitewater rafting, horseback riding, wetlands slowfloating, skiing, and snowmobiling. Outdoor activities can be arranged by the hosts. A base for day trips to Banff, Yoho, and Kootenay national parks. Full breakfast. Cancellation notice five days with 30 percent non-refundable. Cash, traveller's cheques, Visa, MasterCard. French and Polish spoken. Children over five welcome.

Kapristo Lodge

Roswitha Ferstl
1297 Campbell Road
Mail: Box 90
Golden, BC V0A 1H0
(250) 344-6048 fax: (250) 344-6755
web sites: www.kapristolodge.com
www.westrockies.com

- Fourteen kilometres south of Golden and 1.5 kilometres off Highway 95.
- Six rooms and a suite: Two people $170–200. King-sized bed; queen-sized bed; twin beds (or twin beds side by side with king-sized bedding). Ensuite, private, and shared guest bathrooms. Off-season rates.
- A lodge on ninety acres on the side of Kapristo Mountain, close to snowmobiling, dog sledding, ice walks, downhill and backcountry skiing, whitewater rafting, horseback riding, hiking, mountain biking, birdwatching, fishing, and golf. A base for day trips to Yoho, Banff, Jasper, Kootenay, Glacier, and Mount Revelstoke national parks. Lodge has views of mountains and the Columbia Valley. Living room with fireplace. Dining room and adjoining sun room. Hot and cold beverages. Terrace. Sauna and outdoor hot tub. Guest rooms have down quilts. Suite has a kitchen, a fireplace, and a Jacuzzi tub. Host shares knowledge of the area and offers river rafting in the Columbia wetlands, where there is birdwatching. Helicopter landing port on the property. Lunch and dinner available by arrangement. Full breakfast. **In the hosts' own words:** "Our secluded lodge is family owned and operated and is well known for its hospitality and world-class accommodation. Whether you are looking for an outdoor adventure, a quiet getaway, a location for a business meeting, or the perfect spot for a wedding, our lodge is the place for you."

Ruth Lake Lodge

Klaus and Susanna Kaiser
Ruth Lake Road
Mail: Box 315
Forest Grove, BC V0K 1M0
(250) 397-2070 fax: (250) 397-2284
email: ruthlake@bcinternet.net
web site: www.ruthlake.com

• Thirty-two kilometres northeast of 100 Mile House. From Highway 97, turn right onto Canim Lake Road. At Forest Grove, go straight ahead onto Eagle Creek Road and continue for 6.5 kilometres. Turn left onto Ruth Lake Road and continue for 3.5 kilometres.

• Five rooms: One person $59; two people $89. Queen-sized bed; queen-sized bed and sofa bed; bunk beds.
Three self-contained cabins (each sleeps up to six): $130. Queen-sized bed and four mattresses in a loft. Breakfast not included.
Early booking discounts.
Boat, mountain bike, and skidoo rentals.

• A lodge and three cabins separate from the hosts' house, on the shores of Ruth Lake. Fishing, swimming, and hiking from the lodge. Golf, horseback riding, dog-sled rides, and fly-ins by float plane can be arranged by the hosts. Guest sauna by the lake. The lodge has a guest TV and video room and a guest living room with a fireplace. Each cabin has a bedroom with queen-sized bed, a loft with four beds, a bathroom with shower, kitchen facilities, a dining and living area, a wood stove, and electric heaters. A restaurant in the lodge serves European cuisine. Full breakfast is served in the restaurant for lodge guests. For guests staying in the cabins, breakfast is available in the restaurant for an additional fee. Reservations required. Visa, MasterCard, American Express. **In the hosts' own words:** "The sumptuous breakfast we serve in our restaurant will make your day."

Eagle Bluff B&B

Mary Allen and Bryan Cox
201 Cow Bay Road
Prince Rupert, BC V8J 1A2
(250) 627-4955 fax: (250) 627-7945
toll-free from within Canada and the U.S.: 1-800-833-1550
email: eaglebed@citytel.net
web site: www.citytel.net/eaglebluff

• From Highway 16, take the Cow Bay turnoff (Third Avenue East) onto Cow Bay Road. Turn left one block past Smile's Seafood Café. The B&B is next to Cow Bay Wharf.

• Rooms and suite.

Rooms: One person $45–55; two people $55–90. Queen-sized bed and double futon; queen-sized bed and single futon; extra-long twin beds (or extra-long twin beds side by side with king-sized bedding). Ensuite and shared guest bathrooms. Cot available.

Suite: Two people $90. Queen-sized bed, twin beds, and double hide-a-bed.

Additional person $15. Child 7 to 12 $5; children under 6 free. Weekly and winter rates.

• A B&B with a view of a yacht club, on a harbour where cruise ships, sailboats, freighters, and commercial fishing boats come and go. Five minutes' walk from downtown Prince Rupert, the Museum of Northern British Columbia, and Mariner's Park. Ten minutes' walk from a library, tennis courts, an indoor swimming pool, and a performing arts centre. Near a public boat launch and mooring, boat rentals and charters, a hiking trail by the ocean, an eighteen-hole golf course, and a racquet centre. Guest common area. Deck with a view of the harbour. Two of the guest rooms are downstairs, and the other two guest rooms and the suite are upstairs. Suite has a bedroom with twin beds and a sitting room with a queen-sized bed and a hide-a-bed. Laundry facilities available. Within a block of two seaside cafés and a neighbourhood pub. Full breakfast includes muffins and fruit salad. Deposit of one night's rate required to hold reservation. Cancellation notice seven days. Visa, MasterCard. Families welcome. No pets. No smoking. **In the hosts' own words:** "Experience Prince Rupert's waterfront and enjoy the view from our B&B of the sunset over the harbour."

Studio 1735 B&B

Diana Hoffman
1735 Graham Avenue
Prince Rupert, BC V8J 1C7
(250) 622-2787 fax: (250) 622-2787
toll-free: 1-877-922-2787
email: studio1735@hotmail.com
web site: skybusiness.com/studio1735

• Two rooms: One person $40; two people $60. Double bed, ensuite bathroom; double bed, shared bathroom.
Art packages.

• A B&B with an art studio and views of the harbour, ocean, and mountains. Guests can use the art studio, which has a fireplace. Art instruction sessions, art therapy sessions, and art supplies for a fee. One guest room has an ensuite bathroom with a Jacuzzi and skylight. The other guest room has a view of the harbour, a fireplace, a sink, a microwave, a fridge, a patio, and a large sitting area. Both guest rooms have phones and cable hook-ups. Living room with fireplace, TV, games, balcony, and porch with views of the ocean. Sauna. Ten minutes' drive from downtown, golf, a racquet centre, an indoor swimming pool, hiking trails, a performing arts centre, tennis courts, a library, the B.C. and Alaska ferry terminals, and a boat launch. Host is an art instructor and art therapist and provides information about fishing charters, tours, the Museum of Northern British Columbia, the Northern Pacific Cannery, and kayaking. Breakfast, including bread, muffins, waffles, pancakes, bacon, eggs, fruit, juice, tea, and coffee, is served in the dining room, which has a view of the harbour. Children welcome. Pets in residence. No smoking indoors. **In the hosts' own words:** "Passing through. Enjoy the view. Stay a day. Take your own painting away."

LakeHaven B&B

Melanie and Richard Olson
Mail: Box 130
Terrace, BC V8G 4A2
(250) 798-9555 fax: (250) 798-9555
cel: (250) 615-7393
email: lakehaven@telus.net
web site: www.bbcanada.com/2871.html

• Twenty-three kilometres from Terrace, on Lakelse Lake. On the Thornhill side of the Old Skeena Bridge, turn onto Queensway Road, and continue for 6 kilometres. Turn left onto Beam Station Road (chain link fence around the airport) and continue for 14 kilometres to the beam (a tower with a light on top). Turn left onto Catt Point Road and continue up the hill, keeping right. Turn right onto Eagle Ridge Lane. The B&B is a beige house with vinyl siding, 1.4 kilometres from the left turn at Catt Point Road.

• Room and suite.

Room: One person \$60; two people \$65. Queen-sized bed. Private bathroom.
Self-contained suite (sleeps five): One person or two people \$75. Queen-sized bed, double hide-a-bed, and single futon. Bathroom in suite.
Off-season and weekly rates. Additional person \$10.

• A B&B on a lake, with hillside terrace gardens and surrounded by trees. Access to hiking trails, fishing, boating, swimming, and windsurfing. Wildlife viewing in the area. Fire pit and picnic table by the lake. Barbecue. Guest suite has a private entrance, a bedroom, a sitting room, kitchen facilities, a dining area, a fireplace, a TV, a VCR, a covered deck, and a view of the lake. Living room and deck with views. Travel books, other books, and book exchange. Hosts share their knowledge of the area. Laundry facilities. Internet. Pickup and drop-off. Full breakfast. Guest room is wheelchair accessible. Cash, traveller's cheques, Visa. Nonsmoking. **In the hosts' own words:** "Our B&B is ideally suited for people who love the outdoors, beautiful scenery, privacy, peace and quiet, and warm hospitality."

Terrace Mountain B&B

Lance and Sasa Loggin
4512 Cedar Crescent
Terrace, BC V8G 1X6
(250) 635-6940
email: terracemountain@email.com
web site: www.bbcanada.com/terracemountain

• From Prince Rupert, go east on Highway 16. Turn left onto Eby and right onto Lakelse Avenue. Continue through three traffic lights. Turn left onto Atwood Street (Dairy Queen on the corner).
From Prince George, go west on Highway 16. Turn right at the four-way stop onto the old Skeena Bridge. Turn right onto Atwood Street (Dairy Queen on the corner). From either direction, take Atwood Street around a curve and turn onto Cedar, the second street on the left. The B&B is a yellow house, the third on the right.

• Two rooms or suite: One person $50; two people $55. Suite $60–80. Queen-sized beds. Private or shared guest bathroom. Additional person $15. Child over 7 $10; children under 7 free. Double hide-a-bed available. Off-season, weekly, and monthly rates.

• A B&B with a yard in a quiet neighbourhood on a bench, adjacent to a forest. Ten minutes' walk from downtown, a swimming pool, and an arena. Five minutes' walk from hiking trails. Guest living room with satellite TV, books, and games. Guest entrance. Guest suite has an antique bathtub. Toys and high-chair. Internet. Pickup and drop-off for guests travelling by train, bus, or air. Hosts share their knowledge of local attractions. Full breakfast is served in the suite's eating area. Cash, personal cheques, traveller's cheques, MasterCard. Czech spoken. Children welcome. Pets by arrangement; cat and dog in residence. Smoking outdoors.
In the hosts' own words: "Relax in our B&B on a secluded bench above the heart of the city, right at nature's doorstep."

La Mia Casa E'Sempre Aperta

Luciano and Georgina Dotto
2555 Dominion Avenue
Mail: Box 43
Houston, BC V0J 1Z0
(250) 845-7775

• From Highway 16, turn onto Butler Avenue (forestry building on the corner). Turn left onto Eleventh Street. Turn left onto Avalon Avenue. Turn right onto Star Street, which leads to Dominion Avenue. The B&B is on the left and has a tree-lined driveway.

• Three rooms: One person $45; two people $55. Double bed; twin beds. Shared guest bathrooms. Children under 6 free; child 7 to 12 half rate. Queen-sized hide-a-bed available in family room. Highchair and playpen available. Weekly and monthly rates ($35 per person per day including accomodation, breakfast, lunch, and dinner).
Fishing packages.

• A quiet house at the end of a tree-lined driveway, with a yard, a garden, a greenhouse, a patio, a woodworking shop, and a family room with fireplace. Near shopping. Ten minutes from a nature walk along a creek, two nine-hole golf courses, tennis courts, basketball, bowling, fishing, and cross-country skiing. Forty-five minutes from downhill skiing at Hudson Bay Mountain. In the area are sawmill and forestry tours. Coffee, tea, and other beverages are provided when guests arrive. Choice of full breakfast, which includes waffles, fresh strawberries and raspberries with whipped cream, pork sausages, and bacon, or Continental breakfast, which includes toast made with homemade bread, homemade preserves, cereal, and fresh fruit. Other meals by arrangement. Ground floor is wheelchair accessible. Cash, traveller's cheques. Italian spoken. Children welcome. No pets; small dog in residence. Smoking outdoors. **In the hosts' own words:** "Your comfort is our main concern, so come and enjoy your stay in our quiet, peaceful, and friendly house."

Loyola by the Lake B&B

Mary and Noel Dicker
Colleymount Road
Mail: Box 585
Burns Lake, BC V0J 1E0
(250) 695-6396
email: mdicker@futurenet.bc.ca

• Thirty kilometres (20 minutes) south of Burns Lake. From Burns Lake, take Highway 35 south to the Francois Lake ferry landing. Turn west onto Colleymount Road and continue west along the lakeshore for 4.5 kilometres.
• Two rooms: One person \$50–55; two people \$60–65. Queen-sized bed; twin beds. Private and shared guest bathrooms. Additional person \$10.
Family rates.
• A country-style house with an acre of garden surrounded by rolling pastures, woodland, and hills. Guest rooms have a view of Francois Lake with the peaks of Tweedsmuir Park in the distance. In the area are boating, fishing, walking, hiking, cycling, cross-country skiing, and wildlife viewing. Near an alpaca and llama ranch. Living room with satellite TV. Sun room. Full breakfast is served in the dining room or on the veranda. Cash, cheques, traveller's cheques. French and some German spoken. Children welcome. No pets. Smoking outdoors. **In the hosts' own words:** "Our B&B is a perfect retreat from the pressures of the outside world or a place to rest after a long day of travelling."

Bedford Place B&B

Walt and Ruth Thielmann
135 Patricia Boulevard
Prince George, BC V2L 3T6
(250) 562-3269
toll-free from within North America:
1-888-311-9292
email: c/o bedandbreakfastassc@
pgonline.com

- From First Avenue, take Queensway Street. Turn left onto Patricia Boulevard and continue for eight blocks to Taylor Drive.
- Two rooms: One person $65; two people $75. Queen-sized bed. Ensuite and private bathrooms.
- A B&B with a view of the Fraser River and the Yellowhead Bridge. One of the guest rooms has a queen-sized bed that swings up into a cabinet when not in use, maple wainscoting, and an ensuite bathroom. The other guest room has a queen-sized sleigh-style bed and a private bathroom with claw-foot tub. Ten minutes' walk from three parks, regional and railway museums, and the Heritage River Trail. Full breakfast is served in a formal dining room or on the patio. German spoken. **In the hosts' own words:** "Relax and enjoy our beautiful garden and backyard patio."

Huntley Place B&B

Bette and Cy Mackay
218 Huntley Place
Prince George, BC V2M 6W1
(250) 562-4597 fax: (250) 564-2588
toll-free from within North America: 1-877-277-2111
email: huntley@princegeorge.com
web sites: www.bbcanada.com/1774.html
www.princegeorge.com/bnb/huntley.html

- Twelve minutes from the city centre.
- Rooms and suite.

Rooms: One person $50–60; two people $60–75. Queen-sized bed; twin beds (or twin beds side by side with king-sized bedding). Ensuite bathrooms.
Self-contained suite: Two or three people from $65. Queen-sized bed and hide-a-bed. Private bathroom.

- A B&B surrounded by trees, on a quiet cul-de-sac next to a greenbelt. Patchwork quilts, duvets, and maple furniture. Self-contained suite is in the basement and has a kitchen, a gas fireplace, duvets, a telephone, a TV, a VCR, and a private entrance as well as an entrance through the house. Off-street parking. Breakfast is served in the dining room or on the deck. Visa. Adult oriented. No pets. **In the hosts' own words:** "Our patchwork quilts and maple furniture will take you back in time, while you enjoy such modern conveniences as a private phone and a fax machine. The suite is cool in the summer, and the gas fireplace and the duvets will keep you warm on winter nights. We specialize in turning strangers into friends."

Gallery House B&B

Marion and Bernie Nordquist
633 Johnson Street
Prince George, BC V2M 2Z8
(250) 561-2591/564-2216 fax: (250) 564-8998
toll-free: 1-800-511-2725
email: gallery_house@ckpg.net
web site: www.bbcanada.com/3103.html

• Two rooms: One person $50–65; two people $60–75. Queen-sized bed; double bed. Private bathrooms.

• A new house with a water garden, a gazebo, and a deck, all with patio furniture, within walking distance of restaurants and shopping. The guest room that has a queen-sized bed is on the ground floor and has satellite TV and a phone. Living room with TV. Full or Continental breakfast is served in a formal dining room or on the patio. Visa, MasterCard. Children under twelve by arrangement. **In the hosts' own words:** "Enjoy our water garden and our warm hospitality in our centrally located house. Our bedrooms are comfortably and artistically furnished with a Victorian flavour."

South Fort Heritage House B&B

Charlie and Joyce Burkitt
2684 Queensway Street
Prince George, BC V2L 1N2
(250) 563-1374 fax: (250) 563-2632
email: sfhouse@pgonline.com/bnb/sfhouse.html

• Room: One person $40; two people $50. Double bed. Shared bathroom.
Basement room: One person $40; two people $50. Twin beds (or twin beds side by side with king-sized bedding). Private bathroom.
Student rate $30. Additional person $15. Sofa bed and two roll-aways available.

• An older house on a treed lot with a view of the Fraser River. Backyard with lawn chairs and picnic table. Near public transportation to downtown, shopping, restaurants, the airport, the train station, golf courses, a swimming pool, indoor waterslides, the University of Northern British Columbia, a library, theatres, parks, exhibition grounds, bowling, and a railway museum. Within walking distance of the Fraser River. Family room with TV, VCR, and videos. Bike rentals. Laundry services for a fee. Pickup and drop-off for guests travelling by train, bus, or air. Breakfast, with guests' preferences acommodated, is served in a country-style kitchen. Children welcome. Dog and cat in residence. No smoking indoors. **In the hosts' own words:** "We offer friendly, courteous service in our clean, comfortable, older home. Enjoy the warmth and hospitality of your home away from home."

Topo's B&B Gallery

Hilde and Allan Jeffries
10109—105th Avenue (Beattie Avenue)
Mail: Box 696
Hudson's Hope, BC V0C 1V0
(250) 783-5759 or (250) 783-5564

• Four rooms: Two people $40. Double bed. Shared bathrooms. Additional person $10. Weekly and monthly rates.

• A B&B on half an acre, within walking distance of downtown and a take-out restaurant. In the area are hiking and cross-country ski trails, lake and river fishing, a museum in the original Hudson's Bay store, and a log church built in 1938. Deck. Yard with strawberry garden. Living room with TV, futon, rocking chair, armchair, and books. Kitchen facilities. Laundry facilities. Full or Continental breakfast is served in the dining room. German spoken. Smoking in the living room, on the deck, and in the yard. **In the hosts' own words:** "Welcome."

Cascade Court B&B

Clara Tarchuk and John Borisenko
2 Cascade Court
Mail: Box 883
Banff, AB T0L 0C0
(403) 762-2956 fax: (403) 762-5653
email: ctarchuk@telusplanet.net
web site: www.tarchuk.com

• From Banff town centre, go south on Banff Avenue. Cross the Bow River bridge and turn left onto Spray Avenue towards the Banff Springs Hotel. Go through one set of traffic lights and turn right onto Cascade Court.

• Two rooms: One person $60–95; two people $75–125. Queen-sized bed; twin beds. Ensuite bathrooms. Additional person $35.

• A house with a view of Mount Rundle, on a quiet cul-de-sac, a few minutes' walk from Banff town centre and Banff Springs Hotel. Deer and elk can be seen on the property. Within walking distance of Banff Springs golf course, shopping, and museums. Guest living room with TV, books, and a mountain view. Living room with a fireplace and a view of Mount Rundle. TV room with pool table. Family room with Franklin stove and TV. Indoor storage for skis and bicycles. Off-street parking. Breakfast includes fruit, coffee, tea, cereal, and homemade baked goods. Deposit required to hold reservation. Cancellation notice seven days. Check-in between 4:00 p.m. and 6:00 p.m. or by arrangement; check-out until 11:00 a.m. Cash, traveller's cheques. Smoke-free environment. **In the hosts' own words:** "Our friendly, family-oriented B&B can be your base for exploring Banff National Park or a quiet hideaway where you can relax and watch the deer and elk wander through our wooded neighbourhood."

Mountain Home B&B

Lynne and Ecki Treutler
129 Muskrat Street
Mail: Box 272
Banff, AB T0L 0C0
(403) 762-3889 fax: (403) 762-3254
email: info@mountainhomebb.com
web site: www.mountainhombb.com

- Two blocks from Banff town centre.
- Four rooms: In winter (November to April), two people $85–100. In summer (May to October), two people $125–150. King-sized bed; queen-sized bed.
Ensuite bathrooms.
Weekly rates. Ski lift packages.
- A B&B in a quiet neighborhood, half a block from a riverside walk along the Bow River and two blocks from Banff's main street. Guest rooms have down duvets, antique furniture, and ensuite bathrooms with soaker tubs, showers, and Victorian-style pedestal sinks. Living room with a rundlestone fireplace on the main floor. Guest entrance. Parking. In the area are golf, hiking, horseback riding, kayaking, river rafting, fishing, mountain climbing, biking, downhill and cross-country skiing, snowshoeing, ice fishing, dog sledding, heli-hiking, heli-skiing, sleigh rides, art galleries, museums, and the Banff Centre for the Performing Arts. Hosts provide information on the area. Full breakfast, including homemade baked goods and homemade preserves, is served in a breakfast nook. Visa, MasterCard. Not suitable for young children. No pets. Nonsmoking environment. **In the hosts' own words:** "Our B&B offers affordable charm, a relaxed, friendly atmosphere, and Rocky Mountain hospitality."

Cedar Springs B&B

Deborah J. Robillard
426 First Street
Canmore, AB T1W 2K9
(403) 678-3865 fax: (403) 678-1938
email: cedarspr@telusplanet.net
web site: www.cedarspringsbb.com

• On the south side of Canmore (15 minutes from Banff; an hour west of Calgary).

• Rooms and suites.

Rooms: In winter, two people from $100. In summer (May to October), two people from $135. Queen-sized bed; twin beds. Ensuite bathrooms.
Suite and honeymoon suite: Call for information.
Extended stay and group rates.
Special occasion packages.

• A custom-built cedar chalet in a quiet area surrounded by mountains and forest. Views of the Three Sisters Mountains. Guest sitting room has a fireplace, books, a TV, decks, and a fridge with beverages. Guest entrance. Suites have skylights or a fireplace. Wildlife can be seen in the garden area. A few minutes' drive from the Canmore Nordic Centre and Banff National Park. River walkways lead to Canmore's shops, galleries, and restaurants. Host can help plan recreational activities. Marriage commissioner available to perform civil wedding ceremonies. Full breakfast is served in a dining area or on the deck. Deposit of one night's rate required to hold reservation. Visa, MasterCard. French spoken. Adults only. No pets. Smoke-free environment. **In the hosts' own words:** "Come for the mountains and experience our friendly hospitality, affordable luxury, relaxing atmosphere, secluded setting, and spectacular mountain views."

McNeill Heritage Inn

Alan and Sharon Cole
500 Three Sisters Drive
Canmore, AB T1W 2P3
(403) 678-4884 fax: (403) 678-4884
toll-free from within North America: 1-877-MCNEILL
email: info@mcneillinn.ab.ca
web site: www.mcneillinn.ab.ca

• From Highway 1, at Canmore (15 minutes east of Banff; an hour west of Calgary), follow the signs to the Canmore Nordic Centre. After crossing the Bow River, Rundle Drive ends. Turn right onto Three Sisters Drive and continue for 1 kilometre up the hill. The road becomes the B&B's driveway, marked with a stone entrance.

• Five rooms: In summer (June to September), two people $150–175. In winter, two people $110–135. Queen-sized bed; twin beds (or twin beds side by side with king-sized bedding). Ensuite bathrooms. Additional person $25. Closed mid-October to November.

• A 1907 house on a wooded acreage adjacent to trails on the Bow River and the Canmore Olympic Nordic Centre. Hardwood floors, antique pine and oak furniture, and a wraparound veranda with mountain views. Guest living room with books, games table, and stone fireplace. Guest rooms are 250 to 400 square feet and have pine antiques, writing desks, chairs, and down duvets. Hosts are experienced outdoor enthusiasts. Ski and bike storage available. Full breakfast is served in an old-fashioned dining room. Deposit of one night's rate required to hold reservation. Cancellation notice seven days or, for large groups, thirty days; $25 is nonrefundable. Visa, MasterCard. Adult oriented. No pets. Nonsmoking house.

In the hosts' own words: "We offer more than just a room—experience our unique central location in seclusion and quiet, perfect for your vacation in the Rockies."

Enjoy Living B&B

Garry and Nancy Thoen
149 Cougar Point Road
Canmore, AB T1W 1A1
(403) 678-3026 fax: (403) 678-3042
toll-free from within North America: 1-800-922-8274
email: enjoy@telusplanet.net
web site: www.canadianrockies.net/enjoyliving

• From Calgary, take the second exit to Canmore. At the stop sign, turn right. At the traffic light, turn left. Take the next right onto Cougar Creek Drive and the next right onto Cougar Point.
From Banff, take the third exit to Canmore. At the traffic light, turn left. Take the next right onto Cougar Creek Drive and the next right onto Cougar Point.

• Two rooms: $70–100. Queen-sized bed; queen-sized bed and double futon bed. Ensuite bathrooms. Additional person $20. Children's rates negotiable.

• A quiet B&B with mountain views in all directions, ten minutes' walk from downtown Canmore's cafés, specialty shops, art galleries, antiques, and fine dining restaurants. Five minutes' drive from Banff National Park and fifteen minutes' drive from the town of Banff. Near golf courses, ski hills, hiking trails, fishing, climbing, rafting, and sightseeing. Guest rooms have mountain décor. One of the bathrooms has a whirlpool tub. Refreshments area with coffee, tea, and cookies. Guest living room with fireplace, stereo, TV, and VCR. Deck with hot tub. Guest rooms, refreshments area, living room, and deck are on the main floor of the house, which is for guest use only. Phone and fax available. Fire pit for campfires. Ski and bike storage. Full breakfast is served indoors or on the deck. Early breakfast available by request. Cancellation notice seven days. Check-in times flexible. Cash, traveller's cheques. Smoking outdoors. **In the hosts' own words:** "The name of our B&B is more than a name; enjoying living is an attitude that we try to make a way of life. It is our goal to make you feel welcome and at home during your visit to the Rocky Mountains."

Away Inn

Henry and Teresa Kobbero
37 Grotto Way
Canmore, AB T1W 1J8
(403) 678-2198 fax: (403) 678-3362
email: away@telusplanet.net
web site: www.canadianrockies.net/awayinn/

• From Calgary, take Highway 1 to Canmore and take the first exit (the Highway 1A—Exshaw exit). From Banff, take Highway 1 to Canmore and take the fourth exit (the Highway 1A—Exshaw exit). From the Highway 1A–Exshaw exit, turn left onto Highway 1A towards Exshaw. Take the next left onto Elk Run Boulevard and the next left onto Glacier Drive. Continue to the end of the street, turn right, and turn right again onto Grotto Way.

• Two rooms: One person or two people $60–95. King-sized bed; twin beds (or twin beds side by side with king-sized bedding). Ensuite bathrooms. Additional person $15. Extended stay and repeat stay rates.
Two-night minimum stay in summer.

• A quiet B&B in the Bow Valley with a view of Three Sisters Mountain, fifteen minutes from Banff town centre. An hour's drive from Lake Louise, Kananaskis, and Calgary. Guest rooms have TVs. The guest room with twin beds has a semi-private entrance and a view of Three Sisters Mountain. Living room with TV and books. One of the hosts has been a tour-bus operator for over ten years. Hosts share their knowledge of the area and help guests plan activities and sightseeing. Parking. Breakfast. Deposit of one night's rate required to hold reservation. Cancellation notice five days. Visa and MasterCard. Adult oriented. No pets. No smoking. **In the hosts' own words:** "We are tucked away in the best corner of the Rockies. We offer clean, quiet, and comfortable accommodation at sensible rates."

Amble-Inn B&B

Bob and Gabi Ess
438 Second Street
Canmore, AB T1W 2K4
(403) 678-6497 fax: (403) 678-6497
web site: www.cantravel.ab.ca/amble-in.html

- On the south side of Canmore, four blocks from Main Street.
- Two rooms: In winter (November to April), two people $70. In summer (May to October), two people $98. King-sized bed. Ensuite bathrooms.
- A B&B in the Rocky Mountains, with views of the Three Sisters Mountains and Ha'ling Peak. Five minutes' walk from cafés, shops, art galleries, and fine dining. Fifteen minutes' drive from Banff National Park. Living room and dining room with antiques. Honeymoon guest room by arrangement. Full breakfast is served in the dining room at guests' convenience. German spoken. Nonsmoking. **In the hosts' own words:** "We hope you enjoy our warm and friendly hospitality and our gourmet breakfasts. We speak German and English and have a warm smile in every language. We take great pleasure in hosting guests from around the world and look forward to making your stay with us the highlight of your trip."

Reservations Jasper Ltd.

Debbie Taylor
Mail: Box 1840
Jasper, AB T0E 1E0
(780) 852-5488 fax: (780) 852-5489
email: resjas@incentre.net

• A reservation service covering Jasper, Banff, Lake Louise, Canmore, Edmonton, Calgary, and Mount Robson. B&Bs, in-house accommodation without breakfast, hotels, motels, cabins, and bungalows. Booking fee of $20 for one destination and $5 for each additional destination. Additional $5 fee for overseas clients. Visa. Non-commissionable. **In the agents' own words:** "We offer a fast, reliable, and informative service for our clients. You need only make one call for your Canadian Rockies vacation accommodations."